# ST. OSWALD
## *of* NORTHUMBRIA:
### Continental Metamorphoses

# Medieval and Renaissance Texts and Studies

## Volume 297

# ST. OSWALD
## *of* NORTHUMBRIA:
### Continental Metamorphoses

*With an Edition and Translation of*

ÓSVALDS SAGA

*and*

VAN SUNTE OSWALDO DEME KONNINGHE

**Marianne E. Kalinke**

Arizona Center for Medieval and Renaissance Studies
Tempe, Arizona
2005

© Copyright 2005
Arizona Board of Regents for Arizona State University

Library of Congress Cataloging-in-Publication Data

Kalinke, Marianne E.
    St. Oswald of Northumbria : continental metamorphoses : with an edition
and translation of Osvalds saga and Van sunte Oswaldo deme konninghe /
Marianne E. Kalinke.
        p. cm. -- (Medieval & Renaissance Texts & Studies ; v. 297)
    Includes condensed texts of Osvalds saga and Van sunte Oswaldo deme
konninghe in Low German and English.
    Includes bibliographical references and index.
    ISBN-13: 978-0-86698-341-9 (alk. paper)
    ISBN-10: 0-86698-341-4 (alk. paper)
    1. Oswald, King of Northumbria, 604-642--Legends.  2. Osvalds saga
konungs hins helga.  3. Van sunte Oswaldo deme konninghe. I. Osvalds
saga konungs hins helga. English & German. II. Van sunte Oswaldo deme
konninghe. English & German.  III. Title.  IV. Series: Medieval & Renaissance
Texts & Studies (Series) ; v. 297.
PT1631.O7K35 2005
833'.21--dc22
                                                                    2005027822

∞
This book is made to last.
It is set in Reykjavik Times,
smyth-sewn and printed on acid-free paper
to library specifications.
Printed in the United States of America

# TABLE OF CONTENTS

# PREFACE

Oswald of Northumbria, the king and martyr slain by pagans in the year 642, had become a familiar figure in the German-language area by the end of the Middle Ages, a figure quite different from the one portrayed by Bede in his *Historia ecclesiastica*. Through woodcuts and etchings, stained glass and statuary, and the many imprints of the legendaries containing the story of his life and death, Oswald became known on the continent as the king with the raven.

The life and death of St. Oswald inspired two vernacular versions of his life, the one a hagiographic romance in verse, the other a sacred legend in prose. The romance, that is, the *Münchner Oswald*, although extant only in fifteenth-century manuscripts, has in the past been thought to represent the earliest German Oswald legend and to have been composed in the twelfth century. A deviating prose form of the sacred legend circulated in the most popular vernacular legendary of the Middle Ages, the late fourteenth-/early fifteenth-century *Der Heiligen Leben*, but the long version from which this text derived is known today only in an early sixteenth-century Icelandic translation. This version, *Ósvalds saga*, is indispensable for an understanding of the development of the Oswald legend on the continent, yet it is virtually unknown to scholars, despite repeated references to it in editions and studies of the German Oswald tradition. Time and again the Icelandic version has been identified as a translation of the short prose text in the legendaries. This is, however, not the case.

The present monograph is a study of the development of the legend of St. Oswald on the continent. I argue that the oldest vernacular version in the German-language area was the source of *Ósvalds saga*, a text that faithfully transmitted the biographical details of the legend as first told by Bede at the same time that it prefaced Oswald's *vita* with a coronation legend and interpolated a bridal-quest narrative that was generated by Bede's mention of Oswald's marriage to a heathen king's daughter. These innovations were most likely inspired by and composed under the influence of Clovis's baptismal legend, the bridal-quest legend of Henry and Cunegund, and the proselytizing example of both of these Germanic rulers. Despite the injection of ahistorical elements into the German legend, it nonetheless also transmitted the facts of Oswald's life, as told by Bede, and, most importantly, the facts of his death. Oswald died on the battlefield, a martyr for his faith.

This martyr legend was in my opinion the oldest vernacular legend to accompany the developing cult of the Northumbrian king in the German-language area. Once the entertaining bridal-quest plot had been introduced into the legend, it was an easy matter for the bridal-quest narrative to be severed from the rest of the legend and to develop into an independent romance, as happened in the *Münchner Oswald*. Whatever may have motivated the decision—possibly the example provided by Emperor Henry II and Cunegund—the author of this abbreviated metrical version chose to transform Oswald into a virginal confessor, that is, a saint whose heroic chastity could be interpreted as another form of martyrdom. When the motif of conjugal chastity, which first surfaced in Reginald of Durham's Latin Oswald vita but which had already been popularized on the continent in the legend of Henry and Cunegund, was introduced into the *Münchner Oswald*, it generated an entirely new conclusion inconsistent with the facts of Oswald's life: the historical martyr became a fictionalized confessor saint who, having been exhorted by Christ to practice conjugal chastity, dies in bed at the side of his wife.

*Ósvalds saga*, an early sixteenth-century Icelandic translation of a no longer extant German legend, attests that Oswald's bridal quest and conversion of the heathens were inextricably linked to one another in the earliest continental legend of the Northumbrian martyr; that a vernacular Oswald legend circulated in the German-language area that derived from and was faithful to Bede's account; and that this was a conversion legend which culminated in the proselytizing king's martyrdom. While absolute proof of the seniority of the *Ósvalds saga* version—that is, its German source—vis-à-vis the metrical version, that is, the *Münchner Oswald*, is wanting, common sense suggests that the cult of St. Oswald was introduced on the continent through a vernacular legend corresponding to the extant Latin vita in respect to the salient biographical facts, chiefly Oswald's martyrdom, rather than through a legend that silenced his violent death for the faith.

*Ósvalds saga* has been edited here and translated into English in order to make an important but rather difficult text, one laced with a goodly dose of Low German vocabulary and syntax, available to a readership not acquainted with the Icelandic legend, which is crucial to our understanding of the development of the Oswald legend on the continent. Similarly, an edition and translation of "Van Sunte Oswaldo deme konninghe," a condensation of the same German version that was the source of *Ósvalds saga*, follows the Icelandic saga.

In the course of preparing the edition and translation of *Ósvalds saga* I have become indebted to both individuals and institutions, especially the University of Illinois: for a sabbatical leave in fall 2000, which permitted me to work uninterruptedly on this project, and for released time from teaching in spring 2001; additionally, for the services of a research assistant during the academic year 2000–2001, and a generous publication subvention granted to me through the university's Research Board.

In fall 2000 and again in summer 2001 and 2002 I enjoyed the hospitality of the Stofnun Árna Magnússonar á Islandi, where resident and visiting scholars offered not only assistance with recalcitrant readings and linguistic problems in Icelandic but also valuable suggestions for conveying the text in English. I owe special thanks to Sverrir Tómasson for responding to my many queries and giving me access to his hagiographic library. I would not have had the courage to produce an edition in modern Icelandic without the unstinting help offered by Davíð Erlingsson of the Department of Icelandic Literature at the University of Iceland, who guided me through sixteenth-century Icelandic grammar, placed length marks where they were missing and removed misplaced others, and was willing to think and talk with me about the text. Whatever imperfections remain are attributable solely to me.

I am grateful to Ragnheiður Mósesdóttir, librarian at Det Arnamagnæanske Institut in Copenhagen, who provided me with photocopies of the text of *Ósvalds saga* in the manuscript Stockholm Perg. fol. nr. 3.

*Dat Passionael* has never been edited. The edition of "Van Sunte Oswaldo deme konninghe" is based on Steffan Arndes's 1492 Lübeck imprint, a copy of which was available to me at the Royal Library in Copenhagen. I was able to obtain photocopies of the pertinent texts through the good services of Det Arnamagnæanske Institut.

Finally, I am most grateful to Leslie MacCoull, who copyedited my manuscript, and the anonymous readers for their valuable comments and helpful suggestions, especially concerning my English translation of *Ósvalds saga*. The thoughtful feedback of one reader gave me the courage to stop beating about the bush and to express my conviction that the Icelandic translation represents the oldest vernacular Oswald legend on the continent.

Marianne E. Kalinke
Feast of St. Oswald

# ABBREVIATIONS


ÁBM      Ásgeir Blöndal Magnússon. *Íslensk orðsifjabók.* [Reykjavík]: Orðabók Háskólans, 1989.

AA SS      Acta Sanctorum

Bandle      Oskar Bandle. *Die Sprache der Guðbrandsbiblía : Orthographie und Laute. Formen.* Bibliotheca Arnamagnæana 17. Copenhagen: Ejnar Munksgaard, 1956.

Bede, *HE*      Bertram Colgrave and R. A. B. Mynors, eds. *Bede's Ecclesiastical History of the English People.* Oxford: Clarendon Press, 1969.

*HL*      *Der Heiligen Leben.* Vol. 1: *Der Sommerteil.* Ed. Margit Brand, Kristina Freienhagen-Baumgardt, Ruth Meyer, and Werner Williams-Krapp. Tübingen: Max Niemeyer, 1996.

*LMA*      *Lexikon des Mittelalters.* Ed. Liselotte Lutz. 9 vols. Zurich and Munich: Artemis, 1977–1998.

*LTK*      *Lexikon für Theologie und Kirche.* Ed. Josef Höfer and Karl Rahner. 2nd rev. ed. 10 vols. Freiburg: Herder, 1957–1965.

MGH      Monumenta Germaniae Historica

*MNW*      Karl Schiller and August Lübben. *Mittelniederdeutsches Wörterbuch.* 5 vols. Bremen: J. Kühtmann, 1875-1880; repr. Vaduz: Sändig, 1986.

*MO*      *Der Münchner Oswald. Mit einem Anhang: die ostschwäbische Prosabearbeitung des 15. Jahrhunderts.* Ed. Michael Curschmann. Altdeutsche Textbibliothek 76. Tübingen: Max Niemeyer, 1974.

*NT*      Jón Helgason, *Málið á nýja Testamenti Odds Gottskálkssonar.* Safn Fræðafjelagsins 7. Copenhagen: Hið íslenska Fræðafjelag, 1929.

*Pass.*      *Dat Passionael.* Lübeck: Steffen Arndes, 1492.

*Rhb.*      Agnete Loth, ed. *Reykjahólabók: Islandske helgenlegender.* Editiones Arnamagnæanæ A 15, 16. Copenhagen: Munksgaard, 1969, 1970.

*²VL*      *Die deutsche Literatur des Mittelalters. Verfasserlexikon.* 2nd rev. ed. Kurt Ruh et al. 11 vols. New York: Walter de Gruyter, 1978– .

VÓ      Veturlíði Óskarsson. *Middelnedertyske låneord i islandsk diplomsprog frem til år 1500.* Bibliotheca Arnamagnæana 43. Copenhagen: C. A. Reitzel, 2003..

W-N      Christian Westergård-Nielsen. *Låneordene i det 16. århundredes trykte islandske litteratur.* Bibliotheca Arnamagnæana 6. Copenhagen: Ejnar Munksgaard, 1946.

Wolf      Kirsten Wolf, ed. *Saga heilagrar Önnu.* Stofnun Árna Magnússonar á Íslandi 52. Reykjavík: Stofnun Árna Magnússonar á Íslandi, 2001.

# St. Oswald of Northumbria: Continental Metamorphoses

Ave, quondam rex Anglorum, nunc cohæres Angelorum:
placa nobis Regem tuum, qui te fecit civem suum.[1]

(Hail, formerly king of the Angles, now companion of
the angels: reconcile us with your King, who made you
His citizen.)

---

[1] This is a stanza in the hymn at Vespers for the vigil and the feast of St. Oswald. See P. Bayart, "Les Offices de Saint Winnoc et de Saint Oswald d'après le Manuscrit 14 de la Bibliothèque de Bergues," *Annales du Comité flamand de France* 35 (1926): 1–132, here 59, 64.

# I.

## THE TRANSLATION OF
## ST. OSWALD'S RELICS AND LEGEND

On 5 August 642, King Oswald of Northumbria (r. 634–642) was killed in the battle of Maserfelth by Penda of Mercia. Following the battle, Penda had Oswald's head and arms severed and impaled on stakes. Subsequently his head was buried in the cemetery at Lindisfarne, while his arms were sent to Bamborough; there the right arm was placed in a silver shrine, where, in fulfillment of Bishop Aidan's prophecy while Oswald was still alive, it was preserved incorrupt. The mutilated body was taken to the monastery of Bardney in Lindsey by Oswald's niece Osthryth.[2]

The earliest account of Oswald's life, death, and miracles is given by the Venerable Bede (673/674–735) in his *Historia ecclesiastica gentis anglorum* (concluded in 731). The last and longest account of Oswald's life, death, and miracles is found in an Icelandic translation of a Low German redaction of the Oswald legend, namely *Ósvalds saga*, produced ca. 1530–1540, the last decade of the Catholic period in Iceland. Between Bede's eighth-century rather factual account, interspersed in various chapters of Books 2 and 3 of the *Historia ecclesiastica*, and the Icelandic version there exists a German work, the so-called *Münchner Oswald*, thought by most scholars to be the oldest vernacular legend of St. Oswald; scholarly consensus dates the work to the end of the twelfth century.[3]

In Bede's *Historia ecclesiastica* Oswald is presented as a "most Christian king" and "a man beloved of God," a proselytizing king who "held under his sway all the peoples and kingdoms of Britain, divided among the speakers of four different languages, British, Picts, Irish, and English."[4] In a terse statement Bede informs us that Oswald stood godfather for Cynegisl, king of the West Saxons,

---

[2] For the facts relating to Oswald, see D. W. Rollason, "Oswald," in *LMA*, 6:1549–50.

[3] See Michael Curschmann, "Münchner Oswald," in *²VL*, 766–72. Curschmann states that the *Münchner Oswald* "ist der älteste und am nachhaltigsten wirksame Vertreter einer eigentümlich deutschen, breit gefächerten und im ganzen Hoch- und Spät-M[ittel]A[lter] lebendigen Erzähltradition" (766).

[4] Bede, *HE* 2.5; 3.1; "omnes nationes et prouincias Brittaniae, quae in quattuor linguas, id est Brettonum Pictorum Scottorum et Anglorum, diuisae sunt, in dicione accepit" (3.6). References are to *Bede's Ecclesiastical History of the English People*, ed. Bertram Colgrave and R. A. B. Mynors (Oxford: Clarendon Press, 1969).

"the same man whose daughter Oswald was later to receive as his wife."[5] Upon Oswald's death at the hands of the pagan Penda many miracles occurred.

The martyred king's cult spread rapidly. Indeed, by the time of Bede's writing, Oswald's fame as a saint, Bede noted, had reached beyond Britain. Bede reports that "not only did the fame of this renowned king spread through all parts of Britain but the beams of his healing light also spread across the ocean and reached the realms of Germany and Ireland."[6] According to Bishop Acca, a good friend of Bede, Willibrord, archbishop of the Frisians, was wont to recount the miracles that occurred wherever Oswald's relics were venerated in Frisia (3.13). While Alan Thacker remarks on the evidence "that English and Frisian liturgical material combined to make knowledge of Oswald as a Christian saint comparatively widespread in Frisia and parts of Germany along the Rhine in the eighth and ninth centuries," he noted that this is "not, however, proof of an active cult."[7] When Athelstan's half-sister Edith went to Germany to marry the future emperor Otto I in 929/930, "she was described as 'of the blessed line of Oswald'" and her marriage thus reinforced diffusion of Oswald's cult in Germany.[8] In 1038, during the abbacy of Rumoldus (1031–1068), the Benedictine abbey of Bergues-St-Winnoc in French Flanders received relics of several saints, including those of Oswald.[9] At this time Drogo († 1084), one of the monks of St-Winnoc, composed a *Vita Oswaldi*, drawn largely from Bede but also augmented with his own reflections, exhortations to the monks, and slight embellishments of incidents in the martyred king's vita. In the prologue Drogo is quite specific as to what he has done: the vita has been written in response to his fellow monks'

---

[5] "eumque de lauacro exeuntem suscepisse, ac pulcherrimo prorsus et Deo digno consortio, cuius erat filiam accepturus in coniugem, ipsum prius secunda generatione Deo dedicatum sibi accepit in filium" (3.7). According to the twelfth-century "Vita S. Oswaldi" by Reginald of Durham, her name was Kyneburga. See "Vita S. Oswaldi Regis et Martyris," in *Symeonis monachi Opera Omnia. Historia Ecclesiæ Dunhelmensis,* ed. Thomas Arnold (London: Longmans, 1882–1885; repr. Nendeln and Wiesbaden: Kraus, 1965), 1:349.

[6] "Nec solum inclyti fama uiri Brittaniae fines lustrauit uniuersos, sed etiam trans oceanum longe radios salutiferae lucis spargens Germaniae simul et Hiberniae partes attigit. Denique reuerentissimus antistes Acca solet referre, quia, cum Romam uadens apud sanctissimum Fresonum gentis archiepiscopum Uilbrordum cum suo antistite Uilfrido moraretur, crebro eum audierit de mirandis, quae ad reliquias eiusdem reuerentissimi regis in illa prouincia gesta fuerint, narrare" (3.13).

[7] Alan Thacker, *"Membra Disjecta:* The Division of the Body and the Diffusion of the Cult," in *Oswald: Northumbrian King to European Saint,* ed. Clare Stancliffe and Eric Cambridge (Stamford: Paul Watkins, 1995), 97–127, here 117.

[8] Thacker, *"Membra Disjecta,"* 121, 123.

[9] E. P. Baker, "St. Oswald and his Church at Zug," *Archaeologia* 93 (1949): 103–23, here 106, n. 5.

request to bring together in one work the life, martyrdom, and miracles of St. Oswald.[10] Additionally he produced a rhymed office of St. Oswald some time between 1058 and 1070, copies of which reached the German-language area, as attested, for example, in a thirteenth-century manuscript in St. Gall.[11]

Relics of St. Oswald came to southern Germany when in 1071 Judith of Flanders (c. 1027–1094), the widow of Earl Tostig of Northumbria, the brother of King Harold Godwinsson, married Duke Welf IV († 1101) of Bavaria.[12] She brought into her German marriage precious objects, including manuscripts, from England, Flanders, and northern France. In 1094, the year of her death, she bequeathed to the monastery of Weingarten not only liturgical manuscripts but also, more importantly in this context, relics of St. Oswald—"arcellam fabrefactam, plenam reliquiis sancti Oswaldi"[13]—who came to be greatly venerated in the twelfth century and in 1217 joined St. Martin as patron saint of Weingarten.[14] The relics of St. Oswald were presumably accompanied by a *vita Oswaldi*, perhaps Drogo's composition. Subsequently a great number of texts in honor of St. Oswald were composed, including a rhymed office, hymns, prayers, and a sequence.[15] A "vita sancti Osvualdi" in a manuscript produced in Weingarten in the last quarter of the twelfth century compiles, like Drogo, material from Bede relating to Oswald. Unlike Drogo's *vita*, however, this text does not contain the Flemish monk's exhortations to his fellow monks or his amplifications vis-à-vis Bede,

---

[10] ". . . vestræque petitioni voluntatique, fratres, satisfaciens, vitam martyriumque sancti Oswaldi regis, seu miracula ejusdem in uno opere conjunxi" (94). References are to *Acta Sanctorum.* Augusti, 2, 5–12, Aug. 5: 83–103: "De S. Oswaldo rege ac mart."

[11] Bayart, "Les Offices de Saint Winnoc et de Saint Oswald," 57–67; see esp. 33–36.

[12] For a summary of the spread of Oswald's cult in the German-language area to the twelfth century, see Michael Curschmann, *Der Münchener Oswald und die deutsche spielmännische Epik. Mit einem Exkurs zur Kultgeschichte und Dichtungstradition,* Münchener Texte und Untersuchungen zur deutschen Literatur des Mittelalters 6 (Munich: C. H. Beck, 1964), 169–74.

[13] "De Inventione et Translatione Sanguinis Domini," MGH, Scriptores 15, 923; this is cited by Baker, "St. Oswald and his Church at Zug," 106.

[14] See Th. Zotz, "Weingarten," in *LMA*, 8:2132–33; *Weingarten. Von den Anfängen bis zur Gegenwart,* ed. Norbert Kruse et al. (Weingarten: Biberacher Verlagsdruckerei, 1992), 117, 127–29; Dagmar Ó Riain-Raedel, "Edith, Judith, Mathilda: The Role of Royal Ladies in the Propagation of the Continental Cult," in *Oswald: Northumbrian King to European Saint,* ed. Stancliffe and Cambridge, 216–22. Baker reports that a century before Oswald became a patron saint of Weingarten, a chapel was dedicated to him in 1129 in Petershausen, founded in 983 by monks from Einsiedeln ("St. Oswald and his Church at Zug," 104).

[15] *Weingarten,* ed. Kruse et al., 117.

e.g., in recounting Oswald's virtues.[16] Twelfth-century manuscripts, some containing Drogo's *vita*, attest that the Latin legend of St. Oswald was well known throughout the southern German-language area, especially in Regensburg.[17] In the life of Bl. Jutta of Disibodenberg (1092–1136), Hildegard von Bingen's spiritual mother, we even read that St. Oswald appeared to Jutta in a vision shortly before her death to inform her that during this, her last illness, she would die.[18]

Not only did Latin *vitae* of the saint abound but Oswald's life was also vernacularized. Two German versions of his legend have been transmitted, one a metrical romance, the *Münchner/Wiener Oswald*, the other a prose legend current in the most popular vernacular legendary of the Middle Ages, *Der Heiligen Leben*. The romance version departs from Bede's, and consequently also Drogo's, *vita*, inasmuch as the miracles are not transmitted. More strikingly, the saint of the metrical romance does not die a martyr's death. The prose version, however, adheres closely to the account known from Bede: it both transmits the miracle sequence and depicts Oswald's death as a martyr in his struggle against pagan forces.

The German versions transmit an innovation, however, inasmuch as the fact of Oswald's marriage to the daughter of the erstwhile pagan King Cynegisl is expanded into a full-fledged bridal-quest narrative. It is the quest for a pagan princess and the conversion of her people that generates the plot and serves as focal point of the narrative in the vernacular legend. This is especially the case in the metrical romance, for in this version the saint dies a confessor's death at the side of his wife in bed. There is no encounter with Penda's heathen forces and consequently no martyrdom. Therefore, the posthumous miracles recounted by Bede, several attested at the site of Oswald's martyrdom, are also missing.

The interpolated and dominating bridal-quest narrative in the vernacular legend of St. Oswald has led scholars to classify the metrical romance with a group of anonymous, pre-courtly bridal-quest epics known as *Spielmannsepen*, 'minstrel epics'. Although the designation 'minstrel epic' is now generally used with

---

[16] See Wolfgang Irtenkauf, *Stuttgarter Zimelien. Württembergische Landesbibliothek. Aus den Schätzen ihrer Handschriftensammlung* (Stuttgart: Württembergische Landesbibliothek, 1985), 36. Irtenkauf states that the manuscript opens with the lives of Sts. Martin and Oswald, but this is not the case. The "Vita sancti Oswaldi" is found on fols. 90r–99v. The text is incomplete and breaks off at the beginning of the last miracle account. It also contains material not found in Drogo, for instead of relating only the Cynegisl section of Bede, *HE* 3.7, the manuscript continues with the rest of the chapter, even though it has nothing to do with Oswald. I am grateful to the Württembergische Landesbibliothek for making a microfilm of the "Vita sancti Oswaldi" available to me.

[17] See Ó Riain-Raedel, "Edith, Judith, Mathilda," 225–27.

[18] Anna Silvas, *Jutta and Hildegard: The Biographical Sources*, Medieval Women: Texts and Contexts 1 (Turnhout: Brepols, 1998), 78.

the modifier 'so-called' for want of evidence of the existence of such literarily gifted minstrels, scholars posit the production of this group of bridal-quest narratives in the twelfth century, despite the fact that they are extant only in late medieval manuscripts.[19] The metrical *Oswald*, rather than the prose legend, is thought to represent the oldest form of the vernacular legend, the version from which all the others ultimately derive. Consequently, the prototext is assumed to have been a bridal-quest/conversion narrative lacking the account of Oswald's martyrdom and devoid of the miracles. From this protolegend are thought to derive the two fifteenth-century redactions, the *Wiener Oswald* and the *Münchner Oswald*, the latter considered to reflect better the original legend. This metrical version, according to the current scholarly position, is the source of the prose version in *Der Heiligen Leben* (1396/1410), which in turn was translated into Low German and is transmitted in the Low German legendary *Dat Passionael* (1478). Finally, this Low German version was supposed to have been translated into Icelandic and is known as *Ósvalds saga* (ca. 1530). The current scholarly position on the development of the legend can be illustrated schematically as follows:

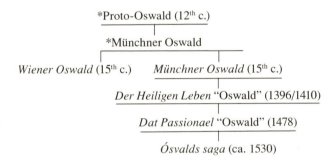

The above scheme visualizes the development of the vernacular legend chronologically. If one now replicates the above from the perspective of content, the development is as follows: A bridal-quest/conversion legend that concludes with a wedding feast and a decision by the couple to lead a chaste married life (*Münchner Oswald*) is the source of a bridal-quest/conversion/martyr legend that concludes with a miracle sequence. In the former, contrary to historical fact, the

---

[19] For a recent summary of the problematic nature of both the designation and the origin of *Spielmannsepen*, see Gisela Vollmann-Profe, *Geschichte der deutschen Literatur von den Anfängen bis zum Beginn der Neuzeit, I/2: Wiederbeginn volkssprachiger Schriftlichkeit im hohen Mittelalter (1050/60–1160/70)*, 2nd rev. ed. (Tübingen: Niemeyer, 1994), 170–75.

saint dies in bed; in the latter he dies on the battlefield, in conformity with the earliest legend recounted by Bede.

Given the lively cult of St. Oswald in the German-language area, it is curious at best that the veneration of this saint, unlike that of other popular German saints, such as Henry and Cunegund, should not early on have been accompanied by a vernacular legend containing evidence in support of Oswald's sanctity; and indeed that the vernacular legend should disseminate a fiction at odds with the facts of Oswald's life and death as transmitted in the Latin legend. The above stemma suggests that late in the development of the vernacular legend, the fictional confessor saint, as known from the metrical romance (*Münchner Oswald*), underwent a transformation in the prose version, so that he regained his martyr status. The German prose version is, however, we shall argue, a significantly condensed account of an older version, which conformed to the Icelandic translation, a text more than twice as long as the German prose legend. Yet this early sixteenth-century Icelandic version has repeatedly and incorrectly been identified as a translation of the prose legend "Van sunte Oswaldo deme konninghe" in *Dat Passionael*.[20]

The Icelandic *Ósvalds saga* plays a central role in our understanding of the vernacular legend of the Northumbrian martyr king. The study of the legend's origins and development will therefore commence with what would appear to be its end, *Ósvalds saga*, the last vernacular representative of the German legend.

---

[20] References are to *Dat Passionael* (Lübeck: Steffen Arndes, 1492), where the Oswald legend is found on fols. C.ii.c–C.v.b.

# II.
## ÓSVALDS SAGA

The earliest record of the legend of St. Oswald in Iceland is found in *Breta sögur*, the Icelandic translation of Geoffrey of Monmouth's *Historia regum Britanniae*, thought to have been translated in the early thirteenth century.[21] A short account of Oswald's life, death, and miracles is found in the manuscript AM 544, 4to, the so-called *Hauksbók* redaction of *Breta sögur*, which was produced in the fourteenth century.

> Eftir hann tok ʀiki en helgi Osvalldr konvngr yfir Norðhvmrv landi. hann var yfir þvi riki .ix. ár, hann var friðgiarn ok fályndr avʀ við fatœkia menn. Kaðall gieck miok a (riki) hans ok letti Osvalldr konvngr vndan til Skotlandz þar er mœttiz ok England. þetta spyr Kaðall ok gerir siþan her a hendr Osvalldi konvngi. var þar formaðr fyri Pendan konvngr. ok er þetta spyʀ Osvalldr konvngr let hann setia niðr a einvm velli kross vars herra Iesv Christi. hann bað þangat sœkia alla sina menn ok bað þa falla a kne ok biðia almatkan gvð at þeir vegi sigr a sinvm vvínvm. þeir gerðv sem hann bavð. Gengv siþan i bardaga ok gerði gvð þat eftir þeira bœn fyri verðleika ens helga Osvallz konvngs at Bretar flyðv. En er Kaðall fra þetta varð hann reiðr miok ok samnar her ok for moti Osvalldi konvngi ok tokz þar harðr bardagi. hafþi Osvalldr ecki liðs við. En er Osvalldr sa at engi viðrstaða mvndi verða settiz hann niðr ok sa i gavpnir ser[22] ok bað til gvðs fyri ollvm þeim er þar borðvz ok siþan let hann þar lif sitt ok for sva til almattix gvðs ok segia menn at Pendan yrði hanvm at bana. flyði þa allt lið hans þat er lifit þa. En efter bardagan geck at konvnginvm ein gamall maðr af monnvm Kaðals hann hafþi fengit mikit sar a hendi. hann skriðnaði ok stack niðr hendinni i bloð Osvallz konvngs ok er hann stoð vpp var heil hondin. margar iartegnir ok storar gerði gvð fyri hans verðleika þo at þær se eigi her ritaðar.[23]

---

[21] Stefanie Würth, *Der "Antikenroman" in der isländischen Literatur des Mittelalters. Eine Untersuchung zur Übersetzung und Rezeption lateinischer Literatur im Norden*, Beiträge zur nordischen Philologie 26 (Basel: Helbing & Lichtenhahn, 1998), 80–82.

[22] The expression "ok sa i gavpnir ser" can mean either that he placed his head in his hands or that he sat with the palms of his hands turned upwards. I choose the latter translation in keeping with Bede, *HE* 3.12.

[23] *Breta sögur*, in *Hauksbók udgiven efter de Arnamagnæanske Håndskrifter No. 371, 544 og 675, 4° samt forskellige Papirhåndskrifter* (Copenhagen: Det kongelige nordiske Oldskrift-Selskab, 1892–1896), chap. 49: "Af Osvalldi konvnge," 298–99.

(After him the holy king Oswald became ruler over Northumbria. He ruled this realm for nine years. He was peace-loving and constant, generous toward the poor. Cædwalla attacked his kingdom severely and King Oswald withdrew to Scotland, where it borders England. Cædwalla learned this and subsequently assembled an army against King Oswald. King Penda was at its head. And when King Oswald learned this, he had the cross of Our Lord Jesus Christ raised on a plain. He asked all his men to assemble there and bade them fall on their knees and ask God to grant them victory over their enemies. They did as he asked. They then went into battle and on account of the worthiness of the holy king Oswald God answered their prayer so that the Britons fled. But when Cædwalla learned this he became very angry and assembles an army and attacked King Oswald and a hard battle ensued. Oswald did not have the army for this. And when Oswald saw that he would not be able to withstand them, he sat down and, with the palms of his hands turned upwards, he prayed to God for all of those who were fighting there, and after this he lost his life there, and thus he went to Almighty God, and people say that Penda was the cause of his death. Then his entire army fled that was still alive. But after the battle an old man, one of Cædwalla's men, went over to the king; he had received a large wound on his arm. He slipped and dipped his arm into the blood of King Oswald and when he got up his hand was healed. God wrought there many great miracles on account of Oswald's merits, though they are not written down here.)

The miracle mentioned here is found neither in Bede nor in the known redactions of Geoffrey of Monmouth's *Historia regum Britanniae*.[24] It is likely that this miracle, like other apparent additions in *Breta sögur*, was found in the manuscript from which the translation was made. As Stefanie Würth has noted, numerous manuscripts of Geoffrey's *Historia* circulated with commentaries, and the above miracle, like other additions in *Breta sögur*, was presumably found in one of these glossed manuscripts.[25]

Oswald's death is recorded in various Icelandic annals, for example in the so-called "Annales regii," which list the "Passio sancti Osvaldi regis filij Elfredi regis Northanhimbrorum," and, immediately following, provides a notice concerning "Kinegils rex Anglorum . . . . Hunc baptizauit sanctus Birinus episcopus.

---

[24] See *The Historia Regum Britanniae of Geoffrey of Monmouth*, ed. Acton Griscom (London: Longmans, 1929; repr. Geneva: Slatkine Reprints, 1977), 525–26. *Breta sögur* has been translated into German; see Stefanie Würth, *Die Saga von den britischen Königen*, in *Isländische Antikensagas*, vol. I (Munich: Eugen Diederichs Verlag, 1996), 51–142.

[25] Stefanie Würth, *Der "Antikenroman,"* 77–78.

quem Honorius papa ad predicandum misit."[26] While there is evidence of the veneration of St. Edmund, the English martyr king († 649), in Iceland,[27] this is not the
case with St. Oswald. Yet that he was known and esteemed in Iceland is attested
by a strange and erroneous bit of genealogical lore in *Njáls saga*, where the great-
great-grandmother of Guðmundr inn ríki, one of the most powerful chieftains of
Iceland who appears in any number of Icelandic sagas, is identified as "Jórunn in
óborna, dóttur Ósvalds konungs ins helga" (Jórunn the Unborn,[28] the daughter of
King Oswald the Saint). Her mother in turn, thus the saga, was Bera, the daughter
of King Edward the Saint. As Einar Ól. Sveinsson wryly noted, given Oswald's
death in 642, this is hardly likely.[29]

It was to be several centuries, however, before an Icelandic version of the legend of St. Oswald was written down. The eve of the Reformation in Iceland saw
the production of a monumental legendary which was not only the last of the Icelandic legendaries but also the last of the great medieval legendaries of Europe.
*Reykjahólabók*, the Book of Reykjahólar, as the legendary has become known
after the place of its origin in the Westfjords of Iceland, has singular value for
our understanding of hagiography in the late Middle Ages inasmuch as twenty-
two of its twenty-five legends are translations of Low German texts that are no
longer extant. They presumably circulated exclusively in manuscript, for there is
no evidence that printed Low German versions of the Icelandic legends had ever
existed. Nor do we know how the compiler of *Reykjahólabók* came to be in pos-
session of the Low German texts that he made available to his countrymen in
translation.

*Reykjahólabók* was written by Björn Þorleifsson († ca. 1554), who was probably the wealthiest Icelander of his time. He belonged to a family well known
for its literary interests, the members of which produced nineteen books in the
period 1420 to 1560.[30] With the exception of Björn Þorleifsson's literary œuvre,
the manuscripts written by the several generations of this family contain copies

---

[26] "Passion of the holy king Oswald, son of King Ælfred, of Northumbria. Cynegisl,
king of the Angles . . . was baptized by the holy bishop Birinus, whom Pope Honorius
sent there to preach": Gustav Storm, ed., *Islandske Annaler indtil 1578* (Christiania: Det
norske historiske Kildeskriftfond, 1888), 93. See also 10, 42, 168, 243, 309. The notice
about Cynegisl derives from Bede, *HE* 3.7.

[27] See Margaret Cormack, *The Saints in Iceland: Their Veneration from the Conversion to 1400*, Subsidia Hagiographica 78 (Brussels: Société des Bollandistes, 1994), 94.

[28] 'Unborn' means born by Caesarean section rather than the normal way.

[29] Einar Ól. Sveinsson, ed., *Brennu-Njáls saga* (Reykjavík: Hið íslenzka fornritafé-
lag, 1954), 284, n. 5.

[30] Marianne E. Kalinke, *The Book of Reykjahólar: The Last of the Great Medieval
Legendaries* (Toronto: University of Toronto Press, 1996), 30–31.

of texts already existing in Iceland, mostly of indigenous literature. In addition
to the legends in *Reykjahólabók*, fragments of four other saints' lives are extant
in Björn's hand, suggesting that he had also produced another legendary, one devoted to the apostles and evangelists.[31] Furthermore, we possess his fragmentary
translation of the Book of Revelation, a translation from German.[32] That the texts
in *Reykjahólabók* were written in Björn Þorleifsson's hand is beyond a doubt,
while circumstantial but nonetheless compelling evidence suggests that he was
not only the scribe but also the translator of the legendary.[33] It is more likely than
not that Björn Þorleifsson was the 'author' of *Reykjahólabók*, that is, its scribe,
translator, editor, and compiler.

The Icelandic legend of St. Oswald, *Ósvalds saga*, is one of the twenty-five
legends in the manuscript Stockholm perg. fol. nr. 3, the so-called *Reykjahólabók*,
preserved in the Royal Library in Stockholm.[34] With the exception of three texts
that are copies of already existing Icelandic translations from the Latin—*Ambro-
sius saga, Laurencius saga*,[35] and *Stefanus saga*[36]—the legends derive from Low
German. They include three legends relating to the life of Christ (the legends of
St. Anne and the Virgin Mary, the Three Wise Men, and Lazarus); seven legends devoted to martyrs, several of them the so-called Holy Helpers (Christopher,
Erasmus, George, Lawrence, Oswald, Sebastian, and Stephen); five Doctors of
the Eastern and Western Church (Ambrose, Augustine, Gregory the Great, Jerome, John Chrysostom); two popes (the aforementioned Gregory and Silvester);
one bishop (Servatius); two friars (the Augustinian Nicholas of Tolentino and the
eponymous founder of the Dominican Order); one desert father (Anthony) and
one hermit (Roch); one martyr king (the aforenamed Oswald); one emperor (the

---

[31] See Mariane Overgaard, ed., *The History of the Cross-Tree Down to Christ's Passion*, Editiones Arnamagnæanæ B 26 (Copenhagen: Munksgaard, 1968), xcix–ciii.

[32] Agnete Loth, "Et islandsk fragment fra reformationstiden. AM 667, x, 4to," *Opuscula* 4, Bibliotheca Arnamagnæana 30 (Copenhagen: Munksgaard, 1970), 25–30.

[33] See Agnete Loth, ed., *Reykjahólabók: Islandske helgenlegender*, Editiones Arnamagnæanæ A 15 (Copenhagen: Munksgaard, 1969), 1:xxix; xxxix–xl; Kalinke, *The Book
of Reykjahólar*, 29–33.

[34] "Osvaldr," in *Reykjahólabók: Islandske helgenlegender*, 1:71–95. Subsequent references are to *Rhb*. In the introduction to her edition, Loth traces the history of references
to and comments about Stockholm 3 fol. I am indebted to her observations for the following. For a fuller accounting of older scholarship and the history of the manuscript, see
*Rhb* 1:xlii–lii.

[35] Marianne E. Kalinke, "Þa kom þar þessi forbrende Lavrencivs: Two versions of
*Laurencius saga*," *Maal og Minne* (1994): 113–34.

[36] Marianne E. Kalinke, "Stefanus saga in Reykjahólabók," *Gripla* 9 (1995):133–87;
eadem, *The Book of Reykjahólar*, 80–95.

aforenamed Henry II) and one empress (Cunegund); and, finally, the apocryphal Barlaam and Josaphat, Gregorius 'peccator', and the Seven Sleepers.

The source of the translated legends in *Reykjahólabók* was until recently thought to have been *Dat Passionael*, the Low German version of *Der Heiligen Leben*. Before Agnete Loth edited the entire Icelandic codex in 1969–1970, only one of its legends had been available in an earlier edition, namely *Ósvalds saga*, which Jón Sigurðsson published in 1854 with a facing translation into Danish.[37] He seems to have considered *Ósvalds saga* an Icelandic composition rather than a translation. He remarked, for example, that the introduction of material not known from Bede into the Icelandic translation of Geoffrey of Monmouth's *Historia regum Britanniae* suggests that several legends about St. Oswald were known in Iceland ("Saga Ósvalds" 17). Similarly, he pointed to the extensive connections between Iceland and England in the first half of the fifteenth century, and concluded by positing extensive knowledge of English legends in Iceland. He thought that Iceland had known the legend of St. Oswald in three English versions: the one reported by Bede; a collection of miracle tales upon which the translator of *Breta sögur* (i.e., the Icelandic translation of the *Historia regum Britanniae*) drew; and the legend that is the immediate source of *Ósvalds saga* (18). Jón Sigurðsson commented on the manner in which the author of *Ósvalds saga* appears to have composed the legend. He considered it reasonable to suppose that the Icelandic author had available, as he worked, written legendaries containing complete *vitae* of St. Oswald; sometimes these agreed in their details with each other, at other times they did not. Access to two or more legendaries, Jón assumed, would explain the author's repeated references to deviating accounts (18–19). As reasonable as Jón's explanation for the origin of *Ósvalds saga* may seem, it was wrong, for the saga, as we shall see, is a translation of a Low German legend.

Once *Ósvalds saga* had been edited by Jón Sigurðsson, it became a source of considerable interest to Germanists. As Agnete Loth pointed out in the introduction to her edition (*Rhb.* 1:xlviii–xlix), Ignaz V. Zingerle was the first to advance the idea that *Ósvalds saga* derives from the German legend found in the widely disseminated legendary *Der Heiligen Leben*. In fact, Zingerle stated that the saga corresponded so exactly to the German version in this monumental compilation that he considered it "eine Uebersetzung der alten deutschen Legende."[38] The same thesis of a High German source was enunciated, but in extended form, by

---

[37]Jón Sigurðsson, "Saga Ósvalds konúngs hins helga," *Annaler for nordisk Oldkyndighed og Historie* (1854): 3–91; the edition and translation are on 24–91.

[38]I. V. Zingerle, *Die Oswaldlegende und ihre Beziehung zur deutschen Mythologie* (Stuttgart and Munich: Scheitlin, 1856), 87, note.

Anton Edzardi in 1876.[39] Despite his conviction that *Ósvalds saga* was translated from the German legend, Edzardi noted that many discrepancies and apparent interpolations in the saga coincide with text known from German redactions of the tale that are older than the version in *Der Heiligen Leben*. Some of these deviations correspond to passages in the *Münchner Oswald*,[40] yet there is also additional text in *Ósvalds saga*, text not found in the Munich redaction, and Edzardi concluded that the saga derives from an older, more complete version of the legend.[41] A year later C. R. Unger included in the introduction to his edition of Old Norse-Icelandic saints' lives an apologia in the form of a footnote for not having made use of the codex Stockholm perg. 3 fol., that is, *Reykjahólabók*.[42] His justification for the omission was the language, which he no longer considered Old Icelandic. He went on to remark that the book was presumably translated from a Low German—as opposed to Edzardi's High German—legendary. In an essay entitled "Om Osvalds saga," published in 1880, Oskar Klockhoff continued the discussion initiated by Edzardi, but came to the conclusion "that the Icelandic Osvalds saga had no other source than the Low German *Passionael*, and that deviations from it are the translator's own arbitrary additions."[43] Klockhoff thus denied the possibility of a source other than the text found in the legendary; furthermore, in accord with Unger, he identified the source as the Low German (*Dat Passionael*)—not the High German (*Der Heiligen Leben*)—compilation. In 1907 Georg Baesecke sided with Klockhoff when he wrote that the saga is a translation of the legend in the Low German *Passionael*.[44] At this point the discussion

---

[39] A. Edzardi, *Untersuchungen über das Gedicht von St. Oswald* (Hannover: Carl Rümpler, 1876), 3–4.

[40] The German metrical *Oswald* is extant in two versions, the one edited by Michael Curschmann, *Der Münchner Oswald. Mit einem Anhang: die ostschwäbische Prosabearbeitung des 15. Jahrhunderts,* Altdeutsche Textbibliothek 76 (Tübingen: Max Niemeyer, 1974), the other edited by Georg Baesecke, *Der Wiener Oswald* (Heidelberg: Carl Winter, 1912).

[41] Edzardi, *Untersuchungen*, 5–8. "Die übereinstimmungen erklären sich also wol daraus, daß die *hauptquelle des sagaschreibers eine ältere vollständigere recension der legende war*" (8; emphasis in original).

[42] *Heilagra Manna søgur* (Christiania: B. M. Bentzen, 1877), ii, note.

[43] Oskar Klockhoff, "Om Osvalds saga," in idem, *Små Bidrag till nordiska Literaturhistorien under Medeltiden* (Upsala: E. Edquist, 1880), 1–22, here 17: "att den isländska Osvaldssagan icke haft någon annan källa än det lågtyska passionalet, och att afvikelserna därifrån äro öfversättarens egna, godtyckliga tillägg."

[44] Georg Baesecke, ed., *Der Münchener Oswald. Text und Abhandlung* (Breslau: Marcus, 1707; repr. Hildesheim: Olms, 1977), 221, n. 2: "Auch ich halte für wahrscheinlich, daß **n** [Ósvalds saga] eine Übersetzung aus dem niederdeutschen Passional ist. . . . Edzardi ist durch Klockhoff widerlegt."

of *Ósvalds saga*, and implicitly of *Reykjahólabók*, came to a standstill. It was not revived until the 1960s when Ole Widding and Hans Bekker-Nielsen published their important studies of *Reykjahólabók*.[45] They too posited the Low German *Passionael* as the chief source of all but one of the translated legends (St. Anne) in *Reykjahólabók*. They too interpreted discrepancies between the Low German and Icelandic texts as the work of the translator. Subsequent scholarship on the transmission of the Oswald legend in the German-language area came to rely on the studies of the two Danish scholars and has repeatedly taken the position that *Ósvalds saga* derives from the *Passionael*.

A detailed study of the translated legends in *Reykjahólabók* and comparison with German antecedents other than *Der Heiligen Leben* has shown, however, that the Icelandic versions, all of which are much longer accounts, are translations not of the short texts in the prose legendary but most likely of the very sources of those texts.[46] In other words, the legends that were condensed by the compiler of *Der Heiligen Leben* in all probability corresponded to the texts that the compiler and translator of *Reykjahólabók* knew in Low German translation. That is the case with *Ósvalds saga*.

The following comparison of *Ósvalds saga* with "Van sunte Oswaldo deme konninghe" in *Dat Passionael* will show on the one hand that there exists a relationship between the Low German and Icelandic legends, but on the other that the Low German text cannot have been the source of the Icelandic translation.

---

[45]Ole Widding and Hans Bekker-Nielsen, "En senmiddelalderlig legendesamling," *Maal og Minne* (1960): 105–28; eidem, "Low German Influence on Late Icelandic Hagiography," *Germanic Review* 37 (1962): 237–62.

[46] See Kalinke, *The Book of Reykjahólar*, esp. 51–77.

# III.
## RELATIONSHIP OF THE LOW GERMAN AND ICELANDIC OSWALD LEGENDS

The German prose legend of St. Oswald is found in *Der Heiligen Leben*[47] and its Low German translation *Dat Passionael*. To judge by its dissemination and impact, *Der Heiligen Leben* is the most important vernacular collection of saints' lives in the Western Middle Ages. The work, which originally included two hundred fifty-one texts, is extant in one hundred ninety-seven manuscripts as well as thirty-three High German and eight Low German imprints.[48] According to Werner Williams-Krapp, *Der Heiligen Leben* was most likely composed between 1396 and 1410 in the context of a reform of the Dominican women's monastery in Nürnberg.[49] The legends in *Der Heiligen Leben*, which were probably intended for reading in the refectory, are drastically reduced versions of older texts.[50] The legends abbreviate their sources so as to transmit the barest of facts. There is no interest in plumbing a character's depths nor in determining the motivation for behavior; dialogue is avoided in favor of third-person narrative; hypotaxis is eschewed in favor of a paratactic style that mimics the undifferentiated presentation of narrative detail.[51] At times the condensation is so drastic and abrupt as to result in an incomprehensible or illogical sequence of events. Werner Williams-Krapp aptly characterized the legends in *Der Heiligen Leben* as "abbreviierte, unkommentierte, zumeist auch völlig enthistorisierte und entrhetorisierte Legendenfassungen."[52] While the

---

[46] See Kalinke, *The Book of Reykjahólar*, esp. 51–77.

[47] "Oswald," in *Der Heiligen Leben*, vol. I: *Der Sommerteil*, ed. Margit Brand, Kristina Freienhagen-Baumgardt, Ruth Meyer, and Werner Williams-Krapp (Tübingen: Max Niemeyer, 1996), 358–68. Subsequent references to the *HL* legend are to this edition.

[48] Werner Williams-Krapp, *Die deutschen und niederländischen Legendare des Mittelalters: Studien zu ihrer Überlieferungs-, Text- und Wirkungsgeschichte* (Tübingen: Max Niemeyer, 1986), 188.

[49] Williams-Krapp, *Die deutschen und niederländischen Legendare*, 300.

[50] Williams-Krapp, *Die deutschen und niederländischen Legendare*, 272.

[51] On the basis of the legends of Henry and Cunegund, George, and Gregorius 'peccator', Volker Mertens summarized the character of the legends as follows: "Kürzung auf die Summa facti, Abbau von individualisierenden Darstellungsmomenten, Ausklammerung einer differenzierten Problematik und im Stilistischen eine vergleichbare Tendenz zur syntaktischen Reihung mit Nivellierung komplexer Abhängigkeitsverhältnisse" : "Verslegende und Prosalegendar. Zur Prosafassung von Legendenromanen in 'Der Heiligen Leben'," in *Poesie und Gebrauchsliteratur im deutschen Mittelalter, Würzburger Colloquium 1978*, ed. V. Honemann et al. (Tübingen: Niemeyer, 1979), 265–89, here 287.

[52] Williams-Krapp, *Die deutschen und niederländischen Legendare des Mittelalters*, 367.

sources of a number of texts in the legendary have not been identified,[53] German scholars nonetheless believe that the greater part of the prose Oswald legend derives from the metrical *Münchner Oswald*,[54] and consequently also *Ósvalds saga*, since, it is claimed, the Icelandic version is translated from the *Passionael*. This is, however, not the case, as will subsequently be demonstrated.

That there exists a relationship between "Van sunte Oswaldo deme konninghe" in *Dat Passionael* and *Ósvalds saga* is beyond a doubt. The Icelandic saga is rife with German loan translations and loan words, which are in some instances hapax legomena in Icelandic and comprehensible only if one knows German.[55] The word *örlög*, for example, recurs throughout the text, but not in its normal Icelandic meaning of 'fate' but rather to mean 'battle', as in Low German. Although the Low German cognate *orloge, orloch* is not found in any corresponding passage in the *Passionael*, the word must have occurred in the source text for Björn Þorleifsson to have been misled into using the Icelandic cognate but in its Low German meaning. Twice the expression *til friða* occurs in the text; while the phrase *til friðar* 'for the sake of peace' does exist in Icelandic, this is not the meaning in our text, which seems to construe the noun as a gen. pl. The phrase *til friðs*, deriving from Low German *tovreden*, is attested in sixteenth-century Icelandic imprints with the meaning of 'at ease', 'satisfied', 'content'.[56] The first time the expression occurs in *Ósvalds saga*, the corresponding passage in the *Passionael* writes: "wes guedes modes" (C.ii.d) 'be in good spirits', which does not solve the puzzle as to how the Icelandic phrase was generated, but the second

[53] Williams-Krapp, *Die deutschen und niederländischen Legendare des Mittelalters*, 269–92.

[54] Curschmann, *Der Münchener Oswald und die deutsche spielmännische Epik*, 206–9. Curschmann's publications are repeatedly cited as the source of the opinion that the prose legend derives primarily from the *Münchner Oswald* but with additional material from Bede. Hence the identification of the source of the Oswald legend in *Der Heiligen Leben* in Williams-Krapp, *Die deutschen und niederländischen Legendare des Mittelalters*, 284.

[55] The case is similar in a sixteenth-century translation of a Low German legend of St. Anne. See Kirsten Wolf, ed., *Saga heilagrar Önnu*, Stofnun Árna Magnússonar á Íslandi 52 (Reykjavík: Stofnun Árna Magnússonar á Íslandi, 2001), cxv–cxxxvi. I am grateful to Kirsten Wolf for having made this edition available to me in proof. References to *Ósvalds saga* are to the edition in modern Icelandic orthography published here. For a justification of this procedure and the editorial principles, see IX: The Edition of *Ósvalds saga*, 105 ff. below.

[56] See Christian Westergård-Nielsen, *Låneordene i det 16. århundredes trykte islandske litteratur*, Bibliotheca Arnamagnæana 6 (Copenhagen: Ejnar Munksgaard, 1946), 134 (hereafter W-N); Oskar Bandle, *Die Sprache der Guðbrandsbiblía: Orthographie und Laute. Formen*, Bibliotheca Arnamagnæana 17 (Copenhagen: Ejnar Munksgaard, 1956), 239, 319 (hereafter Bandle).

time the saga's *vertu vel til friða* mimics the Low German reading *wes to vreden* (C.iii.a). The saga thus simply transfers the Low German phrase *tovrede wesen* 'to calm down', 'to be at ease', 'not to be worried' to an Icelandic cognate.

Twice the word *mak* occurs in the saga, each time with a previously unattested meaning in Icelandic. When the raven returns from his errand to the princess, Oswald "gengur eftirá í sitt heimuglegt mak" ('then goes into his private chamber'). There is no corresponding passage in the *Passionael*. While the Low German loan *mak* is attested in sixteenth-century Icelandic imprints, it was used with the meaning of 'peace', 'quiet' (W-N, 212). Here, however, the word transmits a second meaning of Low German *mak*, that is, 'room', 'chamber'. Similarly, the adjective *heimuglegt* is a borrowing from Low German *hemelik* 'intimate', 'private', 'secret' (W-N, 153; VÓ, 254).[57]

Like *mak* are the words *kram* and *kramverk*, both meaning 'merchandise'. While the word *kramari* 'merchant' is attested in sixteenth-century Icelandic imprints (W-N, 189), the occurrence of *kram* seems to be limited to business documents (VÓ, 269). In *Ósvalds saga* the word *kram,* like the compound *kramverk,* is a loan from Low German *kram, kraem* 'merchandise', 'wares'. In one instance King Oswald asks the heathen king for permission to "selja sitt kram og annan varning er þeir höfðu þangað flutt" 'sell their merchandise and other cargo that they have brought along.' The coupling of *kram* with the Icelandic synonym *varning* suggests that the German loan may have been used here to distinguish *varning* 'cargo' from small merchandise, later referred to as *handsala* and, again with another Low German loan, *klenódía*, that is, jewelry.

Not infrequently one encounters in *Ósvalds saga* examples of unidiomatic syntax, the source of which is German, for example, in the sentence "báðir þessir hlutir eru frá mér fallnir í sjóinn" 'both of these things have dropped off me into the sea' or, in a more roundabout translation that transmits the meaning more exactly, 'I have lost both of these things when they fell from me (that is, out of my claws) into the sea.' The corresponding passage in the *Passionael* reveals the source of the syntax: "dat is my in dat meer gheuallen" (C.iii.b 'that has fallen from me [my claws] into the sea').

One reason earlier scholars were misled into believing that *Ósvalds saga* is a translation of the legend in the *Passionael*—and indeed that most of the texts in *Reykjahólabók* are translated from corresponding texts in the Low German legendary—is that throughout one repeatedly finds not only loan words and expressions but also entire sentences mimicking the Low German text. A few examples of corresponding passages in the two versions will show why earlier scholars concluded that the saga was translated from the Oswald legend in the *Passionael*. When the saga writes "Síðan skrifaði sankti Ósvaldur eitt bréf og setti þar inn þá

---

[57] The phrase *heimuglegt mak* also occurs in other legends in *Rhb*. In *Jóhannes saga gullmunns* (2:173.27), the expression has the same meaning as in *Ósvalds saga*.

tólf parta heilagrar trúar" ('St. Oswald then wrote a letter and put in it the twelve
articles of the holy faith'), its affinity to the corresponding Low German passage
is striking: "Do screeff de leue sunte Oswaldus de .xij. stukke des hylgen louen in
enen breeff" (C.ii.d: 'Dear St. Oswald then wrote the twelve articles of the holy
faith in a letter'). Or, when the raven leaves the princess, and we read in Icelandic, "Eftir þetta hóf krummi sig upp til flugs, en hún bífalaði hann guði í vald og
hans kærustu móður jungfrú Maríu" ('Thereupon the corbie[58] rose up in flight,
and she entrusted him into the care of God and His dearest mother, the Virgin
Mary'), its correspondence to the Low German is remarkable, not least because
of the occurrence of the loan *bífalaði*, which transmits *beuoel* in the following:
"Do vloech de rauen van daer vnde se beuoel ene gode. vnde syner leuen moder
Marien" (C.iii.b: 'The raven then flew away from there and she entrusted him
to God and His dear mother Mary'). A third example is taken from the scene in
which the raven alights before the heathen king Gaudon, asks for permission to
speak, and requests safe-conduct. In the *Passionael* the king responds: "Du hefst
so wol orloff ghebeden vnd gheleyde" (C.iii.a: 'You have asked so well for leave
and safe-conduct'), and this is conveyed in Icelandic by: "Nú þá so að þú hefur
þér so vel orlofs beðið og so þar með frítt leiði" ('Now since you have asked so
well for leave and also for safe-conduct').

A final example of corresponding passages occurs at the very beginning of
the legend, where we read in the *Passionael* that Oswald had become so mighty
that great lords and bishops served him, but then the text continues,

> Der herscop en vorhoff he sik nicht. men he was othmodich. vnde hadde god
> vor oghen. vnde denede em dagh vnde nacht mit grotem vlite. dar vmme
> was got mit em. (C.ii.c)

> (But he did not become arrogant because of his authority, but he was humble
> and had God ever before him. And he served him day and night with great
> diligence. Therefore God was with him.)

The text in *Ósvalds saga* approximates the Low German fairly closely:

> Af þessari mekt og stórri herlegheit upphóf hann sig ekki til neins metnaðar
> eða drambsemi nema að heldur var hann því lítillátari og góðgjarnari í öllu
> og hafði guð jafnan fyrir augum sér. Og þjónaði honum með allri ástúð
> bæði nætur og daga og guð var ætíð með honum.

---

[58] The bird is initially identified as a *hrafn,* cognate with "raven", but subsequently
*hrafn* alternates with *krummi,* an Icelandic nickname for the raven. The word derives from
*krumma, krymma* "to bend", "make crooked", and refers to the bent claws readied for the
catch. Here the Scottish word *corbie* is used for the raven whenever the word *krummi* occurs in the Icelandic text.

(For all of this power and great authority he did not become puffed up with pride or arrogance but rather was all the more humble and benevolent in everything and set his eyes ever upon God. And he served him with great love both night and day and God was ever with him.)

Despite the obvious affinity between the two texts, the Icelandic deviates stylistically by means of semantic couplings—*mekt/herlegheit, metnaðar/drambsemi, lítillátari/ góðgjarnari*—which makes it rhetorically more elaborate compared to the German text, which is terse in the extreme. While passages such as the above led Ole Widding and Hans Bekker-Nielsen to believe that *Ósvalds saga* was translated from the legend in the *Passionael*,[59] they were nonetheless also confronted by some drastic discrepancies between the two texts, and noted that "it was obviously the translator's intention to emphasize important passages through a more elaborate style or the use of the form of dialogue"; nonetheless, they concluded that "in no instances does the Icelandic version differ greatly from the version in the *Passionael*."[60] This is in fact not the case.

The degree of correspondence between the legends in the *Passionael* and the Icelandic translations can differ markedly. This is not owing to inconsistency on Björn Þorleifsson's part as a translator[61]—there is no evidence that he was anything but a careful and exact translator of his sources, although occasionally he did make mistakes—but rather to the nature of the sources used by the compiler of *Der Heiligen Leben*. If Williams-Krapp is right in proposing that the legendary was intended for reading in the refectory and that the aim of the compiler was to produce terse accounts, then the length and style of his source played a role in the condensation. Some legends were reduced more than others simply because they were not only longer but also narratively more sophisticated and therefore further removed from the desired style of a legendary. As Williams-Krapp noted, the *Heiligen Leben* anthology was produced with a view to formal and stylistic uniformity and an eye to the education of the recipients and the intended purpose of the legendary; any element that went beyond the basic plot was eliminated.[62] That was the case with the legend of St. Oswald, which, to judge by the Icelandic translation, was a much longer and narratively more interesting text—in respect

---

[59] Widding and Bekker-Nielsen, "En senmiddelalderlig legendesamling," 113–14.

[60] Widding and Bekker-Nielsen, "Low German Influence," 248.

[61] Widding and Bekker-Nielsen arrived at four groups of legends in *Reykjahólabók* depending upon their textual proximity to the legends in the *Passionael* ("Low German Influence," 247–51); see Kalinke, *The Book of Reykjahólar*, 47–48.

[62] "Bei der Adaptation und Bearbeitung seiner diversen Quellen strebte der HL-Verfasser formale und stilistische Einheitlichkeit an. . . . diese . . . orientiert sich gänzlich an dem Bildungsstand des Rezipientenkreises, der intendierten Gebrauchsfunktion des Werkes und der dezidierten Vorstellung des Verfassers" (*Die deutschen und niederländischen Legendare des Mittelalters*, 271).

to dialogue, motivation, and descriptive as well as other detail, such as temporal and spatial scene shifts—than the legend of St. John Chrysostom, for example, where the correspondence between the Low German and Icelandic versions is much closer. The reason for this is that the legend of John Chrysostom that was the source of the *Heiligen Leben* compiler, and which is presumably represented by the Icelandic version *Jóhannes saga gullmunns*, was much shorter and less complicated than the legend of St. Oswald and therefore needed less cutting and revision for inclusion in the legendary.[63]

Despite recurring correspondences between text in *Ósvalds saga* and the *Passionael* legend, these are limited to isolated vocabulary, phrases, and occasionally several sentences, as the above examples show. Only when one compares entire scenes or episodes, however, does the disparate character of the two versions become evident. The German and Icelandic prose legends differ not only stylistically but also in the amount of information conveyed. In every instance, the saga provides individualizing detail and motivation and dramatizes the plot through dialogue, whereas the *Passionael* strips the legend of all but the barest details. The following example from the very beginning of the legend exemplifies the quite distinct approaches to narrative in the German and Icelandic texts. In the *Passionael* the legend commences as follows:

> De leue here sunte Oswald was eyn gued cristen. vnde was doghentlik. vnde hadde god leeff. vnde gaff vele almissen. vnde beschermede wedewen vnde weyzen. vnde eerde vnde voedede de prester. vnde was hart den vnlouighen. Darumme sach em got voer. vnde wolde em tho enem konnige hebben. vnde do men em wolde to enem konninge kresemen. do tovloet de kresem van godes willen, wente id quam eyn rauen van dem hemmel, vnde brochte ene gulden bussen mit kresem in deme snauele. (C.ii.c)

> (The dear lord St. Oswald was a good Christian and he was virtuous and loved God. And he gave many alms and protected widows and orphans and honored and nourished priests, and he was severe toward unbelievers. Therefore God chose him and wanted him to be king. And when he was to be anointed king, the chrism appeared through God's will, for a raven came down from heaven and brought in its beak a golden phial with chrism.)

---

[63] Not only was the apocryphal legend of St. John Chrysostom included in *Der Heiligen Leben,* as a forestory to the authentic *vita,* but it was also published by Martin Luther in Wittenberg, Augsburg, and Strassburg in 1537. See "Die Lügend von S. Johanne Chrysostomo. 1537," in *D. Martin Luthers Werke, Kritische Gesamtausgabe,* vol. 50 (Weimar: Hermann Böhlaus Nachfolger, 1914), 48–64. For an edition of the Icelandic legend and a translation, see Marianne E. Kalinke, *"Jóhannes saga gullmunns:* The Icelandic Legend of the Hairy Anchorite," forthcoming in *"Beatus vir": Early English and Norse Manuscript Studies in Memory of Phillip Pulsiano,* ed. Kirsten Wolf and Nick Doane.

The above is devoid of suspense. God's choice of Oswald as king is presented just as soberly as the portrait of Oswald. Parataxis prevails not only in the syntax but also in the sequence of narrative units. Every detail presented in the matter-of-fact narrator's voice has identical value.

The case is drastically otherwise in *Ósvalds saga*, which opens with an extended portrait of the saint. This concludes with a remark about the spread of his fame, which functions in turn as the transition to the issue of royal succession and introduces the coronation legend. Here events unfold dramatically and the plot reaches a first climax when no chrism for the royal anointing can be found:

So finnst skrifað í heilagri skrift að í Englandi var einn ágætur herra er Ósvaldur hét og var vel kristinn herra, þvíað hann var dygðugur og góðgjarn við alla þá er þurftugir voru og til hans hjálpar leituðu með orðum og verkum. Ekkjur fátækar og föðurlaus börn tók hann undir sína vernd og varðveislu til allra réttra mála. Hann heiðraði og fæddi alla kennimenn er til hans vildu sækja, en harður og stríður var hann ómildum vantrúöndum og öðrum óráðvöndum mönnum þar sem hann átti yfir að stýra. Hann var og iðjufullur til að fremja góð verk með föstum og vökum so og með guðligu bænahaldi og mildum ölmusugjörðum, so að hann hafði guðs vináttu og góðra manna, og hans góð verk er jafnan framdi hann fóru víða eigi að eins um England nema heldur líka um mörg lönd önnur.

Í þenna tíma var enginn kóngur í Englandi sem að réttum erfðum átti ríkinu stýra. Þá með guðs fyrirætlan og samþykki hinna mektugustu og so vísustu herra í landinu, þá kjöru þeir Osvaldum fyrir einn einvaldsherra yfir sig. Þetta vildi hann ekki og sagðist þar óverðugur til vera í öllum hlutum. En það var ekki so: þó að hann væri og ekki sérlega kóngborinn, þá var hann þó kominn af göfugri ætt bæði að föðurkyni og móður, og so var það ekki á móti guðs vilja þó hann yrði kóngur, sem brátt má heyrast. En er Ósvaldur heyrir að þetta er þeirra fullur vilji til þess að hefja sig til ríkisstjórnar, þá tók hann sig í burtu á laun frá þeim og ætlaði að koma sér með því undan þessari tign, en það hjálpaði ekki þvíað þegar sem þeir vissu af hans burtför sendu þeir eftir honum og báðu hann með allri alúð og koma aftur og vera þeim samþykkur. Þá um síðir mæðir huggæði og kemur inn í staðinn aftur með sendimönnum er til hans voru sendir. Verða allir við það glaðir í staðnum bæði ríkir og fátækir. Þá sem sá dagur kom að hann átti að krýnast til konungs og smyrja hann eftir venju með krisma, þá eftir guðs tilskikkan fannst hvergi krismi að smyrja hann með.

Þá mælti Osvaldus: "Sjáið nú, góðir vinir, að drottinn guð minn birtir nú fyrir öllum að ég er óverðugur til slíks."

Þá þögðu allir þvíað þeir þóttust ekki vita hvað þeir skyldu til gjöra eða hvað guðs vilji mundi vera um þetta. En í þessu kom einn hrafn fljúgandi ofan af himnum og hafði einn buðk fullan af krisma er sankti Pétur hafði sjálfur vígt. Þennan buðkinn hafði hann í nefinu á sér og var gjörður af skíru gulli.

(It is written in a sacred text that there was a noble lord in England whose name was Oswald and he was a good Christian lord, for he was virtuous and kind to all who were needy and who sought his help by word or deed. He took poor widows and fatherless children under his protection and in his safekeeping in all just cases. He honored and fed all priests who wanted to appeal to him, but he was harsh and severe toward all unrighteous disbelievers and other wicked men whom he had to rule. He was also diligent in carrying out good works along with fasts and vigils as well as pious devotions and generous almsgiving, so that he had God's friendship and that of good men, and report of the good works that he always performed spread far and wide not only throughout England but also many other lands.

At this time there was no king in England who was properly in line of succession to rule the realm. Then in keeping with God's providence and the consent of the mightiest and also wisest lords in the land, they chose Oswald to be their ruler. This he did not want and said that he was unworthy of this in every respect. But that was not the case: even though he was not of particularly royal birth, he was still descended from an illustrious family both on his father's and his mother's side, and thus it was not against God's will that he become king, as you will soon hear. And when Oswald hears that it is their definite will to exalt him as their ruler, he secretly stole away from them and thought that in this way he could avoid this honor, but that did not help, for as soon as they found out about his flight, they sent men after him and asked him in all humility to come back and give his consent. Then at last his resolve weakens and he comes back into the town with the messengers who were sent to him. Everyone in the city, both rich and poor, becomes glad at this. Then when the day came on which he was to be crowned king and anointed with chrism, as was customary, then in keeping with God's design no chrism could be found to anoint him with.

Then Oswald spoke: "See now, good friends, that the Lord my God now manifests to all that I am unworthy of this."

All then remained silent since they did not think they knew what they should do or what might be God's will in this matter. But at this moment a raven came flying down from heaven and had a vessel full of chrism which St. Peter himself had consecrated. He had this vessel in his beak and it was made of pure gold.)

The discrepancies between the Icelandic version and the Low German text are not to be attributed to the greater prolixity of the author of *Ósvalds saga*. The Icelandic version most likely represents the German legend that was the source of the *Heiligen Leben/Passionael* redaction, as will be argued subsequently. The *Passionael* redaction clearly reveals—and this applies, of course, in the first instance to the redaction in *Der Heiligen Leben*, of which the text in the *Passionael* is a translation—that in the process of cutting the text to a length appropriate, for example, for reading aloud during meals in a refectory, the author not only eliminated details and dialogue thought to be superfluous, but at times also reduced the text in such a radical manner as to introduce substantive modification into the narrative. The saga, while deferring to God's divine providence, nonetheless grounds in the here and now the events that lead to the day of Oswald's coronation and the dilemma posed by the missing chrism, at the same time that it conveys that what transpires on earth should be seen in the light of God's providence. That is not the case in the *Passionael*, where the extreme condensation of text results in a loss of the very details that account for the dramatic conflict in the coronation legend.

The Low German and Icelandic passages submitted here exemplify the profound differences between the two redactions of one and the same legend. Not only is Oswald allowed to speak in *Ósvalds saga*, but the perplexity and helplessness of the courtiers in face of the missing chrism are also expressed. A remarkable difference becomes apparent in the two versions in respect to God's will. In the *Passionael* the emphasis is on the chrism that appeared in accordance with God's will, whereas in the saga the absence of the chrism is interpreted as a sign of God's will, and this generates Oswald's speech and the courtiers' speechlessness. In the last analysis, however, God's will prevails in either case, but the change introduced in the *Passionael* vis-à-vis its source is drastic: by deleting the retarding element of the missing chrism and Oswald's reaction to this, which is in keeping with his unwillingness to be crowned king in the first place, the *Passionael* transmits a story markedly different from that in *Ósvalds saga*.

The *Passionael* version and the saga diverge from Bede's account not only because of the addition of the prefatory coronation legend but also and especially because of the full-fledged bridal-quest narrative that merited only the terse remark in the *Historia ecclesiastica* that Oswald married the daughter of the pagan King Cynegisl. The extraordinary disparity in the narrative strategy employed in the *Passionael* redaction and *Ósvalds saga* will be illustrated by two episodes, the council scene(s) in which Oswald is advised to take a wife and the confrontation scene between the pagan King Gaudon and Oswald, after the latter has abducted the heathen king's daughter.

In the Low German legend the council episode—with the exception of a single move in space to conclude the scene—consists of a tableau. There is no direct confrontation between Oswald and his counselors as the *Passionael* merely reports that when the king was at the height of his splendor,

> . . . do meneden de heren he scolde ene iuncfrouwe nemen. wente storue he ane erue. so scolde eyn ander syn gued vnde syn rike besitten. deme yd nee sure were gheworden. Do quam alzo drade eyn old man van deme wyllen godes. (C.ii.d)

> (. . . the lords believed that he should take a wife, for if he died without heirs, someone else would possess his wealth and kingdom, someone who had never exerted himself for it. Then suddenly an old man came in accordance with God's will.)

What generates the reaction of the lords and immediately precedes the above is the observation, "Do he nu so doghentlyken vnde salichliken leuede to gode vnde den minschen. . ." ('When he was now living so virtuously and piously in the sight of God and men. . .'). The Low German text relates in indirect discourse the courtiers' opinion that Oswald should marry and their reasons for this, as well as the information that all at once a visitor arrives. The text in the *Passionael* has condensed into two items of information—the courtiers' opinion and the arrival of the old man—an originally lengthy episode, as attested by the saga, consisting of several scenes effectively dramatized through dialogue.

As happens in the Low German legend, the decision by the courtiers in *Ósvalds saga* to counsel the king follows upon an observation concerning Oswald's exemplary rule and virtuous life: "Og þá sem hann hafði nú so prýðilega eflt sitt ríki og sett sína göfuga herra í hvern stað sem hann vildi og öllum þótti so mega fara, þvíað hann var hugljúfi allra manna . . . " ('And now when he had so nobly endowed his realm and set his noble lords in every place he wanted and everyone thought things would go on in this way, for he was beloved by all men . . . '). It is at this point that the courtiers convene (to permit one to see more easily the enormous discrepancies between the Low German and Icelandic texts, passages in the saga that correspond, albeit quite loosely, to those in the *Passional* above have been italicized) :

> *. . . þá eitt sinni tóku sig til samans nokkurir hans trúlegir vinir og gjörðu ráð sín á meðal að þeir skyldi fara á fund kóngsins og ráðleggja honum að fá sér eitthvert sæmilegt kvonfang, so að ríkið stæði ekki so lengur erfingjalaust.*
>
> Þá sem nokkurir dagar voru liðnir frá þessu sem nú var sagt, þá komu þeir til samans aftur herranir með það erindi er fyrr greinir og gengu síðan fyrir Ósvald kóng og biðja hann orlofs að þeir mega bera sitt erindi fram fyrir hann. Hann biður þá skila því er þeir vilja.
>
> Síðan mælti einn þeirra fyrir þá alla, so segjandi: "Verðugi herra, nú frá því að þér hafið sett og samið yðvart ríki með góðri stjórn og nytsemdar verkum so að allir lifa nú með friði og farsæld er undir yðvart vald eru gefnir, þá vonum vér so til að guði muni so líka um yðvart efni sem oss. En þó er eftir einn sjá hlutur er oss þykir á vanta og hans virðist oss með öngu móti mega án vera."
>
> Kóngurinn spyr þá mjög vandlega eftir hvað það væri og sagðist að þeirra ráðum vilja gjöra það mögulegt væri. Þeir þakka kónginum og segja:
>
> "Með yðru orlofi, verðugi herra, *þá þykir oss það helst á vanta að þér eigið öngva drottningu þá er þér megið láta sitja og stjórna yðru ríki eftir yðvarn dag,* þvíað vér vildum ekki gjarnan eiga gefast lengur undir þá herra er ekki eru réttilega komnir til ríkisins; *og þeir hlutir margir sem þér hafið bæði eflt og bætt vort ríki þá skulu aðrir eyða því og spilla í staðinn sem hvorki eiga né so nokkuð ómak hafa fyrir haft. Og viljum vér ekki ef vér skulum ráða."*

En er kóngur hefur gjörla skilið þeirra erindi, þá svarar hann og segist vilja hugsa hér eftir og gefa þeim svar aftur nær sem hann hefur til þeirrar er sig girnti eftir að eiga. En þetta svar gaf hann til þess að hann vildi so með því koma þeim af sér enn með hreinni samvitsku. Var honum í hug að kvongast ekki heldur að halda hreinlífi. Og sem herranir þenktu sér í burtu að ganga, þá var klappað á dyrnar og sá sem klappaði sagðist eiga erindi við kónginn. Þetta er kónginum sagt. Biður hann dyrasvein að láta hann inn og so biður hann herrana að biðleika við og heyra hvað sá vill sem kominn var og so gjöra þeir.

*Síðan gekk þessi maður inn* fyrir kónginn *og sýndist að vilja guðs sem hann væri allur grár af hærum, bæði hár og skegg* og var það mjög langt; og hafði í hendinni annarri einn pálmkvist en í annarri staf og gjörði sig líkan einum pílagrími. En í sumlegum bókum stendur so skrifað að það væri engill guðs. Og þegar að hann kemur fyrir kónginn fellur hann á hné og heilsar honum kurteislega. Kóngur tekur honum vel og bað hann ganga með sér í sína palacia. Það gjörir hann. Og er kóngur var kominn í sitt sæti kallar hann á komumann og fréttir hvað manna hann væri.

Hinn svarar og segist vera einn prophéta "og eru mér kunnig tvö og sjötíu þjóðlönd, og *er ég einn sendiboði af guði sendur.*"

(. . . *then on one occasion some of his faithful friends got together and decided among themselves to go see the king and advise him to find for himself a suitable wife, so that the kingdom would no longer be without an heir.*

When some days had passed after what has just been told, the lords came together again concerning the matter mentioned before, and they then went to King Oswald and ask leave to convey their mission to him. He tells them to state what they want.

One of them then spoke for all, saying: "Worthy Lord, now that you have established and secured your realm with good government and useful works so that all who are subject to you now live in peace and happiness, we expect that God is as pleased by your rule as we are. Yet there is the one thing that to us seems lacking and which we deem to be impossible to be without."

The king then asks very cautiously what that might be and he said that he would act on their advice if it were possible.

They thank the king and say: "With your leave, worthy Lord, *we think what is most wanting is that you have no queen whom you might have preside over and rule your kingdom after your day,* for we would rather not want to have to submit any longer to those lords who have not rightfully obtained the kingdom; *and the many things with which you have strengthened and improved our kingdom, others will then spoil and destroy instead, others who neither have a right to nor for which they have earlier gone to such pains.* And we do not want this if we have a say."

And when the king has fully heard their story, he then answers and says that he wants to think this over and give them an answer when he has thought about her whom he might like to marry. He gave them this answer, however, because he wanted to get rid of them with his conscience still clear. He had in mind not to get married but rather to preserve his virginity instead. And when the lords intended to leave, there was a knock on the door and the one who knocked said that he had a message for the king. The king was told this. He asks the doorkeeper to let him in and asks the lords to stay behind to hear what the newcomer wanted, and they do so.

*Then this man went in* and before the king *and through God's will he appeared to be completely gray, both his hair and beard*, and that was very long; and in one hand he had a palm branch but in the other a staff, and he presented himself as a pilgrim. But in some books it says that he was an angel of God. And as soon as he comes before the king, he falls on his knees and greets him courteously. The king welcomes him and asked him to go with him into his palace. He does so. And when the king had sat down in his seat, he calls on the newcomer and asks who he might be.

He answers and says that he is a prophet, "and seventy-two countries are known to me, and *I am a messenger sent from God.*")

The expansion above is to be attributed partly to the extensive dialogue that takes place between the king and his courtiers, partly to changes of scene. Furthermore, the episode is multi-dimensional, giving full consideration to differences in both time and space. It consists of several scenes requiring the passage of time and a change of place, as the courtiers decide that they should advise the king to marry in order to ensure heirs for the realm. Some days pass before the lords reconvene and seek out King Oswald to ask for permission to address their concerns to him. One of the counselors speaks on behalf of the group and tells King Oswald that only one thing is wanting in him as king. Oswald inquires what that might be and says he will accede to their wishes if at all possible. The courtiers inform him that he needs a queen to rule with him, since they do not wish to submit to a lord who has not acquired the kingdom through rightful succession; furthermore, they point out that it is not proper that others should destroy the realm he has built up. Oswald replies that he will consider their request and give them an answer, but he also tells them that he had actually wished to abstain from marriage and thus preserve his virginity. Just as the lords are to depart, there is a knock on the door and a visitor says he has a matter to bring before the king. Oswald tells the doorkeeper to open the door and asks his courtiers to remain behind in order to witness what is to transpire.

The creator of the above thought in terms of time and space; he permitted the characters to interact and conceived of the episode in dramatic terms: King Oswald is center stage; the other characters are presented in relation to him and must enter and leave his presence. Thus, when a new character, the visitor, enters the scene, the courtiers are not forgotten, but asked by the king to remain. The process leading up to the king's ultimate decision to take a wife evolves over the course of several days. The subsequent scene between the king and the stranger, who identifies himelf as a prophet, is similarly depicted through dialogue.

A third scene, an encounter between the heathen king and Oswald, will offer additional evidence as to the nature of the divergence in narrative strategies, not to mention length, in the German prose legend and the saga. After the princess has escaped from the castle and met up with King Oswald, the couple are pursued by the heathen king, her father. When he finally confronts Oswald, the scene is depicted as follows in the *Passionael*:

> Do sprak he to em. Gy hebben my myne dochter van hijr ghevoert: darumme mothe gy den doet liden. Do sprak sunte Oswald. Ik wil darumme myt iuw stryden. (C.iiii.a)

> (He then spoke to him: "You have abducted my daughter from me. There-fore you must suffer death." St. Oswald then spoke: "I want to fight with you over this.")

The dialogue above follows hard upon the statement that Gaudon pursued Os-wald with a great army "vnde vant syne dochter by em sittende" ('and found his daughter sitting at his side'). The verbal give and take is neutrally introduced by the formulaic "do sprak." In the saga version, however, a rather different scenar-io ensues. Rather than the sober accusation and response, the reader is privy to Gaudon's state of mind; furthermore, it is evident that more is at stake for Oswald than the abduction of the princess:

> Verður hann ákaflega reiður og kallar sem hann má á Ósvald kóng með þessum orðum: "Þú hinn ótrúasti óvinur! Þú og þínir fylgjarar hafa tekið mína dóttur í burtu með flærð og undirhyggju, og fyrir þann skuld verði þér að þola dauða."
> Þá svarar Ósvaldur: "Ef ekki á betra í efni verða, þá er mér það ekki á móti þó að láti líf mitt fyrir minn skapara og heilaga trú skyld og er þér það ið besta ráð, Gaudon, að þú takir heilaga trú og trúir á sannan guð."

> (He gets extremely angry and shouts at King Oswald as loudly as he can with these words: "You most untrustworthy fiend! You and your followers have abducted my daughter with deception and trickery, and for that reason you will have to suffer death."
> Then Oswald answers: "If things are not going to turn out better, then I am not against losing my life for my Creator and for the sake of the holy faith, and it would be best for you, Gaudon, to decide to accept the holy faith and to believe in the true God.")

Oswald refuses to answer to the charge of abduction and thereby he is able to give voice to the real issue in his bridal quest: he has been sent to convert Gaudon and his people and is willing to give up his life for his faith. As will be shown, the fictionalized bridal quest in *Ósvalds saga* is an essential component of the king's conversion politics. The vernacular legend of St. Oswald, its bridal-quest narrative generated by Bede's exceedingly sparse details, nonetheless is faithful to his portrayal of King Oswald as the great proselytizer of his nation.

*Ósvalds saga* is a translation of a rather long Low German Oswald legend, the High German version of which presumably was the source of the severely abridged version found in the *Heiligen Leben/Passionael* legendary.[64] This long vernacular legend transmitted all the factual details of Oswald's life as known from the *Historia ecclesiastica* at the same time that it fictionalized certain aspects of Bede's account through their dramatically narrativized expansion. Ironically, if not surprisingly, when the compiler of *Der Heiligen Leben* condensed the Oswald legend by reducing and omitting detail, dialogue, and motivation and resorted to a largely paratactic style, the vernacular legend actually reverted to a form more in keeping with the earlier Latin *vita* compiled by Drogo from Bede's *Historia ecclesiastica*.

---

[64] Despite its condensation, the Oswald legend is one of the longest texts in *Der Heiligen Leben* (see Williams-Krapp, *Die deutschen und niederländischen Legendare des Mittelalters*, 274).

# IV.
## THE GERMAN OSWALD LEGEND

The continental Latin *vitae* of St. Oswald that were drawn from Bede's *Historia ecclesiastica*—notably the oldest by Drogo—were complemented by two vernacular versions of his legend on the continent, one in verse, the other in prose. The metrical version is represented by the so-called *Münchner Oswald* and *Wiener Oswald*, the former being not only the more important of the two redactions but also, in the judgment of scholars, representative of the source of all the other German Oswald texts.[65] The prose legend is transmitted in three redactions: 1) the legend in *Der Heiligen Leben/Dat Passionael*;[66] 2) the "Budapester Oswald"; and 3) the "Berliner Oswald."[67] There also exists a fragment of a metrical text, the so-called "Linzer Oswald," which contains scenes of a monumental battle between Christians and heathens, in which St. Oswald is identified as being from Norway, though it is clear that the text deals with the Northumbrian king.[68] Finally, in the late thirteenth-century *Märterbuch*,[69] the source of which is a collection of twelfth-century Latin legends, we find "Von sand Oswalden dem chunig,"[70] a legend of 187 verses that includes Oswald's battle against the heathens and a couple of miracles as reported by Bede.

The life of St. Oswald was incorporated into the most popular vernacular legendary of the Middle Ages, *Der Heiligen Leben*, and subsequently into its Low German translation, *Dat Passionael*, the oldest extant imprint of which dates

---

[65] See Curschmann, *Der Münchener Oswald und die deutsche spielmännische Epik*, 2–3; idem, "Münchner Oswald," in *²VL*, 6:766; idem, "'Oswald' (Prosafassungen)," in *²VL*, 7:126.

[66] Curschmann includes *Ósvalds saga* in the *Heiligen-Leben* redaction, for the saga has been considered a translation of the Low German version of the prose legend since the nineteenth century ("'Oswald' (Prosafassungen)," in *²VL*, 7:126).

[67] Curschmann, "'Oswald' (Prosafassungen)," in *²VL*, 7:127–28; for an edition of the "Berliner Oswald," designated 'Oswald-Prosa B' in *Der Münchener Oswald und die deutsche spielmännische Epik*, 3, see the appendix of Curschmann's edition *Der Münchner Oswald. Mit einem Anhang: die ostschwäbische Prosabearbeitung des 15. Jahrhunderts*, Altdeutsche Textbibliothek 76 (Tübingen: Max Niemeyer, 1974), 189–213.

[68] Michael Curschmann, ed., "'Sant Oswald von Norwegen': ein Fragment eines Legendenepos," *Zeitschrift für deutsches Altertum* 102 (1973): 101–14.

[69] Konrad Kunze, "'Buch der Märtyrer' (Märterbuch)," in *²VL*, 1:1093–95.

[70] Erich Gierach, ed., *Das Märterbuch. Die Klosterneuburger Handschrift 713* (Berlin: Weidmannsche Buchhandlung, 1928), 292–96.

from around 1478.[71] The metrical version, that is, the *Münchner Oswald* and the *Wiener Oswald*, diverges from the prose version by lacking two essential components of the legend first told by Bede and compiled by Drogo: Oswald's *passio* and miracles. Loss of the account of Oswald's martyrdom in the two metrical versions resulted in the creation of a fictional saint at odds with the historically attested figure. The case is quite different in the *Heiligen Leben/Passionael* prose version and also the saga, where the legend is quadripartite, consisting of 1) a coronation legend, 2) a bridal-quest and conversion legend, 3) a martyr legend, and 4) a miracle sequence. The metrical version contains only the second part, the bridal-quest and conversion legend.

Almost without exception, scholars follow the judgment of Georg Baesecke, an early editor of the *Münchner Oswald*, in dating the metrical romance to the end of the twelfth century.[72] In 1907 he concluded his analysis of every conceivable aspect of the work—from the language and rhyme schemes of the manuscripts to the author's acquaintance with goldsmithing—with the pronouncement: ". . . lasse O[swald] um 1170 im Bannkreise von Aachen enstanden sein."[73] Michael Curschmann admitted that neither an early dating like Baesecke's nor a later dating to the fourteenth century "fußt auf restlos stichhaltigen Argumenten," but he nonetheless followed Baesecke and proposed that the romance "dürfte in den 70er Jahren des 12. Jahrhunderts entstanden sein."[74] No manuscripts predate the fifteenth century, however, and thus the arguments for placing the proto-Oswald as early as the twelfth century revolve around certain stylistic, motival, and thematic characteristics shared by the *Münchner Oswald*, considered a late-medieval new edition of the work,[75] with the other pre-courtly bridal-quest romances. Or as Gisela Vollmann-Profe argues, common to the *Münchner Oswald* and the other

---

[71] See Williams-Krapp, *Die deutschen und niederländischen Legendare des Mittelalters*, 235.

[72] But see the article by Josef Dünninger, who dates the composition of the *Münchner Oswald* to the middle, perhaps the third quarter of the fourteenth century: "St. Oswald und Regensburg. Zur Datierung des Münchener Oswald," in *Gedächtnisschrift für Adalbert Hämel*, ed., Romanisches Seminar der Universität Erlangen (Würzburg: Konrad Triltsch Verlag, 1953), 17–26, here 26.

[73] Baesecke, ed., *Der Münchener Oswald*, 380.

[74] Curschmann, *Der Münchener Oswald und die deutsche spielmännische Epik*, 82–84; similarly in idem, ed., *Der Münchner Oswald*, xlix; idem, "Münchner Oswald," in *²VL*, 6:768.

[75] Curschmann refers to the *Münchner Oswald* as a "spätm[ittel]al[terliche] Neuauflage" of the twelfth-century work ("Münchner Oswald," in *²VL*, 6:766).

bridal-quest epics is their composition at a transforming moment in German literature, the transition from orality to literacy.[76]

Believing the prose legend to derive from the *Münchner Oswald*, Curschmann interpreted the absence of Christ's apparition to Oswald and exhortation to conjugal chastity in the prose version as a shortening of the source.[77] That is to say, the motif of conjugal chastity was considered to have been part of the original German Oswald legend, since the *Münchner Oswald* is thought to represent this text. Two years after the publication of Curschmann's monograph, Rolf Bräuer published a short article, summarizing the findings of his Berlin dissertation of 1965, on the redactions of the German Oswald narrative.[78] Bräuer remarked on the divergent, indeed contradictory opinions concerning Oswald, and noted that the principal question as to which version represents the original work has not been answered satisfactorily. His analysis of the versions led him to conclude that they derive from the same prototype and that the Low German and Icelandic redactions diverge the most from the original legend ("Die drei Fassungen," 554). While Bräuer believed that the prose version represents a reworking of the metrical version into a martyr's *vita* for a legendary, he posited that the redactor knew and used both "die kirchliche Legende in der Nachfolge Bedas als auch Vorstufen des Münchener und des Wiener Oswald" (554). He concluded that the German Oswald was composed by a cleric at the turn of the twelfth to the thirteenth century in the northwestern part of the German-language area, and that this Ur-Oswald was subsequently adapted, in keeping with the style of the period, as a crusade and bridal-quest romance. Bräuer considered the *Wiener Oswald* the closest relative of the originally hagiographically conceived text.

The *Münchner Oswald*, considered literarily the more important of the two metrical redactions, integrates the figure of the historical king into a bridal-quest narrative, at the conclusion of which Oswald and his wife are exhorted by Christ to live chastely. Indeed, Christ even provides a practical solution to withstanding temptation:

---

[76] Vollmann-Profe writes: "Die entscheidende Gemeinsamkeit der Epen sehen wir darin, daß sie den Moment der Transformation von der Mündlichkeit in die Schriftlichkeit noch festhalten—oder besser: jenen Moment, in dem die Begegnung der beiden literarischen Existenzformen noch offen und im Stadium des Experiments war": *Wiederbeginn volkssprachiger Schriftlichkeit im hohen Mittelalter,* 171.

[77] Curschmann, *Der Münchener Oswald und die deutsche spielmännische Epik,* 209.

[78] Rolf Bräuer, "Die drei Fassungen des Legendenromans vom heiligen Oswald und das Problem der sogenannten Spielmannsdichtung," *Wissenschaftliche Zeitschrift der Ernst-Moritz-Arndt-Universität Greifswald* 15 (1966): 551–55. His dissertation was published subsequently as *Das Problem des "Spielmännischen" aus der Sicht der St.-Oswald-Überlieferung* (Berlin: Akademie-Verlag, 1969).

merk, wie du den sunden solt widerstan:
wasser soltu vor deinem pet han;
wan dich dein manhait wil betwingen,
so soltu in daz wasser springen.
also tuo ouch deu frau dein,
und tuo daz durch den willen mein:
darumb wirt dir geben schon
daz himelreich zuo lon. (vv. 3515–3522)[79]

(Listen to how you are to resist the desire of the flesh. You must have a tub
of water beside your bed and, when your manhood troubles you, jump into
the water; your wife should spring in too. Do this for my sake and the kingdom of heaven will be your reward.)[80]

Unlike the historical Oswald, the protagonist dies peacefully at the side of his
wife in bed:

si chomen des leibs in not,
wan si begraif der hert tod;
der welt muosten si sich verwegen
und begunden sich an ain pett legen.
si saumpten sich nicht mer
und hiessen in pringen zwen priester her:
si erchanten sich ir schuld
und wurben nach gotes huld
und berichten sich mit gots leichnam wert. (vv. 3539–3547)

(Their lives came to an end. When bitter death overtook them and they
suffered bodily distress, they lay down in bed and renounced the world.
Sending for two priests without delay, they confessed their guilt, prayed for
God's mercy, and received the sacrament. [118])

There is no indication in the *Münchner Oswald* that the protagonist is remembered as the historical figure who died in battle against heathen forces. Yet this
is what Curschmann claimed: "Im *Münchener Oswald* ist das Wissen um die
historische Person Oswalds noch unmittelbar lebendig, genauso wie das Wissen
um die Eigenschaften, die ihn zum heiligen Herrscher erhoben: Oswald ist als im
Heidenkampf Gefallener Märtyrer und Missionsförderer, also *quasi sacerdos*,

---

[79] All references to the *Münchner Oswald* are to Curschmann's edition, *Der Münchner Oswald*.

[80] "The Munich Oswald," in *The Strassburg Alexander and the Munich Oswald. Pre-
Courtly Adventure of the German Middle Ages*, trans. and with an introduction by J. W. Thomas (Columbia: Camden House, 1989), 118. Subsequent references are to this translation.

zugleich *rex iustus* und Fürsorger der Armen. . . ."[81] While the hagiographic features are somewhat more pronounced in the *Wiener Oswald* and the issue of conjugal chastity is at the forefront throughout, the Viennese redaction tells much the same story as the Munich version. Unlike the latter, however, the *Wiener Oswald* concludes with the mass baptism of the heathens. While the reader can assume that Oswald and the princess will marry and live a life of conjugal chastity, the author of the *Wiener Oswald* is content to lay the story to rest as soon as Oswald has succeeded in converting the heathens.

Here it is argued conversely that the prose version and not the metrical version represents the original vernacular legend; in other words, that the metrical, not the prose, version is derivative. Central to our understanding of the nature of the proto-Oswald is the Icelandic translation of a Low German version. *Ósvalds saga* does not derive from the German prose legend that is transmitted in *Der Heiligen Leben/Dat Passionael*, as scholars have in the past repeatedly asserted.[82] Rather, the saga is a translation, via a Middle Low German text, of a fairly long quadripartite Middle High German legend, which was condensed for inclusion in *Der Heiligen Leben*. This ultimate source of *Ósvalds saga* represents, in my opinion, the oldest version of the legend in the German-language area, while the metrical version, that is, the *Münchner Oswald* and *Wiener Oswald*, is a derivative work that transmuted a martyr's *vita* and *passio* into a hagiographic romance inspired by and emulating the legends of virginal royal saints. This transformation came about through the abbreviation of the account of Oswald's proselytizing efforts; the modification of the historically attested martyr's death into that of a confessor who embraces conjugal chastity; and the exclusion of the miracle sequence that affirms Oswald's sanctity.

In effect, the German Oswald narratives transmit two models of sanctity, the older model corresponding to historical fact in which Oswald attains sanctity through martyrdom, and the younger, fictionalized model that proposes virginal marriage rather than martyrdom as the source of Oswald's sanctity.[83] The oddity of the Oswald legend in the German-language area is that one and the same royal saint served as a model for two distinct paths to sanctity, the historical Oswald through

---

[81] Curschmann, *Der Münchener Oswald und die deutsche spielmännische Epik,* 180.

[82] When Curschmann, in his article on the prose redactions of the Oswald legend, in the second edition of the *Verfasserlexikon,* writes that the Icelandic version derives from the legend in the *Heiligen Leben* via the Low German redaction—"Diese Prosa, aus der später noch—über die nd. Fassung des Legendars—eine isländische Bearbeitung hervorging" ("'Oswald' (Prosafassungen)," 126)—he is merely repeating what generations of Germanists have claimed before him.

[83] See Dyan Elliott, *Spiritual Marriage: Sexual Abstinence in Medieval Wedlock* (Princeton: Princeton University Press, 1993), 127, where she states: "When saintly kings made their painful transition from martyrs to confessors, in the process they appropriated the virginal marriage model, hitherto the exclusive preserve of their regal consorts."

his martyrdom, the traditional means, and the fictionalized Oswald through his spiritual marriage, a more recent road to sanctity, as exemplified and popularized by the lives and legend of Emperor Henry II and Cunegund at the very time that the Oswald legend was presumably developing in the German-language area.

The thesis that the sacred legend derives from the hagiographic romance, that is, the *Münchner Oswald*, and not the other way around, is not compelling. Such a derivation demands a complicated reconstruction, with recourse to a variety of texts. The latter thesis, however, that the hagiographic romance derives from the sacred legend, posits the simple severance of one structural element, the conversion/bridal quest plot, and the composition of a new conclusion introduced by Christ's test of Oswald's willingness to give up all, including his wife, and to preserve conjugal chastity (v. 3510). This final narrative element is notably lacking in the *Wiener Oswald*, which concludes with the baptism of the heathen princess, her father, and his people (vv. 1430–1437) and the drowning of all those who refuse baptism (vv. 1446–1453). Deriving the romance from the sacred legend, as we maintain, supports Bräuer's thesis that the *Wiener Oswald* is a closer relative of the original German legend than the *Münchner Oswald*, especially since the latter so obviously moves into the sphere of the comical, even burlesque, especially in the characterization of the raven.[84]

How likely is it that a romance which ignores the protagonist's martyr status and chooses not to transmit the miracles confirming his sanctity would have been the earliest vernacular text accompanying the cult of St. Oswald in the German-language area? To be sure, the "authentic" Latin *vitae* existed, but for the saint's cult to reach the populace at large, vernacular versions of Oswald's *vita* and *passio* were called for. Furthermore, how plausible is it that an author who wished to compose the sacred legend in the vernacular would have used the bridal-quest romance as a basis but reconstituted and reinterpreted it with elements from Bede? Or, to ask with Achim Masser: "War sie [die Oswald-Dichtung] sozusagen 'rein spielmännisch' angelegt und ist dann die legendenhafte Komponente erst später hinzugekommen, oder ist vielleicht umgekehrt anzunehmen, daß ein als wirkliche Legendendichtung konzipiertes Werk in spätmittelalterlicher Fabulierlust zu dem geworden ist, als was es sich uns zuletzt darstellt?"[85] To answer Masser: the most likely origin and development of the German Oswald legend is to be sought in an originally hagiographically conceived work, a vernacularization of an existing Latin legend, such as Drogo's composition, with its *vita, passio,* and miracles.

---

[84] Cf. Walter Haug, "Das Komische und das Heilige. Zur Komik in der religiösen Literatur des Mittelalters," *Wolfram-Studien* 7 (1982): 8–31; repr. in idem, *Strukturen als Schlüssel zur Welt. Kleine Schriften zur Erzählliteratur des Mittelalters* (Tübingen: Max Niemeyer, 1989), 257–74; see esp. 268–73.

[85] Achim Masser, *Bibel- und Legendenepik des deutschen Mittelalters,* Grundlagen der Germanistik 19 (Berlin: Erich Schmidt, 1976), 163.

This was expanded through the addition of a prefatory coronation legend and the development of the bridal-quest narrative. Subsequently, this vernacular Oswald legend became bifurcated, when the version extant in the *Münchner Oswald* eliminated the prefatory and concluding sections of the legend, that is, the coronation legend on the one hand, and Oswald's death at the hands of pagan forces, as well as the miracles attesting his sanctity as a martyr, on the other, so that a hagiographic bridal-quest romance emerged in which the historical martyr king was in the end transformed into a fictional confessor king.

*Ósvalds saga* is not a translation of the *Heiligen Leben/Passionael* legend, as the passages adduced above in section III amply attest. Although *Ósvalds saga* has repeatedly been mentioned in discussions of the German Oswald legend, the place of the Icelandic translation among the German redactions has consistently been misrepresented for the simple reason that no previous scholar has ever conducted a systematic comparative analysis of the saga and the German prose legend. What is presumably true for the other legends translated from Low German into Icelandic that are found in the *Reykjahólabók* legendary applies to *Ósvalds saga* as well: not the *Heiligen Leben/Passionael* version is the source of the saga, but rather the long German version that was condensed for inclusion into *Der Heiligen Leben*. Given that the saga's source was beyond a doubt Low German, the long vernacular Oswald legend must have existed in both High and Low German redactions. The Middle High German redaction was condensed for the *Heiligen Leben* legendary, while its Middle Low German variant was the source of the Icelandic saga.

In keeping with the above, the stemmatic relationship traditionally assumed for the development of the Oswald legend in the German-language area, as depicted earlier (see p. 7), no longer holds true. Instead, the following most likely represents the evolution of the vernacular legend:

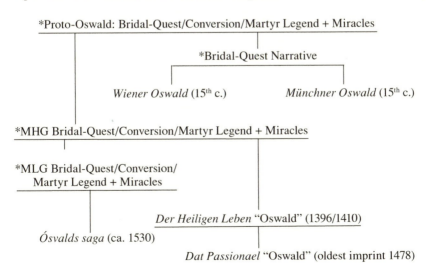

\*Proto-Oswald: Bridal-Quest/Conversion/Martyr Legend + Miracles

    \*Bridal-Quest Narrative

    *Wiener Oswald* (15th c.)      *Münchner Oswald* (15th c.)

\*MHG Bridal-Quest/Conversion/Martyr Legend + Miracles

\*MLG Bridal-Quest/Conversion/
    Martyr Legend + Miracles

    *Der Heiligen Leben* "Oswald" (1396/1410)

*Ósvalds saga* (ca. 1530)

    *Dat Passionael* "Oswald" (oldest imprint 1478)

It is impossible to establish the date of the Middle Low German translation. Its Middle High German source, however, that is, the source of the condensed text in *Der Heiligen Leben*, has to antedate the production of the legendary; thus it had to have been produced before the period 1396–1410. If the legend was composed to accompany the developing cult of St. Oswald, as is most likely, then there is no reason not to posit the origin of the vernacular legend in the twelfth century, especially if the legend of Henry and Cunegund, as will be argued below, played a central role in the development of the bridal-quest narrative in the Oswald legend. Presumably the Proto-Oswald was a metrical legend, like any number of other vernacular legends produced in the twelfth century.[86] While at first it may seem odd that a twelfth-century legend does not surface except in reduced form at the turn of the fifteenth century, and in its complete form only in Icelandic translation in the early sixteenth century, one ought to recall the fate of other early hagiographic literature. For example, the only complete text of Heinrich von Veldeke's twelfth-century legend of St. Servatius is found in a manuscript dated to the second half of the fifteenth century.[87] For its part, Ebernand von Erfurt's legend of Heinrich and Cunegund, dated to around 1220, is transmitted in only one manuscript thought to have been produced in the second quarter of the fifteenth century.[88] The situation is similar in respect to secular literature: Hartmann von Aue's *Erec* and the anonymous *Moriz von Craûn*, among others, are extant only because these works were transmitted in the early sixteenth-century manuscript known as the *Ambraser Heldenbuch*.[89] Not one manuscript of Konrad von Würzburg's *Engelhard* exists; we know the romance only in a 1573 Frankfurt imprint.[90]

The German Oswald legend represented by *Ósvalds saga* did not derive from the metrical version, that is, the *Münchner/Wiener Oswald*, but rather antedated it and was its source. This German version, known today only because it was translated into Icelandic in the early sixteenth century, represents the original vernacular legend, consisting of the coronation, bridal-quest/conversion, and martyr narratives and concluding with a miracle sequence. The original German life of

---

[86] A similar case has been made for the unknown source of another legend, that of John Chrysostom, found in *Der Heiligen Leben/Dat Passionael* and also *Reykjahólabók*. Charles Allyn Williams's analysis of the prose legend in *Der Heiligen Leben* revealed "traces of older rimed verse" of which "enough are left to make plausible the existence of an earlier German version in rimed couplets": *The German Legends of the Hairy Anchorite*, Illinois Studies in Language and Literature 18 (Urbana: University of Illinois Press, 1935), 38–39.

[87] "Heinrich von Veldeke," in ²*VL* (1981), 3:904.

[88] "Ebernand von Erfurt," in ²*VL* (1978), 2:291.

[89] "Ambraser Heldenbuch," in ²*VL* (1978), 1:323–27.

[90] "Konrad von Würzburg," in ²*VL* (1984), 5:294-95.

Oswald was quadripartite; it expanded Bede's account in the *Historia ecclesias-tica* with the coronation and bridal-quest narratives. The version transmitted in the *Münchner Oswald* and *Wiener Oswald* derives from this quadripartite legend; it omitted all but the conversion/bridal-quest story and, in the case of the Munich redaction, transformed the historically attested martyr into a fictionalized vir-ginal confessor. The following pages explore the hagiographic context that made possible the evolution of the German Oswald legend from a staid Latin martyr legend into a vernacular version fictionalized through the introduction of a brid-al-quest narrative featuring a most unusual proxy wooer, a talking raven.

# V.

# THE CORONATION LEGEND AND DEVELOPMENT OF THE BRIDAL-QUEST NARRATIVE

The original German legend of St. Oswald, which, it is here claimed, is represented by the Icelandic *Ósvalds saga*, has a quadripartite structure and consists of three legends—the coronation legend, the bridal-quest/conversion legend, and the martyr legend—and a series of miracles. The first two parts of the *vita* exist solely *in nuce* in Bede's account in the *Historia ecclesiastica*, which relates that Oswald became king after the death of his brother Eanfrid and after the "savage tyrant" Cædwalla's death in battle against him (3.1), and that he married the daughter of the West Saxon King Cynegisl after the latter's baptism (3.7). In the Icelandic saga, which represents the original German legend, Bede's characterization of Oswald as an exemplary Christian king—"Christianissimus rex Nordanhymbrorum" (3.9)—and the facts of Oswald's coronation and marriage to an erstwhile pagan king's daughter have been transmuted into fully developed narratives. How did this come about?

The extant Latin texts offer evidence that from its beginnings the legend contained material constituting a portrait of Oswald as a Christian king. Bede's information is sketchy, and we learn about Oswald more from his deeds than from the historian's own appraisal of the saint. He merely remarks that "though he wielded supreme power over the whole land, he was always wonderfully humble, kind, and generous to the poor and to strangers," a characterization also transmitted by Drogo in his *Vita Oswaldi*.[91] This very comment, that Oswald remained humble even though he came to wield supreme power over the whole land, occurs in the saga after Oswald has been crowned and has subjected mighty lords and lands to his rule:

Af þessari mekt og stórri herlegheit upphóf hann sig ekki til neins metnaðar eða drambsemi nema að heldur var hann því lítillátari og góðgjarnari í öllu og hafði guð jafnan fyrir augum sér. Og þjónaði honum með allri ástúð bæði nætur og daga og guð var ætíð með honum. (1:73.5)

(For all of this power and great authority he did not become puffed up with pride or arrogance, but rather was all the more humble and benevolent in everything and set his eyes ever upon God [Psalm 25:15], and he served him with great love both night and day and God was ever with him.)

---

[91] "quo regni culmine sublimatus (quod mirum dictu est) pauperibus et peregrinis semper humilis benignus et largus fuit" (3.6). Cf. "De S. Oswaldo rege ac mart.," *Acta Sanctorum*. Augusti, II, 5–12, Aug. 5, 97. Subsequent references to Drogo's *vita* are to this text.

Drogo's *vita*, written for the monks' edification, expands Bede's characterization of Oswald considerably by focusing on the virtues that distinguished him—and which presumably were meant to be emulated by the monks:[92]

> At idem Rex insignis virtutibus, Christique præclarus athleta, Spiritu sancto regente omnes actus ipsius, semper in melius proficiebat, de virtute in virtutem ibat, ut mereretur assequi quod sequitur; Videbitur Deus deorum in Sion [Psalm 84:7]. Dein usque actu suo, tum autem mente quattuor virtutes, prudentiam, justitiam, fortitudinem, temperantiam amplexabatur, & quasi quoddam sanctum justumque, per quas acquiritur cælum, aditur Deus, præ se ferebat: tum autem memoriæ quasi charissima pignora fixas tenebat. Semper denique bonus, pius, mansuetus bonis habebatur: ferus verò, asper, & velut arrogans impiis videbatur, ut bonitas illius bonis, & asperitas, uti videbatur, impiis prodesset. Verùm id quidem norma justitiæ tenet, ut blandiantur & hortentur justi exemplo, miti verbo, bono opere; injusti quoque deterreantur aspera invectione. Sic utique actus suos, sic mores, sic vitam instituit, ut sibi, & omnibus prodesse optaret. (99)

> (Moreover the king, remarkable for his virtues and a splendid champion of Christ, all his deeds guided by the Holy Spirit, advanced steadily in becoming better; he went from strength to strength, so as to merit attaining what follows: "the God of gods will be seen in Zion" [Psalm 84:7]. Then ever in his deeds, moreover with his mind he embraced the four virtues, prudence, justice, fortitude, and temperance, and bore them before him as something holy and just, by means of which heaven is gained and God is approached: moreover, he firmly remembered them as most loving pledges. In fine, he was always good, kind, and gentle to the good, but fierce, harsh, and haughty to the wicked, so that his goodness was of benefit, so it seemed, to the good, and his harshness to the wicked. In truth he observed the precepts of justice, so that the just were persuaded and exhorted by example, by gentle words, by good works; but the unjust were deterred by fierce verbal attacks. That is how he undertook his deeds, his habits, in sum his life, for he desired to be of benefit to himself and all.)

While the portrait in *Ósvalds saga* corresponds only in general outline to the above, the two texts nonetheless similarly present Oswald as the virtuous Christian king who practiced good works but was stern and harsh toward the wicked.

It strikes one as somewhat odd that Bede should not have depicted the martyr king more fully in the *Historia ecclesiastica*, especially since he does so in the case of King Oswine. He ruled the kingdom of Deira after Oswald's death, and his portrait is devoted to both his physical and spiritual qualities:

---

[92] "Ces gloses ajoutées par Drogon, et avec discrétion, ne touchent en rien à l'histoire: elles ne veulent qu'être édifiantes": Bayart, "Les Offices de Saint Winnoc et de Saint Oswald," 14.

Erat autem rex Osuini et aspectu uenustus et statura sublimis et affatu iu-
cundus et moribus ciuilis et manu omnibus, id est nobilibus simul atque ig-
nobilibus, largus; unde contigit ut ob regiam eius et animi et uultus et meri-
torum dignitatem ab omnibus diligeretur, et undique at eius ministerium
de cunctis prope prouinciis uiri etiam nobilissimi concurrerent. Cuius inter
ceteras uirtutis et modestiae et, ut ita dicam, specialis benedictionis glorias
etiam maxima fuisse fertur humilitas. (*HE*, 3.14)

(King Oswine was tall and handsome, pleasant of speech, courteous in
manner, and bountiful to nobles and commons alike; so it came about that
he was beloved by all because of the royal dignity which showed itself in his
character, his appearance, and his actions; and noblemen from almost every
kingdom flocked to serve him as retainers. Among all the other graces of
virtue and modesty with which, if I may say so, he was blessed in a special
manner, his humility is said to have been the greatest.)

Oswine was treacherously murdered by Oswy, Oswald's brother, "in the ninth
year of his reign" (3.14) and was subsequently canonized, "probably as a result of
Bede's encomiums."[93]

One explanation for the extended portrayal of Oswine on the one hand but the
terse characterization of Oswald on the other as "humble, kind, and generous to
the poor and to strangers" may be that in this case Bede preferred to illustrate the
character of the king by including an exemplum. For, immediately following the
remark concerning the generosity of the king, Bede relates how Oswald one Easter
Day ordered that the food which was set before him be distributed to the poor and
the silver dish containing it broken into pieces and similarly distributed. This happened in the presence of Bishop Aidan and merited Aidan's memorable blessing
and prayer: "Numquam inueterescat haec manus" ('may this hand never decay'
[3.6]). And Bede goes on to record that this did indeed come true for the relic.

The saga's introductory portrait of Oswald, cited above in section III, is followed by the remark that "" þenna tíma var enginn kóngur í Englandi sem að réttum erfðum átti ríkinu stýra" ('at that time there was no king in England who was
properly in line of succession to rule the kingdom' [*Rhb.*, 71:13–15]), and the saga
continues by reporting that the mightiest and wisest lords of the land agreed that
Oswald should be their ruler. But he fled, wishing to avoid this honor. Only after
repeated entreaties by the emissaries sent after him does Oswald consent to become
king. None of this material comes from Bede. What is the hagiographer's source?

The development of the vernacular Oswald legend may be understood in the
context of existing saints' lives, chiefly the lives of royal saints. The legends produced to accompany and support a saint's cult followed well-established narrative

---

[93] *Bede's Ecclesiastical History of the English People*, ed. Colgrave and Mynors,
256, n. 2.

models and were responsive to audience expectations.[94] Unlike more modern medieval saints, that is, eleventh-, twelfth-, and thirteenth-century saints, hagiogra-
phers had no canonization acts to fall back upon in the production of Oswald's
*vita*. What they did have, however, were already existing *vitae*, and it is most
likely that Oswald's portrait as a Christian king as well as various other "fictionalized" parts of his *vita* are indebted to the life of another royal saint.

The saga's portrayal of Oswald—and, as we shall see, the composition of
the bridal-quest narrative—was most likely inspired by the life of the emperor
Henry II (1002–1024), whose *vita* was being shaped at around the same time that
Oswald's relics came to Weingarten, and the fictional aspects of which—such as
his virginal marriage to Cunegund—had become incorporated into his legend
early on. Already around 1060 Leo of Ostia refers to the virginal marriage in the
monastic chronicle of Monte Cassino.[95] The story belonged to the material col-
lected for furthering Henry's canonization[96] and is mentioned in the bull of canonization of 1146.[97] In the third Nocturn of Matins for the feast of St. Henry, the
virginal marriage and Cunegund's subsequent chastity test are the subject of one
of the responses.[98] The legend of Henry and Cunegund immediately precedes
that of Oswald in *Reykjahólabók* and it is tempting to interpret this juxtaposi-
tion as a German compiler's indication of their affinity as royal saints, that is, if
these two *vitae* were actually found together in Björn Þorleifsson's Low German
source.[99] Indeed, a relationship between the two saints is attested by the earliest
reliquary of Henry II from the last quarter of the twelfth century, produced in
Hildesheim. This cruciform reliquary, which depicts Christ on one side and Hen-

---

[94] See Thomas J. Heffernan, *Sacred Biography: Saints and Their Biographers in the
Middle Ages* (New York and Oxford: Oxford University Press, 1988), 14–15.

[95] *Chronicon monasterii Casinensis,* MGH, Scriptores 7 (Hannover: Hahn, 1846),
658. Cf. Renate Klauser, *Der Heinrichs- und Kunigundenkult im mittelalterlichen Bistum
Bamberg* (Bamberg: Selbstverlag des Historischen Vereins, 1957), 33; Robert Folz, *Les
saints rois du Moyen Âge en Occident (VIe – XIIIe siècles)*, Subsidia Hagiographica 68
(Brussels: Société des Bollandistes, 1984), 87.

[96] Klaus Guth, *Die Heiligen Heinrich und Kunigunde* (Bamberg: St. Otto-Verlag,
1986), 78.

[97] MGH, Scriptores 4 (Hannover: Hahn, 1841), 813b. See also Hans-Jürgen Schröpfer, *"Heinrich und Kunegunde". Untersuchungen zur Verslegende des Ebernand von Erfurt und zur Geschichte ihres Stoffs* (Göppingen: Alfred Kümmerle, 1969), 22–25.

[98] Robert Folz, "La légende liturgique de saint Henri II empereur et confessor," in
*Clio et son regard: Mélanges d'histoire de l'art et d'archéologie offerts à Jacques Stien-
non à l'occasion de ses vingt-cinq ans d'enseignement à l'Université de Liège*, ed. Rita
Lejeune and Joseph Deckers (Liège: Pierre Mardaga, 1982), 245–58, here 253.

[99] In one of the manuscripts listed by Klauser as containing the legend of Henry, a
fourteenth-century manuscript of unknown provenance and containing about fifty saints'
lives, the *Vita Heinrici* is immediately followed by "Beda in historia Anglorum de sancto
Oswaldo" (*Der Heinrichs- und Kunigundenkult*, 207).

ry on the other, shows three kings bowing before their heavenly king. The one on Christ's right, receiving Christ's blessing as it were, is Oswald.[100] While Oswald represents the older path to sanctity, martyrdom, Henry's life illustrates the more modern approach through virginity. Like Oswald, Henry subjected other peoples to his royal authority and like him he is remembered for his conversion efforts, notably in Hungary, which earned him one hagiographer's appellation "Apostle of the Hungarians."[101]

*Hendreks saga og Kunegundis*, like *Ósvalds saga*, opens with a portrait of the saint:

> Upp í Ofurlandi liggur eitt land er þeir kalla Bæjeren.[102] Í þessu landinu var einn so megtugur hertogi er Hendrikus hét. Þessi hertogi var einn góðkristinn herra og óttaðist guð. Hann var og vel lærður á heilagri skrift. Hann var mildur og góðgjarn, hægur og lítillátur við alla fátæka og auðmjúka, en þó harðrægur og réttlátur við ómilda og drambláta. Hann elskaði vel guðsþjónustu bæði nótt og dag, með föstum og vökum, með bænum og mildum ölmusugjörðum. Og fyrir þessa hluti og marga aðra er hann framdi í guðs augliti, þá vildi guð almáttugur ekki láta minnka hans heiður og tign hér fyrst á jarðríki, og var hann kjörinn af öllum herrum og forstjórum heilagrar kristni til eins keisara yfir allt rómverskt ríki. Af þessari tign og verðugheit uphóf hann sig ekki í neinu drambi eður ofmetnaði so það mátti nokkur finna, heldur kallaði hann sig vera með öllu óverðugan í augliti guðs til slíks embættis, en eftir guðs tilskikkan þá varð so að vera sem alþýðan og herranir vildu.[103]

(In the highland area there is a country called Bavaria. In this country there was a very powerful duke whose name was Henry. This duke was a deeply Christian lord who feared God. He was also very learned in sacred scripture. He was generous and kind, gentle and humble toward all those who

---

[100] *Kaiser Heinrich II. 1002–1024*, ed. Josef Kirchmeier et al., Veröffentlichungen zur Bayerischen Geschichte und Kultur 44 (Augsburg: Bayerisches Staatsministerium für Wissenschaft, Forschung und Kunst, 2002), 364–66; cf. illus. 189. It is noteworthy that around this same time an Oswald reliquary was donated to the cathedral chapter in Hildesheim, presumably a gift of Henry the Lion and his wife Mathilde (365).

[101] Folz, *Les saints rois du Moyen Âge*, 88–89. The reference is to Ebernand von Erfurt's metrical legend, *Heinrich und Kunigunde*, where we read: "Ungerlant dô heiden was, / der keiser ir apostel wart, / er wîstes an die rehte vart / kristenlîcher dinge" (Ebernand von Erfurt, *Heinrich und Kunigunde*, ed. Reinhold Bechstein [Quedlingburg and Leipzig: G. Basse, 1860], vv. 2100–3). The martyrology relates that "sanctum Stephanum Hungarorum regem cum universo fere ejus regno ad fidem Christi suscipiendam perduxit" (AA SS, July 3.714a).

[102] The manuscript writes *Beijeren*, transmitting the German form. This text, like that of *Ósvalds saga*, is here given in modern Icelandic orthography.

[103] "Hendreks saga og Kunegundis," *Rhb.*, 1:35.1–16.

were poor and meek, but severe and righteous toward the unrighteous and arrogant. He loved serving God both by day and night, with fasts and vigils, with prayers and generous alms. And for these things and many others that he carried out in God's sight, God did not want to have his honor and high station diminish here on earth, and he was chosen by all the lords and leaders of holy Christendom as emperor over the entire Roman empire. On account of this high station and merits he did not become puffed up with arrogance or overweening pride so that anyone could fault him; rather he considered himself in every way unworthy in the sight of God for such an office, but in keeping with God's providence things turned out as the common people and the lords wanted.)

Here we need to recall that *Hendreks saga*, like *Ósvalds saga*, is translated from a Low German source, and as is the case with the prefatory portrait of Oswald, the portrait of Emperor Henry in the *Passionael* is characterized by a similar parataxis of style and reduction of narrative detail:

Keyser Hinrik was eyn hertoghe in Beyeren. vnde he wart keyser na der bort Cristi dusent iar. vnde was ein cristen. vnde vurchtede got. vnde was wol ghelert in der hyllighen scrift. vnde was othmodich. vnde vorhoef syck nycht in synen eren. vnde was rechtuerdich. vnde denede gode dach vnde nacht. mit bedende. mit vastende. mit wakende. vnde mit vele ander guder ouinghe. (lviii.a)

(Emperor Henry was a duke in Bavaria. And he became emperor one thousand years after the birth of Christ. And he was a Christian, and he feared God, and he was very learned in sacred scripture. And he was humble, and he did not become arrogant on account of his honors. And he was righteous, and he served God day and night, with prayer, fasting, vigils, and with many other pious devotions.)

Unlike Oswald, in the Icelandic legend Henry does not flee when he is chosen emperor; the *Passionael* is silent concerning Henry's choice as emperor. Recall that when Oswald learns that he is to be chosen king, he considers himself unworthy and secretly steals away, hoping that he could thus avoid the honor (see p. 24). Oswald's behavior is in the best tradition of saints who flee in order to escape high office. That is the story told, for example, about Gregory the Great when the people of Rome elected him to be their bishop. In the *Legenda aurea* we read:

. . . fugere voluit, sed nequivit, quia die noctuque portas urbis propter eum vigiles observabant. Tandem mutato habitu a quibusdam negotiatoribus obtinuit, ut in quodam dolio super quadrigam de urbe educeretur. Qui mox sylvam expetiit, cavernarum latibula requisivit ibique tribus diebus latuit.

Verumtamen dum sollicite quaereretur, columna lucida perfulgida a coelo dependens super locum, in quo latitabat, apparuit, in qua columna angelos descendentes et ascendentes quidam reclusus aspexit, moxque ab universo populo capitur, trahitur et summus pontifex consecratur.[104]

(. . . Gregory tried to flee from home but could not, because they watched for him day and night at the city gates. At length he changed his clothes and persuaded some tradesmen to hide him in a wine cask and get him out of the city in a wagon. When they reached a forest, he made for a hiding place in the caves and hid there for three days. A relentless search for him was under way, and a bright column of light beamed down from the heavens and appeared over the place where he had concealed himself: a certain hermit saw angels descending and ascending [cf. Genesis 28:12] in this beam. Of course this led the pursuers to Gregory, and they carried him back to Rome and consecrated him as supreme pontiff.)[105]

While the flight motif in *Ósvalds saga* could have been borrowed from any number of existing saints' lives, the impulse for the inclusion of the coronation legend proper and the following bridal-quest story should be sought in existing legends popular in the German-language area. In all probability the legends associated with two powerful Germanic rulers and their saintly queens, Clovis, king of the Franks, and Clotild, and Emperor Henry II and Cunegund, were the chief donors in the development of the Oswald legend, as we shall see.

By means of the coronation legend that prefaces Oswald's *vita*, the Northumbrian martyr is drawn into a wider complex of already existing narratives about historical royal figures and in the process he gains a proxy wooer, a staple of Germanic bridal-quest narrative. The story of the missing chrism when Oswald is to be anointed as king and the miraculous delivery of the same by a heavenly-sent raven is an analogue to a legend told in connection with another Germanic king, like Oswald a convert from paganism and like him engaged in conversion politics, namely Clovis. The story of this Frankish king's baptism in 496 is documented in the legend of St. Remigius, which attests the fifth-century missionizing activity

---

[104] "De sancto Gregorio," Jacobi a Voragine *Legenda Aurea vulgo Historia Lombardica dicta*, ed. Th. Graesse, 3rd ed. (Bratislava: Koestner, 1890; repr. Osnabrück: Otto Zeller Verlag, 1969), 191. Cf. the account in the "Vita sancti Gregorii papae," in Boninus Mombritius, ed., *Sanctuarium seu Vitae Sanctorum* (Paris: Albert Fontemoing, 1910; repr. Hildesheim and New York: Georg Olms, 1978), 1:590–91.

[105] Jacobus de Voragine, *The Golden Legend. Readings on the Saints,* tr. William Granger Ryan (Princeton: Princeton University Press, 1993), 1:173. Jacobus goes on to note that it is clear from Gregory's writings that he accepted this highest honor against his will, and he cites excerpts from Gregory's letters and the prologue to his Dialogues in support of the statement (in idem, *The Golden Legend*, 173–74).

of the Church. The story of the missing chrism surfaces in the life of Remigius
by Hincmar of Reims († 882)—the story is not found in Gregory of Tours's *History of the Franks*—and gained general currency when the legend was transmitted in the popular Latin and vernacular compilations of saints' lives. Hincmar's
legend of Clovis's baptism, which "rests on no known historical foundation,"[106]
relates that when no sacred chrism could be found, St. Remigius lifted his eyes
and hands to heaven and tearfully prayed for help,

> Et ecce subitò columba nive candidior attulit in rostro ampullulam, chrismate sancto repletam, cujus odore mirifico super omnes odores, quos antè
> in baptisterio senserant, omnes, qui aderant, inæstimabili suavitate repleti
> sunt. Accipiente autem sancto Pontifice ipsam ampullulam, species columbæ disparuit: de quo chrismate fudit venerandus Episcopus in fontem sacratum. Viso autem rex tanto miraculo, abnegatis diaboli pompis & operibus
> ejus, petiit, se à sancto Pontifice baptizari.[107]

> (And behold suddenly a dove, whiter than snow, arrived, bearing in its beak
> an ampulla filled with sacred chrism, whose fragrance, wondrously surpassing all fragrances and replete with inestimable mildness, reached all present
> in the baptistery. When the holy bishop had taken the ampulla, the dove disappeared, and the venerable bishop placed the contents of this chrismatory
> into the sacred font. Moreover, the king having seen such a great miracle,
> abjured the pomps and works of the devil and asked to be baptized by the
> holy bishop.)

Robert Folz's suggestion that the legend of Clovis's baptism most likely inspired
Oswald's coronation legend is persuasive.[108] Acquaintance with the Remigius leg-

---

[106] J. M. Wallace-Hadrill, *The Long-Haired Kings and Other Studies in Frankish History* (New York: Barnes & Noble, 1962), 103. While Gregory of Tours gives an account
of Clovis's baptism in the *Historia Francorum* (2.31), it does not include the story of the
missing chrism.

[107] AA SS, Octobris 1:146–47.

[108] Robert Folz, "Saint Oswald roi de Northumbrie: Étude d'hagiographie royale,"
*Analecta Bollandiana* 98 (1980): 49–74, here 58. The connection between Oswald's coronation and Clovis's baptism was already suggested by Ignaz V. Zingerle in 1856 in *Die
Oswaldlegende und ihre Beziehung zur deutschen Mythologie*, 67: "Was Punkt I. betrifft [i.e., the raven brings the chrism for the coronation], so scheint die Legende vom h.
Remigius hier benützt worden zu seyn. Die Taube, die bei der Taufe des Chlodwig den
Chrisam brachte, *musste* hier als Rabe erscheinen. Eine solche Verwechslung des Raben und der Taube findet sich in den Volkstraditionen öfters." The *Handwörterbuch des
deutschen Aberglaubens* (ed. Hanns Bächtold-Stäubli [Berlin: Walter de Gruyter, 1935–
1936], 7:435) writes: "In St. Oswald mit dem R[abe]n Wodan sehen zu wollen, ist wohl
verfehlt."

end was widespread in the German-language area; vernacular versions are found in many legendaries—although not all versions contain the story of Clovis's baptism—including *Der Heiligen Leben* and *Dat Passionael*,[109] and the great *Vers-Passional*, dating from the end of the thirteenth century. In this work we are told that when Remigius was to anoint Clovis with the sacramental oil at his baptism,

> . . . seht wo des gebrach!
> wand man nindert ensach
> alda olei so bereit.
> diz was dem bischove leit,
> des in doch wol machte vri,
> ein wize tube quam im bi,
> mit der in got bedachte,
> diu ein ampullen brachte,
> darinne er schonen cresmen vant.
> zu gote neic er alzuhant
> und salbete den kunic mite
> als im wisete der site
> von der ecclesien ufgeleit.
> noch hute ist ein gewonheit
> des landes zu Vrancriche,
> daz man erliche
> die ampullen behaldet
> und dran nicht verschaldet,
> man ersalbe damite
> die kunige noch, daz ist ir site.
> Clodoueus der kunic hiez,
> dem got dise genade liez,
> daz im diz olei wart gesant.[110]

(. . . behold, it was missing! Nowhere could the chrism be found. The bishop was upset at this, but he was saved when a white dove appeared, sent by God, which brought an ampulla in which there was fine chrism. He bowed down before God and anointed the king, as church tradition demanded. To this day it is the custom in France to preserve the ampulla and not to misuse

---

[109] Williams-Krapp, *Die deutschen und niederländischen Legendare des Mittelalters*, 455, lists thirteen legendaries—in addition to *HL* and *Pass.*—that contain the legend of St. Remigius.

[110] Karl Köpke, ed., *Das Passional. Eine Legenden-Sammlung des dreizehnten Jahrhunderts* (Quedlinburg and Leipzig: Gottfr. Basse, 1852), 95:19–41. According to Williams-Krapp, *Die deutschen und niederländischen Legendare des Mittelalters*, 287, the *HL* Remigius derives from *Vers-Passional*, #7, *Legenda Aurea*, CXLVII, and *Märterbuch*, # 82. The last, however, does not contain the story of Clovis's baptism.

its contents; with it the kings are still anointed; that is their custom. Clovis was the name of the king, to whom God granted this favor, that this chrism was sent for him.)

The link between the baptismal chrism and that used in the coronation liturgy is clearly established, for the German legend relates that the chrism for Clovis's baptism came to be identical with the chrism subsequently used to anoint French kings. Thus it is not surprising that the story of the missing chrism at Clovis's baptism should be appropriated for another king, the Northumbrian Oswald, as a sign of divine approval of his royal election.

In Oswald's *vita* the story of the missing chrism may be considered an appropriate narrative element in a legend focusing at the outset on the issue of royal succession. In the legend of Oswald, a raven with chrism for the coronation is substituted for the dove in the story of Clovis's baptism. That the hagiographer might have been inspired to incorporate into the legend of St. Oswald material from the baptismal legend of Clovis and the derivative coronation legend of the French kings is not extraordinary. The similarity between Clovis (466–511), founder of the Frankish kingdom—convert to Christianity, champion of orthodoxy, and intrepid warrior—and the Northumbrian martyr king could not have been lost on the hagiographer.[111] Like Clovis, Oswald was concerned about the consolidation of Christianity in his realm and, like the Frankish king, the Northumbrian was born a heathen and converted to Christianity. Whereas Oswald, the Christian, married a pagan princess, whom he converted, Clovis, the pagan, married a Christian, the Burgundian princess Clotild (Chrodechild), who was instrumental in his conversion and came to be venerated as a saint.[112] The queen's efforts at converting her husband are no less diligent than Oswald's in seeking to convert the pagan princess, her father, and his people. Hincmar mentions Clotild's repeated attempts to convert her husband:

Regina enim cotidie illi prædicabat eum: at ille nolebat eam audire. . . . Regina quoque non cessabat regi prædicare, ut Deum verum coleret, & idola, quæ colebat, vana derelinqueret; sed nullo modo animum ejus ad credendum poterat commovere. (AA SS Oct. 1:145)

(For the queen did not cease exhorting him daily, but he did not want to listen. . . . Nonetheless, the queen did not cease exhorting the king, that he worship the true God, and that he cease worshipping his empty idols, but she was in no way able to move his heart to believe [in the true God].)

---

[111] See "Chlodwig," in *LMA*, 2:1863–1868. Cf. Gregory of Tours, *Historia Francorum*, 2.30–31; Wallace-Hadrill, *The Long-Haired Kings,* chap. 7.

[112] See Robert Folz, *Les saintes reines du Moyen Âge en Occident (VIe – XIIIe siècles)*, Subsidia Hagiographica 76 (Brussels: Société des Bollandistes, 1992), 9–13.

Not until Clovis prepares to fight against the Alemanni, and his counselor urges him to turn to the Christian God, does the king promise God

> ut, si mihi victoriam super hostes dederis, & expertus fuero illam virtutem, quam de te populi prædicant, credam tibi, & in nomine tuo baptizabor. Invocavi enim deos meos, &, ut experior, elongati sunt ab auxilio meo: unde credo, eos nulla potestate esse præditos, qui sibi credentibus non succurrunt. Te verum Deum ac Dominum invoco, & in te credere desidero; tantùm ut liberer ab adversariis meis. (AA SS, Oct. 1:145)

> (that if you give me victory over the enemy, and I experience that power about which the people preach, I shall believe in you and will be baptized in your name. For I have called upon my gods and have realized that they are far from granting me assistance. Hence I believed that they have no power if they do not assist those who believe in them. I call upon you, the true God and Lord, and I desire to believe in you if you deliver me from my enemies.)

God hears Clovis's prayer and the Alemanni are routed. The victorious Clovis returns to tell his queen what has happened and the latter implores St. Remigius "ut regi salutis viam prædicaret" ('to teach the king the way of salvation' [AA SS, Oct. 1:145]). Clovis in turn decides to preach to his people who do not want to follow him into Christianity, and we read: "Et veniens rex ad populum cœpit hortari eos, ut in Deum, qui eis victoriam dederat, crederent; quoniam dii illorum in tribulatione sua nichil eis prodesse potuerunt" ('And when the king came to the people, he began to exhort them to believe in the God who had given them victory, since their gods were not able to aid them in their tribulation' [AA SS, Oct. 1:146]). The convert Clovis, as subsequently the convert Oswald was to do, thus participates in proselytizing his pagan people.

Once the raven was introduced into Oswald's legend as the bearer of the divine chrism, it was only natural for the bird to become the proxy wooer. Unlike Clovis's white dove, Oswald's black raven has the gift of speech and becomes his proxy wooer, a task not as remarkable as one might think, if one considers that the raven also figures in other sacred texts as a messenger from God.[113] In the life

---

[113] See "Rabe" in *Handwörterbuch des deutschen Aberglaubens*, 7:443, for references to the raven as a wise and advising bird; also Curschmann, *Der Münchener Oswald und die deutsche spielmännische Epik*, 15–16. Curschmann notes that there is no clear explanation as to how the raven was introduced into the German legend (60, n. 1), and he refers to Reginald's twelfth-century *vita* (174–75), in which a large bird—"eratque ales ipsa, ut putabatur, corvini generis" ("Vita S. Oswaldi Regis et Martyris," 1:356)—is depicted snatching up Oswald's right arm. Reginald goes on, however, to state: "sed pro grandibus rostro et unguibus aquilarum similitudini conformis fuisse videbatur" (1:356). I consider it most unlikely that the inspiration for the raven in the Oswald legend came from Reginald's Latin *vita* rather than the account of Clovis's baptism in the Remigius legend, especially since the function of the bird is completely different in this Latin Oswald *vita*.

of the hermit St. Paul, for example, a raven provides nourishment for him and St.
Anthony in the desert, an incident presumably inspired by Elijah's experience in
1 Kings 17:4–6. In the German *Vitaspatrum* we learn that as Anthony and Paul
are conversing,

> . . . so komet en rappe geflogen, vnd brâcht en ganzes brot in dem munde,
> vnd leit es fúr sú beide. Do sprach Paulus: "O Anthoni! Got hat vns von
> siner erbemde einen imbis gesant. Es sint sechzig iar, das er mir alle tage en
> halbes brot bi disem vogel gesent hat. Nu ist ovch din tail húte komen, den
> hat got dar zuo geleit."[114]

> (. . . a raven comes flying, and brought an entire loaf of bread in its mouth,
> and laid it in front of the two. Then Paul spoke: "O Anthony! In His mercy
> God has sent us some food. It has now been sixty years that He has been
> sending me every day half a loaf of bread by means of this bird. Now today
> your portion too has arrived, which God has added.")

As for the life of St. Oswald that Bede told, it is clear that he was interested only
in the fact that Oswald married a pagan king's daughter. This is told in the context
of Oswald's missionary activity with a focus on the conversion of a pagan king
and his baptism. For Bede Oswald's marriage to this king's daughter is incidental,
since Cynegisl has already been converted. This is not to say that Bede is totally
uninterested in marriage politics—but only as a means to conversion. Thus he
includes the story of the bridal quest of Peada, the son of King Penda, at whose
hands Oswald was slain:

> Qui cum esset iuuenis optimus, ac regis nomine ac persona dignissimus,
> praelatus est a patre regno gentis illius, uenitque ad regem Nordanhymbro-
> rum Osuiu, postulans filiam eius Alchfledam sibi coniugem dari. Neque
> aliter quod petebat inpetrare potuit, nisi fidem Christi ac baptisma cum
> gente cui praeerat acciperat. At ille, audita praedicatione ueritatis et promis-
> sione regni caelestis speque resurrectionis ac futurae inmortalitatis, libenter
> se Christianum fieri uelle confessus est, etiamsi uirginem non acciperet,
> persuasus maxime ad percipiendam fidem a filio regis Osuiu, nomine Alch-
> frido, qui erat cognatus et amicus eius, habens sororem ipsius coniugem,
> uocabulo Cyniburgam, filiam Pendan regis. (*HE*, 3.21)

> (As he was a most noble youth, worthy both of the name and office of king,
> he was placed by his father on the throne of the kingdom of the Middle An-
> gles. He thereupon went to Oswiu, and asked for the hand of his daughter

---

[114] "Paulus Eremit," *Die >Alemannischen Vitaspatrum<. Untersuchungen und Edition*, ed. Ulla Williams (Tübingen: Niemeyer, 1996), 8:14–18.

Alhflæd. But his request was granted only on condition that he and his nation accepted the Christian faith and baptism. When Peada heard the truth proclaimed and the promises of the kingdom of heaven, the hope of resurrection and of future immortality, he gladly declared himself ready to become a Christian even though he were refused the hand of the maiden. He was earnestly persuaded to accept the faith by Alhfrith, son of King Oswiu, who was his brother-in-law and friend, having married Penda's daughter, Cyneburh.)

Peada's bridal quest is worth telling, since it provides the impetus for his conversion. In the case of Cynegisl and his daughter, the potential conflict does not exist, since Oswald's marriage follows upon Cynegisl's baptism, and implicitly his daughter's as well. The author of the German Oswald legend presumably considered Cynegisl's baptism and Oswald's marriage to his daughter to be inextricably linked and an aspect of the saint's missionizing activity. Such reasoning would demand that Oswald's bridal quest be generated by his desire to convert the heathen peoples. Indeed, that is how *Ósvalds saga* motivates the wooing of the pagan princess.

The author of the German version of the Oswald legend decided that the king's need for a wife was worth pursuing and adapted a bridal-quest model well known in the Germanic realm.[115] Since the author of the Oswald legend knew the story of Clovis's baptism, he presumably also knew other details of the king's life. The story of Clovis's quest for Clotild may have played a role in the composition of the bridal-quest narrative, especially since proselytization was a key element.

The story of Clovis's wooing of Clotild became ever more fictionalized in the course of time and accumulated motifs that became stock features of Germanic bridal-quest narratives. The account by Gregory of Tours is still quite laconic; he tells us that Clovis

> . . . dum legationem in Burgundiam saepius mittit, Chrotchildis puella reperitur a legatis eius. Qui cum eam vidissent elegantem atque sapientem et cognovissent, quod de regio esset genere, nuntiaverunt haec Chlodovecho regi. Nec moratus ille ad Gundobadum legationem mittit, eam sibi in matrimonio petens. Quod ille recusare metuens, tradidit eam viris; illeque accipientes puellam, regi velotius repraesentant.[116]

---

[115] For the following discussion of the bridal-quest narratives in the Franconian chronicles, I am indebted to Claudia Bornholdt, *Engaging Moments: The Origins of Medieval Bridal-Quest Narrative*, Ergänzungsbände *zum Reallexikon der Germanischen Altertumskunde* 46 (New York: Walter de Gruyter, 2005), 17–41.

[116] *Gregorii Tvronensis Opera*, ed. W. Arndt and Br. Krusch, I. *Historia Francorum*, MGH, Scriptorum rerum Merovingicarum 1 (Hannover: Hahn, 1885), 90.

(. . . often sent envoys to Burgundy and they saw the girl Clotild. They observed that she was an elegant young woman and clever for her years, and
they discovered that she was of royal blood. They reported all this to Clovis
and he immediately sent more messengers to Gundobad to ask for her hand
in marriage. Gundobad was afraid to refuse them and he handed Clotild over
to them. They took her back with them, and presented her to their king.)[117]

The story was spun out by Fredegar in his chronicle of the Merovingians, the
*Chronica Fredegarii,* and in the *Liber Historiae Francorum.* As Wallace-Hadrill
has noted, some of Fredegar's interpolations vis-à-vis Gregory of Tours are of a
"purely factual nature," but others "look rather like additions from folk-tale or
hearsay" and among these is "Clovis' wooing of the Burgundian Chrotechildis."[118]
The relatively terse account by Gregory develops into extended, self-contained
bridal-quest narratives in these two later chronicles.[119] Of particular interest from
our perspective is the figure of Aurelian who, in Fredegar's chronicle, becomes the
proxy wooer. When he manages to speak with Clotild in private, he says:

"Chlodoveus rex Francorum me direxit; si voluntas Dei fuerit, te vult cul-
minis sui sociare coniugum. Ut certe ficeris, hoc anulum tibi direxit." Quem
illa accipiens, gaviso gaudio magno, dixitque ad eum: "Accipe centum sole-
dus pro laboris tui munere et anolum hoc meum."[120]

("Clovis, the king of the Franks, has sent me; if it is the will of God, he
wants you to become joined to him in marriage. In testimony of this he has
sent you this ring." She accepted this with great joy and said to him: "Accept
one hundred solidi as reward for your efforts and also my ring.")

As we shall see, the motif of the exchange of rings is appropriated by the Oswald
legend, as is another, found in the *Liber Historiae Francorum,* namely Clotild's
request upon marrying Clovis to submit to specific articles of faith. When Clovis
informs her that he will grant anything she asks, Clotild says:

"Primum peto, ut Deum caeli, Patrem omnipotentem credas, qui te creavit.
Secundo confitere dominum Iesum Christum, filium eius, qui te redemit,
Regem omnium regum, a Patre de caelis missum; tertio Spiritum sanctum
confirmatorem et inluminatorem omnium iustorum. Totam ineffabilem ma-

---

[117] Gregory of Tours, *The History of the Franks,* trans. with an introduction by Lewis
Thorpe (Harmondsworth: Penguin, 1974), 2.28, 141.

[118] Wallace-Hadrill, *The Long-Haired Kings,* 84.

[119] Bornholdt, *Engaging Moments,* 33.

[120] *Fredegarii et aliorum chronica. Vitae sanctorum,* ed. Bruno Krusch, MGH, Scriptorum rerum Merovingicarum 2 (Hannover: Hahn, 1888), 99.

iestatem omnipotentiamque coeternam agnosce et agnitam crede et idola vana derelinque, qui non sunt dii, sed sculptilia vana, incendeque ea (cf. Deuteronomy 7:5, 25) et ecclesias sanctas, quas succendisti, restaura."[121]

(I ask first that you should believe in God in heaven, the almighty Father who created you. Second, that you acknowledge Jesus Christ his son, who redeemed you, the King of all kings, sent down from heaven by the Father. Third, [that you believe in] the Holy Ghost, who strengthens and enlightens all the just. Acknowledge their inexpressible majesty and coeternal omnipotence, and having acknowledged, believe in it. Abandon your useless idols, which are not gods but vain images. Burn them, and rebuild the holy churches you once set on fire.)

Joaquín Martínez Pizarro has remarked on the "organized, comprehensive statement of Trinitarian orthodoxy" in Clotild's speech, which is so at odds with its "anecdotal, romantic context."[122] In *Ósvalds saga*, the figures are, of course, reversed: the Christian king seeks the hand of a pagan princess. Unlike Clotild, Oswald asks for acceptance of the articles of the faith prior to marriage, which are found in the letter that the proxy wooer, that is, the raven, is to bring to the princess together with a ring. Unlike the persons of the Trinity, who are enumerated in Clotild's speech, the articles of faith in Oswald's letter are merely referred to, not listed for the reader, for when the princess receives the letter,

> . . . finnur þar eins sem hrafninn hafði sagt henni og það með hversu að hún skyldi frjálsast frá eilífri pínu og dauða ef hún vildi snúast frá heiðni og villu en trúa á sannan guð og halda þessa tólf parta heilagrar trúar.

> (. . . she finds there what the raven has told her and in addition how she would be saved from eternal punishment and death if she converted from paganism and error and believed in the true God and accepted these twelve articles of the holy faith.)

There is no reason to believe that Björn Þorleifsson's Low German source had actually enumerated the articles of faith as found in the Apostles' Creed (see p. 71, n. 142). The hagiographer most likely assumed that his audience would have known exactly what this part of the letter contained and therefore considered it unnecessary to spell out the details. In any case, it is clear that Oswald's bridal quest must be understood in the context of conversion, for when the stranger arrives at

---

[121] *Liber Historiae Francorum*, ed. Bruno Krusch, MGH, Scriptorum rerum Merovingicarum 2 (Hannover: Hahn, 1888), 257–58.

[122] Joaquín Martínez Pizarro, *A Rhetoric of the Scene: Dramatic Narrative in the Early Middle Ages* (Toronto: University of Toronto Press, 1989), 91.

Oswald's court, just after the king's counselors had asked him to take a wife, he says that he is a prophet,

". . . og eru mér kunnig tvö og sjötíu þjóðlönd, og er ég einn sendiboði af guði sendur að kunngjöra þér að þú skalt taka þér til drottningar eina jungfrú og er eins heiðins konungsdóttir og heitir hann Gaudonus en þessi jungfrúin dóttir hans heitir Pia og er harla mjög væn og hyggin. Og guð býður þér að þú skalt halda mikið örlög fyrir hennar skuld og koma henni til heilagrar trúar og guð drottinn hefur hana út valið til þessa."

(". . . and seventy-two countries are known to me, and I am a messenger from God sent to make known to you that you are to take as your queen a maiden who is the daughter of a heathen king, and his name is Gaudonus, but this maiden, his daughter, is called Pia and she is exceedingly beautiful and wise. And God commands you to wage a great battle for her sake and to convert her to the holy faith, and the Lord God has chosen her for this.")

As we shall see, the battle that Oswald is to wage against her father becomes a battle for the faith, so that the bridal quest for the heathen princess has truly become the means to convert not only her but also her father and all those subject to him.

In considering the development of Clovis's bridal quest from the terse account by Gregory of Tours into the elaborate narratives in Fredegar's chronicle and the *Liber Historiae Francorum* one might bear in mind that Fredegar's additions "probably stem from quite reputable sources, oral and written."[123] Similarly, it is not out of the question that what appears to be pure fabrication in Oswald's legend was based on reputable sources, not sources of ascertainable fact but rather hagiographic sources that provided a model for generating the material that Bede did not include in the life of Oswald.

Although the author of the German Oswald legend was familiar with some aspects of Clovis's life, at least with the story of his baptism, which he integrated into the coronation legend, the immediate impulse for the bridal-quest story most likely came from contemporary imperial history rather than the chronicles of the Franks. In the same period that acquaintance with the details of Oswald's life and death may be assumed for parts of the German-language area because of the composition and transmission of his *vita* to the continent, another royal saint and his queen became the subject of hagiography, namely Emperor Henry II († 1024) and his wife Cunegund († 1033). Henry was canonized in 1146, Cunegund in 1200.

Already by the time of Henry's canonization, not to mention Cunegund's, their lives had undergone extraordinary fictionalization in Latin accounts. The mid-twelfth-century "Vita Heinrici II. Imperatoris" written by the Bamberg deacon Adalbert incorporated the historically unattested motifs of the *Josephsehe*

---

[123] Wallace-Hadrill, *The Long-Haired Kings,* 87.

or spiritual marriage—to explain their lack of progeny—and Cunegund's chastity test.[124] The somewhat later *Additamentum* to the *Vita Heinrici* explained the saints' conjugal chastity as another form of martyrdom.[125] Ebernand von Erfurt's metrical legend *Heinrich und Kunigunde*, thought to have been composed around 1220, transmits what was already found in Latin, a bridal-quest narrative in which the obstacle to marriage is a vow of perpetual virginity by each of the prospective partners, and where the solution to the dilemma is the mutual decision to preserve conjugal chastity.[126] Given the ready insertion of fantastic matter into the biographies of the imperial couple, the development of whose legend was contemporaneous with the acquisition of Oswald's relics in Bergues-St-Winnoc and Weingarten, the transmission of his Latin *vita*, and the ensuing cult, it is not at all remarkable that in the case of the distant figure of St. Oswald a tiny detail of his life, his conversion of a pagan king and marriage to his daughter, should have blossomed into a full-fledged bridal-quest narrative—but with a proselytizing focus.

It is clear that the German hagiographer wanted to expand one aspect of Oswald's life that is barely touched upon either by Bede or in the Latin *vitae*, namely his marriage to Cynegisl's daughter. Although the popularity of bridal-quest narrative in the German-language area is assumed by scholars for the twelfth century, the hagiographer did not need to go to secular sources for inspiration as to how to construct the bridal quest: it was right there in the legend of Henry and Cunegund.

One of the episodes adduced by Anton Edzardi for arguing that the Icelandic Oswald legend actually represents an older and longer version of the legend than that found in the *Passionael* is the council scene, in which Oswald's men urge him to marry.[127] This is not found in the *Münchner Oswald*, where Oswald himself initiates the quest for a wife, but the *Wiener Oswald* relates that the king's courtiers approach him about the matter:

do der milde sinte Oswalt
gewuchs unde wart so alt,
daz im kunige gefuge

---

[124] "Adalberti Vita Heinrici II Imperatoris," MGH, Scriptores 4 (Hannover: Hahn, 1841), 805. Subsequently, Bk. 3 of the *vita*, the "Vitae S. Heinrici Additamentum," thought to have been composed around 1200, transmits an extraordinarily elaborated account of the bridal-quest and chastity-test narratives (816–20), and this was the source of Ebernand's account. Concerning the scholarly discussion of the redactions of the legend, their dating, and Adalbert's role, see Schröpfer,"Heinrich und Kunegunde," 61–63.

[125] In the *Additamentum* we read: "et cum preter sanguinis effusionem duo sint genera martirum, scilicet castitas in iuventute et abstinentia in habundantia, beatos coniuges, quorum preconia non tacemus, gemina martirii corona coronatos esse confidimus, qui et castitatem omni vite sue tempore et abstinentiam summopere studebant conservare" (818a).

[126] See vv. 897–924; 933–956.

[127] Edzardi, *Untersuchungen über das Gedicht von St. Oswald*, 5–6.

sin swert na trugen,
do riten im alle sine man,
her solde daz mit nichte lan,
her enneme endelich
eine frouwen lobelich,
die im wol gezeme
unde ir geburt im eben queme. (vv. 31–40)

(When the gracious saint Oswald had grown up and become old enough
that kings fittingly carried his sword for him, all his men advised him that
he should at last marry a praiseworthy wife, who was suitable and equal to
him in birth.)

The scene above is entirely devoid of drama; this is also the case in the *Passionael* redaction of the Oswald legend. In the Icelandic Oswald legend, however,
and also that of Henry II, the deliberations surrounding each king's lack of a wife
are presented in the best tradition of bridal-quest narrative.

The similarity between the council scene in *Hendreks saga og Kunegundis*
and that in *Ósvalds saga* is so pronounced that the Swedish scholar Oskar Klockhoff sought to rebut Edzardi's thesis that *Ósvalds saga* derives from a longer German legend than that in the *Passionael* by arguing that the Icelandic translator
of the Oswald legend actually expanded and augmented the same with material
from *Hendreks saga*. Klockhoff pointed out that *Hendreks saga* immediately precedes *Ósvalds saga* in the legendary and that therefore it was quite natural for the
compiler of *Reykjahólabók* to carry over and repeat some of the material from the
legend of Emperor Henry.[128] The relationship between the two council scenes is
unmistakable, expressed through a similar structure and phraseology (italicized),
as the following texts show:

| **Hendreks saga og Kunegundis,** 1:42.24–43.9: | **Ósvalds saga,** 1:73.20–74:3: |
|---|---|
| The counselors approach Henry and say: *"Verðugasti herra, nu eftir því* að guð hefir gefið yður so fagran sigur og mikinn sem þér sjálfir vel vitið *og so hafið þér samið og sett ydvart ríki* nú í góðan máta, | The counselors approach Oswald and one of them says: *"Verðugi herra, nú frá því að þér hafið sett og samið ydvart ríki* með góðri stjórn og nytsemdar verkum so að allir lifa nú með friði og farsæld er undir |

---

[128] Klockhoff, *Små Bidrag till nordiska Literaturhistorien under Medeltiden,* 16:
"Den naturliga förklaringen härtill är, att sagosamlaren, då han nyss förut behandlat Hen-
riks historia, lät de tankar, som han där framstält, återkomma äfven i Osvalds, som i några
afseenden bildar ett motstycke till den förres."

**Hendreks saga og Kunegundis**

**Ósvalds saga**

yðvart vald eru gefnir, þá vonum vær so til
að guði muni so líka um yðvart efni sem
oss. En þó er eftir einn sjá hlutur er oss
þykir á vanta og hans virðist oss með öngu
móti mega án vera. . .

þá *með yðru góðu orlofi, kærasti herra,*
höfum vær hugsað um nokkuð efni á yðra
vegna að so megi ekki standa að *þér eigið
ekki drottningu en ríkið erfingjalaust,
en vær viljum þo allra helst eiga að
vera undirgefnir yðru afkvæmi og vort
afspringi,* einkannlega þó fyrir þann
skylld eigi síður en aðra að vær vitum að
guð drottinn er með yður."

*Með yðru orlofi, verðugi herra,* þá þykir
oss það helst á vanta að *þér eigið öngva
drottningu þá er þér megið láta sitja og
stjórna yðru ríki eftir yðvarn dag, þvíað
vær vildum ekki gjarnan eiga gefast
lengur undir þá herra er ekki eru réttilega
komnir til ríkisins;* og þeir hlutir margir
sem þér hafið bæði eflt og bætt vort ríki
þá skulu aðrir eyða því og spilla í staðinn
sem hvorki eiga né so nokkuð ómak hafa
fyrir haft. Og viljum vær ekki ef vær
skulum ráða."

*En sem kaisarinn hafði heyrt þeirra orð
og erindi* og so fastlegt ráð er þeir vildu
að hann tæki upp, þá varð hann hljóður
við þetta og bles af nokkuð so þunglega
og mællti síðan. "Kæri vinir, slíkt erindi
hefði ég ekki ætlað að þér munduð að
sinni frami hafa, þvíað *ég hefir enn ekki
um hugsað mig um slíkt mál, og mun ég
gefa yður hér svar upp á seinna meir."* . . .
Leið en so nokkura stund að *keisarinn enn
um þetta efni mjög hugsandi . . . . hugsar
hann og um það, hverju að hann hefði
lofað guði.*

*En er kóngr hefur gjörla skilið þeirra
erindi,*

þá svarar hann og *segist vilja hugsa hér
eftir og gefa þeim svar aftur* nær sem hann
hefir <hugsað> til þeirrar er sig girnti eftir
að eiga. En þetta svar gaf hann til þess að
hann vildi so með því koma þeim af sér
enn með hreinni samvitsku.
*Var honum i hug að kvongast ekki heldur
að halda hreinlífi.*

*"Most worthy lord, now since* God has
granted you such a fair and great victory,
as you yourself know, *and you have now
secured and established your realm in
good fashion,*

*"Worthy lord, now that you have
established and secured your realm with
good government and useful works,* so
that all who are subject to you now live in
peace and happiness, we expect that God
is as pleased by your rule as we are.
Yet there is one thing that to us seems
lacking and which we deem not to be able
at all to be without . . .

| *Hendreks saga og Kunegundis* | *Ósvalds saga* |
|---|---|
| *With your good leave, dearest lord*, we have thought about a matter concerning you, *namely that things cannot continue as they are, that you do not have a queen and the empire is without heirs*; *we want most of all to be subject to your descendants as we want our heirs to be,* and especially for that reason no less than others that we know that the Lord God is with you." | *With your leave, worthy lord, we think what is most wanting is that you have no queen whom you might have preside over and rule your kingdom after your day, for we would rather not want to have to submit any longer to those lords who have not rightfully come by the kingdom,* and the many things with which you have strengthened and improved the kingdom, *others will then spoil and destroy instead,* others who neither have a right to it nor for which they have earlier gone to such pains. And we do not want this if we have a say." |
| *And when the emperor had heard their words and story* and also the earnest advice that they wanted him to take, he became quiet and sighed deeply and then spoke: "Dear friends, I had not thought that you would be proposing such advice at this time, for *I have not yet thought about such a matter, and I shall give you an answer to this later.*" Some time passed while the emperor kept thinking about this a great deal. . . . *he also thinks about what he had promised God.* | *And when the king has fully heard their story,*<br><br>he then answers *and says that he wants to think this over and give them an answer when he has thought about her whom he might like to marry.* He gave them this answer, however, because he wanted to get rid of them with his conscience still clear. *He had in mind not to get married but to preserve his virginity instead.* |

We know now that while Björn Þorleifsson may occasionally have made mistakes in translation, he did not engage in creative writing. The explanation for the similarity in the construction and wording of the council scenes is to be sought in the German sources themselves. Henry's seemingly vague "he also thinks about what he had promised God" is not vague at all in the context of his legend. Some years earlier Henry had one night experienced a vision in which he found himself in the church of St. Emmeram in Regensburg, where he sees St. Wolfgang standing beside the saint's grave. On the wall above the grave he reads a cryptic message: "Eftir sex" ('After six'). As Henry is trying to understand what this might mean, he wakes up. He interprets the two words to mean that he would die in six days. He confesses, gives alms to the poor, and makes out his last will. When he does not die, however, he thinks the words must refer to six weeks, then six months, and finally six years. At this point, Henry promises God that if he lets him live another six years, he will remain chaste for the rest of his life:

"Og skal ég so heita guði, ef lifir so lengi, þá skal ég halda hreinlífi alla mína daga" (1:36.22–23).[129]

The similarity of the two council scenes already existed in the German sources of *Hendreks saga* and *Ósvalds saga*. The bridal-quest narrative of the German Oswald legend developed under the impact of the legend of Henry and Cunegund, and the Icelandic translations of the two legends suggest that the influence of Henry's legend went beyond inspiring the transformation of the fact of Oswald's marriage into a bridal-quest tale: it actually was the donor of both the chastity motif and the council scene.

The council scenes in *Ósvalds saga* and *Hendreks saga* are composed according to the same model: the courtiers observe that their lord lacks a wife; they recommend that he marry to obtain heirs; and the protagonist replies that he had not intended to do so. The difference between the episode in the *Passionael*'s "Van Keyser Hindrick" and *Hendreks saga* is similar to that between the Low German and Icelandic redactions of the Oswald legend: a flat, one-dimensional account—albeit with some dialogue—in "Keyser Hindrick" on the one hand, but on the other hand a multi-scenic depiction in *Hendreks saga* that traverses time and space. The council scene is reported as follows in the Low German redaction:

> vnde beden den keiser dat he ene vrouwen neme. dar vmme leghen se em an. Dat was em swar. wente he hadde vnsen heren Jhesum cristuz vterkoren to eneme eruen. dat wisten se nicht. vnde spreken ouer to deme keyser. Dat enbethemet deme ryke nicht. vnde is nycht wontlyk dat gy dat allene hebben. vnde do gy des nicht. so mote gy vnsen vnwillen hebben. Do trostede sik de keyser godes. deme he syne kusckheyt hadde gelauet beth in syneme doet vnde sprak to den heren. dat se em gheuen ene vrouwen. de em vnde deme ryke bequeme were. Do worden de heren alle vro. (lviii.c)

> (And they asked the emperor to take a wife; that is what they begged him to do. That was difficult for him, since he had chosen Our Lord Jesus Christ to be his heir. They did not know this and censured him: "That is not fitting for the empire and it is not customary for you to reign alone, and if you do not do as we wish, you will earn our displeasure." Then the emperor placed his hope in God, to whom he had vowed chastity until death, and he said to the lords that they should find him a wife who was fitting for him and the empire. Then the lords all rejoiced.)

Although the above is more verbose than the corresponding episode in the Low German Oswald redaction and includes some dialogue, a comparison of this

---

[129] Ebernand was the first to report that after his dream vision Henry decided to remain a virgin (*Heinrich und Kunigunde*, vv. 281–282), but the causal link found in the saga is missing.

council scene with that in *Hendreks saga* shows that a disparity similar to that between the Low German and Icelandic redactions of the Oswald legend obtains.

In the Icelandic version, the author permits Henry to explore his dilemma as he
ponders the conflict between the lords request on the one hand and his vow to God
on the other. The nature of his deliberations slips almost imperceptibly from third-
person authorial narrative into a third-person monologue, that is, *erlebte Rede*:

> Af þessu hvorutveggju var keisarinn harðla mjög hugsjúkur hvað hann
> skyldi af ráða. Og væri það so að hann giftist ekki sem þeir vildu, þá væri
> það jafn víst að sundurþykki mundi mikið verða í ríkinu, þvíað þeir sem
> megtugir væri og af stórum ættum komnir mundu taka sig upp hver í móti
> öðrum þegar að hans missti við. En þó víst og óvíst hvort það bíði so lengi
> og væri það þá mikil ábyrgð fyrir sig við guð ef það bæri til af hans völdum
> að sá hefði sízt er helzt ætti. í annan stað setur hann og í sinn hug ef hann
> verður þeim samþykkur í þessu að þá mundi hann styggja mjög guð er hann
> rýfur sitt heit er hann hefir lofað, nema hann gæti því so af stað komið að til
> þeirrar lofunar yrði heldur tvö en einn. Og með það seinasta tekur hann það
> upp að eiga allt sitt mál undir guði almáttugum. (*Rhb.* 1:43.9–22)

> (Because of these [conflicting demands] the emperor was very sad wondering
> what he should do. And should it be that he did not marry, as they wanted
> him to, then it would be quite certain that the empire would be greatly torn
> apart, since those who were mighty and came from great families would
> rise up against each other as soon as he was gone. And yet the odds are
> even whether it would take so long, and he would be greatly answerable to
> God if it were to happen on his account that the one who least deserved the
> empire were to get it. On the other hand, he reflects that if he agrees with
> his counselors in this matter, then he will make God very angry by breaking
> the vow that he has made, unless he could get around it in such a way that
> in respect to this vow there might be two rather than one. And in the end he
> decides to place his entire case in the hands of God Almighty.)

The Icelandic *Hendreks saga* attests that there existed a German legend of Henry
and Cunegund that was expansive and permitted Henry to explore his quandary
at length. The extended debate within himself does not exist in Ebernand von
Erfurt's *Heinrich und Kunegunde*, where Henry's dilemma is given short shrift as
he makes a decision to acquiesce to the wishes of his counselors:

> úf gotes trôst er ez tete.
> er dâhte: 'er sol mich wol bewarn,
> daz ich mit kûscheit vollenvarn
> hin biz an mîn ende.' (vv. 790–793)

> (He did so trusting in God. He thought: "He is going to watch over me so
> that I can preserve my virginity until the end of my life.")

Oswald finds himself in a similar dilemma, and it may very well be that the legend of Henry and Cunegund provided the model. To be sure, the solution to the problem is realized quite differently in *Ósvalds saga*, since there is direct intervention from above. Before Oswald has a chance to give his courtiers a reply and as he is still faced with his desire to remain a virgin rather than marry, the divine messenger arrives to inform him that it is God's will that he marry a heathen princess in order to convert her and her people. In effect, the vernacular Oswald legend takes what is accorded but a brief notice by Bede, that is, that Oswald stands godfather to the king whose daughter he will subsequently marry, and transforms it into a major crusade, generated by a bridal quest, to convert an entire people.

The episode in *Ósvalds saga* diverges from that in the *Passionael* inasmuch as the Low German legend lacks the chastity motif; thus Oswald raises no objection to marriage in the German prose version. That the chastity motif should have been dropped when the German Oswald legend was condensed for inclusion in the *Passionael* is strange, since the motif recurs at the end of the legend as an explanation for the childless marriage of Oswald and Pia. Nonetheless, this kind of internal inconsistency does occur in the *Heiligen Leben*/*Passionael* legends as a result of their having been so drastically reduced vis-à-vis their sources. In any case, the Icelandic Oswald legend attests that the chastity motif did exist in the vernacular legend, making it all the more likely that the bridal-quest narrative in the Oswald legend was inspired by and derives in large part from the legend of Emperor Henry. At the very time that the bridal-quest and chastity-test narratives of the legend of Henry and Cunegund were developing in the eleventh century—Henry's canonization bull of 1146 gives his absolute chastity as one of the reasons for his canonization[130]—Oswald's relics and cult came to Flanders and the German-language area.

It should be noted, however, that the chastity motif is also found in the "libellus in honorem Sancti Oswaldi" that was compiled around 1165 by Reginald of Coldingham, a monk at the monastery of Durham.[131] While his *vita* is indebted to Bede, he also adds new material deriving from oral tradition. Folz characterized the work as ". . . pleine de digressions, écrite dans une langue prolixe, débordant de rhétorique et surchargée d'images, on ne retiendra ici que les éléments qui ont confirmé ou enrichi le portrait d'Oswald."[132] Reginald reports that after a vision in which he learns that he will not die of the plague, Oswald brought it about

> ut Kyneburgam sponsam suam, regis Kynegulsi filiam, post hanc visionis
> gloriam ab unius thori communione sejungeret, et deinceps castitatis illiba-

---

[130] The bull states: "integritatem castimoniae usque in finem vitae conservavit" (MGH, Scriptores 4, 813b). See Folz, *Les saints rois du Moyen Âge*, 90.

[131] "Vita S. Oswaldi Regis et Martyris," in *Symeonis monachi Opera Omnia*, ed. Arnold, 1:338.

[132] Folz, "Saint Oswald roi de Northumbrie," 54.

tae munditiam conservaret. Prius tamen de ea sobolem procreaverat, quem unicum tantum in terra filium possidebat. (349)

(that Kyneburg his wife, the daughter of King Kyneguls, after this favor of a vision was separated from sharing with him the marital bed, and thence he preserved the purity of untainted chastity. Nonetheless prior to this he had engendered from her an offspring, which was the only son he had on earth.)

While the notion that Oswald and Kyneburg—the name, which is not found in Bede, is Reginald's contribution to the legend—observed conjugal chastity after the birth of a son may have been transmitted to the continent through Reginald's *vita*, the very prominence of the chastity motif in the contemporary legend of Henry and Cunegund presumably contributed to realizing its narrative potential in the vernacular lives of St. Oswald.

The motif plays a central role in the *Wiener Oswald*,[133] where the king tells his retainers that he has not intended to marry because he desires to lead a life of chastity. Oswald inquires of the pilgrim whether he knows of a maiden he might marry, but with a stipulation: she has to be someone,

> da her mit bliben mochte
> kusche biz an sin ende
> ane alle missewende. (vv. 56–58)

(with whom he might remain absolutely chaste until the end of his life.)

And the same concern recurs:

> kennst du in dinen sinnen
> irne eine kuniginne,
> die mir zum wibe tochte
> und kusche mit mir leben mochte? (vv. 83–86)

(do you know of a queen who would be fitting to be my wife and who might want to live chastely with me?)

While the Viennese metrical redaction, like *Ósvalds saga*, amply attests the existence of the chastity motif in the vernacular legend of St. Oswald, the motif does not fully surface in the *Münchner Oswald* until the end of the romance, when Christ appears to Oswald and demands a virginal marriage of him and his wife.

---

[133] The chastity motif occurs in vv. 40a–b, 56–58, 86, 90, 100, 104, 176, 758, 912–913, 1110, 1119–1120, 1137–1138, 1143, 1365–1370, 1378–1384.

It is noteworthy that the council scene in the *Münchner Oswald* is very different from that in the *Wiener Oswald*, the *Heiligen Leben/Passional* redaction, and *Ósvalds saga*. Not the counselors approach their king to urge him to marry, but instead Oswald himself convenes them to inform them that he intends to get a wife and that he needs their advice in this matter. In the *Münchner Oswald*, unlike the other vernacular versions, Oswald himself reaches the decision to marry, and in prayer he expresses his intention to God:

> er sprach: "solt ich mich sein nicht schämen,
> so wolt ich geren ain frauen nemen.
> nun pin ich ain kindischer man:
> herr, wie sol ich ez greifen an?
> ich näm geren ain magedein,
> möcht es nür an sund gesein.
> ei himlischer furst her,
> nu gib mir rat und ler!" (vv. 35–42)

> (Then he added: "I would gladly take a wife if I could do so without loss of honor. Lord, I am still young and wanting in knowledge. How shall I begin? I would like to have a maiden if this could be without incurring sin. O Ruler of Heaven, counsel me!" [83])[134]

And one night he himself makes a decision— "er gab im selber rat und ler" (v. 51)—that it is his duty to marry so that when he dies his kingdom will not be without heirs (v. 49). Here the *Münchner Oswald* deviates drastically from the other vernacular versions; indeed, the divergence becomes even more pronounced when the pilgrim arrives. Unlike the stranger in the prose legend, the pilgrim named Warmunt in the *Münchner Oswald* is not sent from God to inform Oswald that he is to marry a pagan princess in order to convert her to Christianity; instead, he informs Oswald that the pagan princess, here named Paug, already believes "an got und an die muoter sein" (v. 244 'in God and His mother'), but that she and her handmaidens "wolten zuo der tauf keren / und kristenleichen glauben meren" (vv. 251–252 'want to be baptized and to spread the Christian faith'). They need someone to help them achieve this (v. 254), however, and Oswald declares his willingness to undertake the quest even if it means losing his life (vv. 257–258).

The vernacular legend of St. Oswald developed during the same time as or in the wake of the canonization processes of Henry II and Cunegund, a considerable part of whose popular legend was devoted to Henry's bridal quest, the couple's

---

[134] I have revised Thomas's translation of v. 40, which reads: "if this would not be a sin." I believe Oswald's prayer is somewhat more subtle: he does not believe that to marry is a sin, but rather that sin, presumably devolving from sexual intercourse, is incurred in marriage.

vow to preserve a virginal marriage, and Cunegund's demonstration of her in-
nocence by means of a chastity test in response to Henry's accusation of adul-
tery. This part of their legend, which is entirely fictional and which one scholar
dubbed a "Klosterroman,"[135] may have provided some of the narrative details and
structure for the introductory portion of the bridal-quest plot of the Oswald legend. Not only the royal status of the saints links them to each other but also their
considerable efforts on behalf of the church, as evidenced by the conversion motif
in both legends.

The greatest discrepancy from a historical and hagiographic perspective between *Ósvalds saga* and the German prose legend on the one hand and the *Münch-
ner/Wiener Oswald* on the other relates to the king's death. Whereas Oswald dies
a martyr at the hands of the heathen Penda in the German/Icelandic prose version,
just as in Bede, in the *Münchner Oswald* he dies in bed at the side of his wife (the
*Wiener Oswald* concludes with the baptism of the pagans). When their end came,
Oswald and his wife took to their bed and sent for two priests; they confessed their
guilt, prayed for God's mercy, and received the sacrament (see p. 34). The king
who died a martyr on the field of battle has become a confessor saint who gently
enters eternal rest in his bed. This divergence from fact, which dehistoricizes the
Northumbrian king and takes away his martyr's crown, should be a major consideration in attempting to establish the nature of the earliest vernacular text accompanying the cult of St. Oswald in the German-language area.

Repeatedly scholars have lamented the lack of cohesion in the structure of
the *Münchner Oswald*. While Curschmann argued that the *Münchner Oswald*
represents a balanced combination of the sacred legend and the bridal-quest narrative—"völlige Gleichwertigkeit der Gattungen Legende und Brautwerbungs-
erzählung in der stofflichen Zusammensetzung des Werkes"—he noted at the
same time an extraordinarily complex relationship of the two genres to each other—"ein bei engster Verschmelzung äußerst kompliziertes Verhältnis der beiden
zueinander."[136] Oswald's original qualms concerning marriage—he had said he
wanted to marry only if thereby he would not incur sin—play no role whatsoever
in the course of the bridal quest, but the issue surfaces again at the end of the romance when Christ appears to Oswald and challenges him to conjugal chastity.
And Christ comes with specific instructions as to how the king and his wife are
to resist temptation: they are to have a vat of water at their bedside, into which
they are to jump whenever the urgings of the flesh threaten to overpower them
(see p. 34), and that is indeed what happened according to the legend.

---

[135] Heinrich Günter, *Kaiser Heinrich II., der Heilige* (Kempten and Munich: Jos.
Kösel'sche Buchhandlung, 1904), 80.
[136] Curschmann, *Der Münchener Oswald und die deutsche spielmännische Epik*,
72–73.

Curschmann argued that the depiction of Oswald's chaste marriage at the end of the romance suggests that in the last analysis the work is concerned with the problem of a sanctified marriage as expressed through conjugal chastity. Nikolaus Miller objected to such an interpretation of the *Münchner Oswald*, which does not resolve the conflict between the implicit goal of the bridal-quest plot, marriage for the sake of heirs—Oswald specifically considers the importance of heirs for the kingdom (vv. 45–49)—and the exhortation to conjugal chastity at the conclusion of the legend. The *Josephsehe* at the end of the romance, avers Miller, puts the bridal quest in question, and therefore he proposed that Oswald's proselytization and sanctification, and not marriage, were at the heart of the romance; that the bridal quest was to be understood as an essential element of Oswald's conversion efforts. Miller remarks: "Gottesvertrauen und Missionierungsauftrag bilden gewissermaßen den religiösen Bewußtseinshintergrund, auf welchem die gefährliche Brautwerbung ihren höfischen Regeln gemäß abläuft." [137] He goes on to note that the conversion episode—or, as he puts it, "der plötzliche Einsatz einer Legendenhandlung" ("Brautwerbung und Heiligkeit," 238)—interrupts the bridal-quest plot before the marriage can take place. Miller concludes: "Der Schluß des *Münchner Oswald* hat deshalb auch eine doppelte Funktion: er erzählt erstens das Brautwerbungsschema zu Ende und liefert zweitens die Heiligkeitsbewährung nach, die der Bekehrungshandlung vorausgesetzt aber nicht erzählerisch realisiert wurde" (239).

Miller's thesis is well taken and his argument makes sense. His analysis, which points in the direction of what must have been the original Oswald legend, goes only so far, however, for it is predicated on the fictionalization of Oswald's death. Not one scholar has remarked on the inexplicable shift of status of the Northumbrian saint. While conjugal chastity is the means to sanctity in the *Münchner Oswald*, it is in conflict not only with the implied object of the bridal quest, marriage and thereby the continuation of the royal line, but also with the historical facts of Oswald's life and death.

The figure of Oswald transmitted in the vernacular German legend is a split personality: in the prose versions Oswald marries and dies on the field of battle; in the *Münchner Oswald* he dies in bed at the side of his wife. Nonetheless, the *Heiligen Leben* legend reports that after the wedding Oswald and his bride

---

[137] Nikolaus Miller, "Brautwerbung und Heiligkeit: Die Kohärenz des *Münchner Oswald*," *Deutsche Vierteljahresschrift* 52 (1978): 226–40, here 237. Claudia Bornholdt notes that "the final part of the work is entirely devoted to Oswald's sanctity and his chaste marriage. The latter is at odds with the very purpose of his journey, assuming the bridal quest is indeed his true goal and not the rescue of Pamige, who secretly believes in the Christian God. One can argue that Oswald's true intention is to save Pamige and convert her and her heathen father and his men to Christianity. In this case, the work is more the description of Oswald's crusade and mission", Engaging Moments, 142–143.

"lebten raineklichen vnd kevschleichen vnd verzerten ir zeit mit got vnd noch seinem lob"[138] ('lived purely and chastely and were devoted to God and sought his praise'). While the *Passionael* has a corresponding passage, following the account of Oswald's martyrdom the Low German legend nevertheless interjects a remark concerning deviating information: "Ok vint men in etliken hystorien van Sunte Oswalde. Dat he nee ene vrouwe hadde. Men he leuede kuscklyken de daghe synes leuendes" (C.iiii.d 'And in some accounts of St. Oswald one reads that he never had a wife and that he lived chastely to the end of his life'). The reference to Oswald's not having had a wife is most likely corrupt, the victim of thoughtless condensation, for, to judge by the saga, the variant version originally must have related that Oswald did not have sexual relations with his wife and therefore no offspring:

> So finnst og í sumlegum historíum af sankti Osvaldo að hafi aldregi þýðst neina kvinnu utan haldið hreinlífi alla sína daga—og kemur þetta þá og vel til saman þvíað hvergi finnst það að hann hafi átt nokku<r>t barn—og so það að hann hafði fallið í stríði jafnt og hér segir.

> (One also reads in some accounts about St. Oswald that he never knew woman but that he preserved his virginity his entire life—and this also makes sense, for nowhere does it say that he had a child—and that he fell in battle, just as is told here.)

The comment suggests that this particular hagiographer was not convinced by accounts of Oswald's conjugal chastity, but that for the sake of the record he should mention the claim made by some sources—and this seems reasonable to him. The final comment contradicts Bede, who mentions one son, Ethelwald (*HE*, 3.14.24). In any case, by the time the long German redaction that was the source of the Icelandic translation was composed, there already existed a tradition that, like Henry and Cunegund, Oswald and his wife preserved conjugal chastity.

---

[138] *Der Heiligen Leben*, Band 1: Sommerteil, 364.

# VI.
## *ÓSVALDS SAGA:*
## A CONVERSION AND MARTYR LEGEND

The vernacular Oswald legend deviates from Bede's sober account inasmuch as it incorporated an introductory coronation legend and developed the fact of Oswald's marriage to a pagan princess into an extended bridal-quest narrative. The fictionalization of Oswald's *vita*, it was argued above, occurred in the context of the developing legend of Henry II and Cunegund. Not only the preliminaries to the bridal quest itself, that is, the council and deliberation scenes with the central chastity motif, would seem to be indebted to the legend of the saintly German emperor but also the portrayal of Oswald's bridal quest as principally a proselytizing endeavor. The distinguishing feature of *Ósvalds saga*—and the German prose legend—is its emphasis on establishing and strengthening the Church and converting the heathens, in the pursuit of which Oswald becomes a martyr. Indeed, Oswald's quest for a wife is explicitly linked to the king's missionizing activity and readiness to suffer martyrdom.

Following the story of Oswald's coronation, the saga reminds us that the historical Oswald is remembered for his having completed the construction of St. Peter's church in York, the upkeep of which he supported with tithes, and that he furthermore provided for priests to serve there.

> Þá lét hann byggja eina kostulega kirkju guði til heiðurs ok sankti Pétri postula. Og lagði þar til mikla rentu til uppheldis. Þar með fékk hann þangað kennimenn er þar skyldu þjóna guði og heilagri kirkju. (*Rhb.*, 1:72.23–26)

> (Then he had a precious church built in honor of God and St. Peter the Apostle. And he provided much income toward its upkeep. In addition he obtained priests for it who were to serve God there and the Holy Church.)

This corresponds to what Drogo tells us; Bede mentions only that Oswald completed building the church begun by Edwin[139]—"Construxit namque templum honorabile beati Petri Apostoli, quod mirificè decoravit, & dignos ministros, qui ibidem Deo deservirent, regio usu deliberavit" ('And he honorably constructed a church dedicated to the blessed apostle Peter, which he adorned magnificently,

---

[139] Cf. Bede, *HE* 2.20: "Adlatum est autem caput Eduini regis Eburacum, et inlatum postea in ecclesiam beati apostoli Petri, quam ipse coepit, sed successor eius Osuald perfecit" ('The head of King Edwin was brought to York and afterwards placed in the church of the apostle St. Peter, which he himself had begun to build and his successor Oswald completed').

and he consulted worthy clergy, who served God there, concerning royal practice' [95]). It is noteworthy that King Oswald's efforts on behalf of the Church
are quite similar to those reported about Henry II and his wife Cunegund. In
*Hendreks saga og Kunegundis* we read that Henry founded the bishopric of Bamberg and several monasteries (*Rhb.*, 1:48). Furthermore, we are told that he and
Cunegund

> létu þau upphefja og endurbæta mörg önnur klaustur og kirkjur er skemdar og
> niðurbrotnar höfðu verið af ómildum tírannum og öðrum heiðingjum. . . . og
> til þessara staða allra gaf hann stórar eignir og rentu til uppheldis þeim er
> þar þjónuðu. En til allra þeirra staða og klaustra sem keisarinn lét efla eða
> nokkurn styrk veita, þá lagði hann og af sínum peningum þar til guði til lofs
> og hans helgum mönnum. (*Rhb.*, 1:48.29–49:9)

> (had raised up and restored many other monasteries and churches which had
> been damaged and destroyed by ruthless tyrants and other heathens. . . . and
> to all those places he gave great possessions and tithes for the maintenance
> of those who served there. And to all those places and monasteries which
> the emperor had founded or endowed, he contributed from his own money
> for the praise of God and His holy saints.)

The Northumbrian Oswald and the German Henry are cut from the same cloth
and generate similar depictions of royal munificence vis-à-vis the Church.[140]
While the depiction of Oswald's program of construction and his efforts in support of the administration of the church of St. Peter derive from Bede, it is clear
that in the vernacular legends of Oswald and Henry we are dealing with one and
the same motif of royal support of the Church.

Already at the outset, the conversion/martyr narrative is anticipated in *Ósvalds saga* by the report that hard upon his coronation the king begins to wage
war on heathen peoples for the sake of the Christian faith and that he forces both
mighty lords and towns to submit to Christianity and to his authority: "heldur lætur hann vaxa stór örlög við heiðnar þjóðir fyrir skuld heilagrar trúar og þvingaði
bæði mektuga herra og stóra staði undir heilaga kristni og sig" ('he also waged
great battles against heathen peoples for the sake of the holy faith, and he subjected both mighty lords and large towns to Christianity and to his rule'). When
his unmarried state becomes a matter of concern to his counselors, he hesitates
to respond to their exhortations to seek a wife, for, we are told, he was considering not marrying at all in order to remain a virgin. This immediately becomes a
moot issue, however, for a pilgrim arrives, a heavenly messenger, who conveys an
unequivocal message from God:

---

[140] Cf. "H[einrich] II," in *LMA*, 4:2037–2039.

þú skalt taka þér til drottningar eina jungfrú og er eins heiðins konungsdóttir og heitir hann Gaudonus en þessi jungfrúin, dóttir hans, heitir Pia.
. . . Og guð býður þér að þú skalt halda mikið örlög fyrir hennar skuld og
koma henni til heilagrar trúar og guð drottinn hefir hana út valið til þessa.
(74:19–24)

(you are to take as your queen a maiden who is the daughter of a heathen
king, and his name is Gaudonus, but this maiden, his daughter, is called Pia.
. . . And God commands you to wage a great battle for her sake and to convert her to the holy faith, and the Lord God has chosen her for this.)

Thus from the outset the quest for a wife is linked to conversion, which will not
take place without war. This is not the case in the *Münchner Oswald*, however, where the princess and her maidens are already Christians (vv. 244–245).[141]
While it is true that the immediate cause of Oswald's confrontation by heathen
forces is his abduction of the princess, as will be seen, the battle itself with the
heathen king actually results from Oswald's attempt to convert him.

The significance of conversion for the quest emerges in the letter that Oswald
sends the princess via the raven. The letter, according to the saga, contains nothing but the essentials of the Christian faith, for we read that Oswald listed in it
"þá tólf parta heilagrar trúar" (75:22), that is, the articles of faith in the Apostles'
Creed (see p. 123);[142] at the same time, the raven is instructed to inform the princess that he, Oswald, has chosen her as his beloved and that she is dearer to him
than any other woman on earth.[143] When the princess reads the letter, we learn
that the articles of faith are accompanied by Oswald's exhortation "að hún skyldi
frjálsast frá eilífri pínu og dauða ef hún vildi snúast frá heiðni og villu en trúa á
sannan guð og halda þessa tólf parta heilagrar trúar" ('that she would be saved
from eternal punishment and death if she converted from paganism and error and
believed in the true God and accepted these twelve articles of the holy faith'). The
effect of the letter on the princess is immediate and inspired by the Holy Spirit:

---

[141] The *Münchner Oswald* is not consistent, however, for when Oswald gets ready to
sail to heathen territory, he informs his men that he wants to spread the Christian faith and
also to obtain for himself a heathen queen (vv. 1533–1539).

[142] The reference is to the twelve "articuli fidei" of the Apostles' Creed, which originated in the baptismal liturgy, and which required an expression of belief. See J. N. D.
Kelly, "Apostolisches Glaubensbekenntnis," in *LTK*, 1:760–62; H. Bacht, "Glaubensartikel," in *LTK*, 4:934–35; A. Stenzel, "Glaubensbekenntnis," in *LTK*, 4:935–39.

[143] In the *Münchner Oswald* the letter also contains a brief reference to the princess
accepting Christianity: "si sol, ob got wil, wer[d]en mein weib. / wil si cristen glauben
han, / daz sol si mich wissen lan" (vv. 598–600 'God willing, she shall become my wife.
If she will accept the Christian faith, she should let me know' [89]).

. . . þá af miskunn heilags anda uppkveikist hennar hjarta með þeirri logandi ást til guðs so að hún sagðist gjarnan öllu því trúa er hann vildi sér
til þeirra hluta kenna og lyfti sínum augum upp til himna samaleiðis sínum
höndum so mælandi: "Faðir á himnum, þér gjör ég þakkir fyrir þína mildi er
þú mér virðist að veita," og féll á sín hné með tárum og lá so nokkra stund.
(77:19–25)

(. . . then by the mercy of the Holy Spirit her heart was kindled with a burning love for God so that she said that she would gladly believe everything
that he wanted to teach her about these things, and she lifted up her eyes
and hands to heaven, speaking thus: "Father in heaven, I give you thanks for
your kindness which you have vouchsafed to grant me," and she fell on her
knees in tears and lay thus for a while.)

The saga depicts here a case of spontaneous conversion through the workings of
divine grace, the *gratia illuminans* of the Holy Spirit.[144] We do not learn the contents of the princess's written response to Oswald, but the letter presumably includes affirmation of her acceptance of the Christian faith. She replies to Oswald's
declaration of love in kind: the raven is to inform Oswald that she holds him dearer
than any other man on earth and that he is to ask God "að allt það verði sem hann
vill honum og mér á milli og hann finnur skrifað í bréfinu" ('that everything turn
out between him and me as he wants and finds written in the letter' [78:1–2]).
    It is noteworthy that when Oswald summons his retainers, the mighty lords
of his realm, including clergy—twelve bishops and nine abbots—he outfits them
as crusaders: each is to wear a cross on his garments. In his address to the as-
semblage prior to departure, not one word is uttered concerning the bridal quest.
Instead, Oswald exhorts his men to fight for the faith and promises eternal life to
all who fall in battle:

"Kærustu vinir og dýrlegir herrar, allir sem hér eru nú í guðs augliti til samans komnir eftir minni bæn og boði: Hafið þér yður vel hvað sem fram kann
koma fyrir oss í þessari vorri reisu og stríðið mannlega fyrir trú heilagrar
kristni ef þess kann við að þurfa þvíað guð vill vera með oss. Og hver sem
síðan deyr af oss í réttu stríði og í þessari reisu, þá hefur sá eilíft líf og ríki
með honum og hans útvöldum vinum í himiríki utan enda." (80:5–12)

("Dearest friends and noble lords, all who have now assembled in God's
sight in accordance with my request and command, behave well no matter what may befall us on our expedition and fight manfully for the faith of
holy Christianity if this becomes necessary, for God shall be with us. And
whoever among us dies in the just fight and on this expedition, that one will

---

[144] See I. Auer, "Erleuchtungsgnade," in *LTK*, 3:1015–16.

have eternal life and rule with Him and His chosen friends in the heavenly kingdom without end.")

Despite the incorporation of the bridal-quest narrative in *Ósvalds saga*, the author of this version clearly adhered to the spirit of Oswald's *vita* which portrays him as a proselytizing king. The bridal quest seems to have been forgotten, and instead the focus is solely on fighting for the faith. While in the *Münchner Oswald* the king announces: "ich wil in die haidenschaft ker[e]n / und cristenleichen glauben meren" (vv. 1533–1534 'I want to sail across the sea to heathendom to spread the Christian faith' [99]), he immediately follows up with the real reason for the journey across the sea:

"ain haidmische kunn[i]ginne
die wil ich uber mer her pringen.
es sai den wilden haidem[145]
lieb oder laid[e], ( )
( ) ich muoß haben die kungin guot!" (vv. 1535–39)

("and bring back a heathen queen; I must have her whether or not her uncouth countrymen are willing." [99])

That the bridal quest is the means of proselytization in *Ósvalds saga* is strikingly evident in the scene in which the pagan king Gaudon confronts Oswald and informs him that he will suffer death for having abducted his daughter. Oswald's reply ignores what is foremost in Gaudon's mind, the abduction. Instead of responding that he is willing to risk his life for the princess, as one might expect in a bridal-quest narrative, Oswald talks past the heathen king and asserts that he is risking his life for the sake of his faith. Furthermore, he exhorts Gaudon to accept the faith and believe in the true God:

Þá svarar Ósvaldur: "Ef ekki á betra í efni verða, þá er mér það ekki á móti þó að láti líf mitt fyrir minn skapara og heilaga trú skyld og er þér það hið besta ráð, Gaudon, að þú takir heilaga trú og trúir á sannan guð." (86:10–14)

(Then Oswald answers: "If things are not going to turn out better, then I am not against losing my life for my Creator and for the sake of the holy faith, and it would be best for you, Gaudon, to decide to accept the holy faith and to believe in the true God.")

---

[145] Curschmann's edition consistently writes *-m, -m-* (*haidmische* [v. 1535] and *haidem* [1537]) where one would expect to find *-n, -n-*.

It is this rejoinder and not the abduction that provokes the ensuing combat. Twice the Christian forces turn out to be superior to those of the pagans; twice Oswald threatens to kill Gaudon if he does not accept the faith; twice Oswald asks God to perform a miracle—to resurrect Gaudon's and his own fallen warriors and to have a spring gush out of a rock—before the pagan king finally submits to baptism and receives a new name, Símon, possibly an allusion to the latter miracle and its etymological connection to Peter.[146] Surprisingly enough, the last persons to be baptized are the princess and her following; this takes place on the third day after her father and his men have accepted the faith. The bridal-quest/conversion narrative concludes with King Símon's return to his kingdom, where he speaks so much about the new faith that his wife has herself baptized along with everyone else in the kingdom. The saga reports that within eighteen days the entire country has been converted to Christianity.

Most of this account is of course a fictionalized and dramatized elaboration of what Bede and his successors tell about the baptism of Cynegisl, here named Gaudon. Noteworthy is the context of the account of Cynegisl's conversion in Drogo's *vita*. He relates the episode as an example of Oswald's proselytizing efforts:

> Non solùm autem Oswaldus rex gloriosissimus suæ gentis sollicitus fuit; verum etiam aliarum gentium, quæ sub extero jure regum erant constitutæ, volens omnes ad cultum unius veri Dei, veræque religionis tramitem adducere, quapropter suos ecclesiasticos nuntios ad amicissimos sibi reges mittebat, ad fidei suæ lumen provocans; tum verò litteris, tum autem regiis xeniis animos eorum sedulò alliciebat. Nonnumquam per se, suique præsentiam eos monebat, uti religionem suam pio quidem animo amplecterentur, Deoque omnipotenti colla submitterent; eo victores hostium gloriosè existerent; in quo sperare, sive inniti, veram semper victoriam esse affirmabat. (98)

> (The most glorious king Oswald was solicitous not only of his own people, however, but also of other peoples who were ruled by foreign kings, wanting to lead all to the worship of the one true God and the path of the true faith; for this reason he sent his ecclesiastical emissaries to the kings most favorably disposed to him, urging them to accept the light of his faith; he diligently attracted their souls now through letters, now through royal gifts. Sometimes he admonished them himself and by his presence to embrace his faith with a devout heart and to subject themselves to the omnipotent God; that they might show themselves victorious over the enemy; he affirmed that to hope in Him, or to rely upon Him, was always the true victory.)

---

[146] In the *Münchner Oswald* he takes the name Zentinus (v. 3127), but the Innsbruck manuscript gives this as *zenzim,* possibly a corrupt reading of an original Simon/Symon as in the saga and *HL/Pass.*

And Drogo immediately offers a specific example of Oswald's general efforts to convert the heathens—"Unde unum de multis exemplum ponemus. Et id quidem sufficiat tam gloriosa facta tanti Regis legentibus" (98: 'and we provide one of many examples of this: And let this suffice of the glorious deeds of such a king for the readers')—and the monk goes on to tell the story of the West Saxons and their king Cynegisl, who "fidem Christi suscepit, hortante ad eam ipsam Oswaldo sanctissimo rege, ac prædicante illis Byrino episcopo" (98: 'received the faith of Christ at the urging of Oswald, the most holy king, and through the preaching of Bishop Birinus'). And Drogo continues with Bede's account:

> Contigit tunc temporibus sanctissimum ac uictoriosissimum regem Nordanhymbrorum Osualdum adfuisse, eumque de lauacro exeuntem suscepisse, ac pulcherrimo prorsus ac Deo digno consortio, cuius erat filiam accepturus in coniugem, ipsum prius secunda generatione Deo dedicatum sibi accepit in filium. (*HE*, 3.7)

> (It so happened that at the time Oswald, the saintly and victorious king of the Northumbrians, was present and stood godfather for him. Lovely indeed and well-pleasing to God was their relationship; that same man whose daughter Oswald was later to receive as his wife, that day, after his new birth and dedication to God, was received by Oswald as his son.)

Considering that with Cynegisl's baptism Oswald also acquired a wife, it is understandable that one hagiographer was inspired to seize on this important event and expand it into a full-fledged bridal-quest/conversion narrative with the requisite miracles to convince Cynegisl, alias Gaudon, to accept Christianity.

In the *Münchner Oswald* a verbal confrontation between the pagan king, who is here called Aron, and Oswald does not occur until after thirty thousand heathen warriors have lost their lives and Aron has been captured. The latter promises to accept baptism if his men are raised from the dead, and Oswald works this miracle, but now that he has his full force again Aron wants to engage in battle once more. His men refuse to do so, however, for, as they say,

> . . . "her, lat von eurem zoren!
> ir sult von dem krieg lan,
> wir wellen euch nicht pei bestan!
> wir sein gewesen an dir stund
> pei der haissen helle grunt,
> do ist uns also we geschehen,"
> begunden die haiden all[e] jehen:
> "habt ez auf all[e] unser er,
> an Machmeten gelauben wir nimmer mer!
> er mag niemant nicht pai bestan,

wir wellen an Jesum Crist gelauben han;
dem wellen wir ( ) dienen fur aigen,
der mag uns hilf erzaigen." (vv. 3026–3038)

("Don't be angry, lord," said those who had been dead. "You must give up
the fight, for we will not stand by you. We have just now been in the depths
of fiery hell, where we suffered greatly. You may take our word for this: we
shall never again believe in Mohammed. He can't help anyone. We want to
put our faith in Jesus Christ and serve Him as vassals, for He can give us
aid." [112])

The upshot of this incipient mutiny is that Aron promises to receive baptism if
Oswald can work the miracle of having a cliff exude water, for, as he argues, he
does not want to be baptized in the sea because it is not only salty but also bot-
tomless, and he fears drowning in it (vv. 3041–3050). God comes through with a
miracle the effect of which reaches epic proportions. With his sword Oswald cuts
a swath into the rocky wall:

daz schwert im aus der hent prach
(von gottes chrefte daz geschach)
ab durch den herten stain.
gotes kraft da wol erschain:
von des schwertes ort
sich die stain[e]s want enpart:
nu lie sich ain schiel her dan
(daz sahen haiden und cristenman):
der was so groß, als wir noch horen sagen,
tausent wagen möchten in nindert haben getragen.
gottes craft die was groß:
aus der stain[e]s want ain prun gefloß,
der waz zehen klafter weit
(sait uns das täutsch puoch seit)
und nür ainer tief. (vv. 3083–3097)

(God's might was then revealed. It caused the sword to leap from the king's
hand down into the hard stone. The point opened up the cliff and out fell
a piece of the rock so large—they still tell of it—that a thousand wagons
could not have carried it; both Christians and heathens saw this. God's power was indeed great. From the cliff flowed a spring that, according to the
German book, was ten fathoms wide and only one fathom deep. [113])

The miracle in the *Münchner Oswald* undoubtedly would originally have evoked
the biblical provision of water for the Israelites, when God told Moses to strike
the rock at Horeb (Exodus 17:1–6), an event that is recalled by the Psalmist: "He

cleft rocks in the wilderness, and gave them to drink abundantly from the deep.
He made streams come out of the rock, and caused waters to flow down like riv-
ers" (Ps. 78:15–16). Nonetheless, the unmistakably comic tone of this miracle
tale in the *Münchner Oswald*—produced partly by its extraordinary, Hollywood-
extravaganza-like proportions[147]—places it in stark opposition to the corresponding account in *Ósvalds saga*. Gaudon's response to Oswald's exhortation to accept the Christian faith is a refusal to do so,

> ". . . nema guð þinn sé so kraftauðigur að hann láti þann harða steininn er
> þar liggur gefa vatn af sér so að ég sjái það." Ósvaldur segir: "Sannlega er
> mínum guði þetta ekki meira en það fyrra er hann hefur tvisvar sýnt þér og
> meiri er dýrð hans og góðsemi ef hann vil sér sóma láta og birta þér slíka
> hluti og aðra þvílíka heldur en þú ert verður til. En til þess að hans guðleg
> mekt verði að ljósari fyrir þeim sem áður eru blindir, þá biður ég hans
> háleita mildi að reiðast mér ekki þó að ég freista enn þessa." Og gekk að
> einum miklum steini og sté á með fæti sínum og mælti síðan: "Þú steinn,"
> sagði hann, "gef þú vatn af þér so að allir þeir er hér standa megi sjá guðs
> dýrð." En jafnsnart heyrði guð hans ákall so að steinninn varð so blautur
> sem leir og spratt þar út skírt vatn.

> (". . . unless your God is so powerful that he has water gush out of this hard
> rock that is lying there as I watch." Oswald says: "Truly this is no greater
> thing for my God than what He has already twice shown you,[148] and His glo-
> ry and goodness are greater if He deigns to manifest to you such things and
> others like them of which you are not worthy. But so that His divine power
> might become all the more manifest to those who otherwise would be blind,
> I ask of His great mercy not to be angry with me though I try Him once
> again." And he went to a large rock and placed his foot on it and then spoke:
> "You rock," he said, "let water gush out so that all those who are standing
> here may see God's glory." And God heard his prayer at once, for the rock
> became as soft as loam and out of it spurted pure water.)

---

[147] On humor in the *Münchner Oswald* in general, see Haug, "Das Komische und das
Heilige. Zur Komik in der religiösen Literatur des Mittelalters."

[148] This and the subsequent reference to two miracles suggests that the text is corrupt.
While one might here interpret the statement to God's manifesting His power twice as an
indication that Oswald considers the resurrection of Gaudon's and his own men as two
separate miracles, this is not the case subsequently, where the text clearly indicates that
Gaudon's men were raised from the dead on two occasions. It is likely that the original
legend had three miracles—a twofold resurrection of Gaudon's men and the miracle of the
rock exuding water—but the second resurrection got lost in transmission. Such a second
miracle occurs neither in the *HL/Pass.* nor the *Münchner Oswald*.

And with this miracle, Gaudon now agrees to be baptized and his people with him.

Unlike the *Münchner Oswald*, the prose legend does not conclude with the immediate aftermath of the above, that is, the wedding, Christ's testing of Oswald, and his peaceful death at the side of his wife. Instead, *Ósvalds saga* goes on to depict the encounter in battle between the Northumbrian king and several pagan kings, foremost among them Penda, whom Bede portrays as being "cum omni Merciorum gente idolis deditus, et Christiani erat nominis ignarus" (*HE* 2.20: 'like the whole Mercian race . . . idolaters and ignorant of the name of Christ'). It was by this pagan people and their king—"ab eadem pagana gente paganoque rege Merciorum" (*HE* 3.9)—that Oswald was slain on 5 August 642. It is noteworthy that Bede does not unambiguously portray Oswald's final battle as a battle for the faith; he refers to Maserfelth as the place where "pro patria dimicans a paganis interfectus est" ('he was slain by the heathens fighting for his fatherland' [*HE* 3.9]). And the question is whether for Bede *patria* refers to Northumbria or to heaven, the *patria aeterna*.[149] There is absolutely no doubt in the vernacular version, however, as to what is meant, for this interprets Oswald's strife with the pagan kings as being "fyrir heilagrar trú skuld" ('for the sake of the holy faith'). Indeed, Oswald is challenged by the pagan kings "að kasta heilagri trú og dýrka goð þeirra" ('to renounce the holy faith and to worship their gods'), and as he sees his men being slain, Oswald prays to God to take to Himself the souls of the men who "hér í dag láta sitt líf fyrir þíns helga nafns skuld" ('lose their lives here today for the sake of Your holy name'). The king who wooed a pagan princess in order to convert her to Christianity, and who engaged her pagan father in battle for the sake of the faith, now takes his men into his final battle, prior to which a heavenly voice addresses him as "píslarvottur guðs" ('martyr of God'). Unlike the Greek loan word used in English, the meaning of the Icelandic *píslarvottur* is self-evident: by means of his suffering—*písl*—Oswald becomes a witness—*vottur*—of his faith.

As is the case with the narrativization of Cynegisl's conversion through the creation of the figure of Gaudon, the account of Oswald's last battle against pagan forces is greatly embellished in *Ósvalds saga*, but derives ultimately from Bede. The latter informs us that it normally was Oswald's custom

> . . . a tempore matutinae laudis saepius ad diem usque in orationibus persteterit, atque ob crebrum morem orandi siue gratias agendi Domino semper, ubicumque sedens, supinas super genua sua manus habere solitus sit.

---

[149] J. M. Wallace-Hadrill, *Bede's Ecclesiastical History of the English People: A Historical Commentary* (Oxford: Clarendon Press, 1988), 103, note to *HE* 3.9: "Cuius quanta fides . . . satis duximus."

Vulgatum est autem, et in consuetudinem prouerbii uersum, quod etiam inter uerba orationis uitam finierit; namque cum armis et hostibus circumseptus iamiamque uideret se esse perimendum, orauit pro animabus exercitus
sui. Vnde dicunt in prouerbio: 'Deus miserere animabus, dixit Osuald cadens in terram.' (*HE* 3.12)

(. . . that very often he would continue in prayer from matins until daybreak;
and because of his frequent habit of prayer and thanksgiving, he was always
accustomed, wherever he sat, to place his hands on his knees with his palms
turned upwards. It is also a tradition which has become proverbial, that he
died with a prayer on his lips. When he was beset by the weapons of his
enemies and saw that he was about to perish he prayed for the souls of his
army. So the proverb runs, "'May God have mercy on their souls', as Oswald
said when he fell to the earth.")

Bede interjects the above into the miracle tale of a little boy who is cured of a
fever at the tomb of St. Oswald. In *Ósvalds saga*, however, the corresponding
passage occurs immediately before the battle in which the king is to suffer martyrdom. The hagiographer depicts the saintly king in prayer the night before the
encounter with Penda, when he entrusts himself and his men to God and the
Virgin Mary.

Og um nóttina áður en stríðinn átti að vera um morguninn eftirá, lá Ósvaldur
kóngur alla nóttina á bænum og bífalaði sig og sína menn undir miskunn og
umsjón almáttugs guðs og hans signaðrar móður jungfrú Maríu og bað þau
um að það skyldi ske sem þau vildi.

(And during the night before the morning on which the battle was to take
place, King Oswald was prostrate the whole night in prayer and commended
himself and his men to the mercy and providence of almighty God and His
blessed mother, the Virgin Mary, and prayed that their will be done.)

Not unexpectedly, a voice from heaven hails Oswald as a martyr and noble
knight—"Eyja, þú píslarvottur guðs og ærlegur riddari Osvalde"—and exhorts
him not to fear, rather to rejoice, "for already tomorrow you shall be sitting and
ruling with God and His chosen in the heavenly kingdom, and not you alone but
also all your followers."

A saintly king's solitary prayer during the night before a battle is a common-
place. In *Hendreks saga ok Kunegundis*, too, the ruler absents himself from his
men to implore God's assistance:

Þegar að varla var komin miðnótt stendur hann upp aftur so að það vissu
öngvir í hernum nema hans heimuglegir vinir og fer einsaman íburtu frá
sínum mönnum og fellur til bænar og kallar enn til guðs sér til fulltings af

öllu hjarta so segjandi: "Heyr þú mig, drottin guð minn, þú ert mín hjálp og mitt örugt traust. Veittu mér, drottin, að þínir þjónustumenn sem bæði líf og sál vilja í þitt vald gefa og fyrir þitt helgasta nafn skuld vilja bæði lifa og deyja, gef þú þeim þá hjálp og styrk so þeir megi því öruggara skilja að þú ert alveldugur guð og herra yfir öllum." (*Rhb.*, 1:39.16–25)

(When it was not yet quite midnight he gets up again without anyone in his army knowing this except his close friends and he goes away alone from his men and falls to praying and calls on God again with all his heart for assistance, speaking thus: "Hear me, God, my Lord, you are my help and my secure support (cf. Psalm 115:9, 10, 11). Grant me, Lord, that your servants who want to entrust to you both their lives and souls and want both to live and die for the sake of your holy name, give them help and strength so that they may more confidently understand that you are the all-powerful God and Lord over all.")

And the narrator interjects to relate that even before the emperor had finished his prayer, an angel appeared to tell him that God had heard his prayer; he should not fear his enemies for he will obtain divine help. In the ensuing battle the emperor sees—when his eyes are opened "spiritually" (1:40.3: "keisarans augu lukust upp andlega")—that an army of young men on white horses has come to help his forces. The pagans are routed. Except for the fact that Henry is victorious, the similarity to the corresponding episode in *Ósvalds saga* is unmistakable, and while the ultimate source for the scene transmitted in the saga is Bede's account, the development of its dramatic potential presumably occurred in the context of vernacular hagiography, in which the legend of Henry II would have been a likely donor in the German-language area.

Oswald decides to have a cross set up as his army's standard, and this agrees with Bede's account: ". . . ubi uenturus ad hanc pugnam Osuald signum sanctae crucis erexit, ac flexis genibus Deum deprecatus est, ut in tanta rerum necessitate suis cultoribus caelesti succurreret auxilio" (*HE* 3.2: 'Oswald, when he was about to engage in battle, set up the sign of the holy cross and, on bended knees, prayed God to send heavenly aid to his worshippers in their dire need'). Bede reports this incident as occurring not prior to Oswald's last battle, however, but rather before the battle of Hefenfeld. Before this same battle Oswald is reported by Bede as having exhorted his army as follows:

"Flectamus omnes genua, et Deum omnipotentem uiuum ac uerum in commune deprecemur, ut nos ab hoste superbo ac feroce sua miseratione defendat; scit enim ipse quia iusta pro salute gentis nostrae bella suscepimus." (3.2)

("Let us all kneel together and pray the almighty, everliving, and true God to defend us in His mercy from the proud and fierce enemy; for He knows that we are fighting in a just cause for the preservation of our whole race.")

Oswald's erection of the cross resulted in the liturgy's celebrating the saint as a second Constantine. A responsory in the Second Nocturn of Matins for the Vigil of his feast reads:

Gloriosus es, æterne Rex,
    Qui sicut tuum quondam Constantinum,
    Sic per signum crucis
    Oswaldum regem triumphare facis.

(You are glorious, Eternal King, who through the sign of the cross, like another Constantine, had King Oswald triumph.)[150]

In *Ósvalds saga* and its presumed German source—the *Heiligen Leben/Pasionael* has an abbreviated version—the prayer before the battle of Hefenfeld is relocated to the morning of the king's final battle. Oswald encourages his men to be strong in their faith and God's voice affirms in the presence of the entire army that Oswald will enjoy eternal life:

Um morguninn snemma þegar í ár vakti kóngur allt sitt lið og taldi fyrir þeim heilaga trú og mörg önnur stórmerki drottins er hann hafði veitt og sýnt sínum ástvinum bæði fyrir hingaðburðinn og so eftir á og styrkti sitt fólk bæði með þessu og mörgu öðru. Og mælti þá til þeirra sjálfra, so segjandi: "Heyrið þér, hinir allra sterkastir riddarar Jesu Christi; verið öruggir og styrkir í heilagri trú í þessari stríð. Og stríðið mannlega á móti guðs óvinum og yðrum og fyrir það skulu þér eiga að sitja eilíft ríki með sjálfum guði og hans helgum mönnum. Hér fyrir, þér allra kærustu vinir, útréttið nú yðrar hendur og hjörtu til guðs og biðjið hann að hjálpa yður með sínum englum." En þá sem kóngur hafði þetta mælt, þá kom ofan af himni yfir hann mikið ljós og úr því ljósinu heyrði hann rödd drottins so segjandi: "Osvalde, þú verður eilíflega lifandi með mér."

(And early in the morning as soon as day broke, the king awakened all his men and spoke to them of the holy faith and many other great signs the Lord had granted and shown His beloved friends both before His birth and after, and he encouraged his men both with these words and many others. And he spoke to them, saying: "Listen, you strongest of knights of Jesus Christ, be fearless and strong in the holy faith during this battle. And fight manfully against God's enemies and yours, and in return you will enjoy eternal life with God Himself and His saints. Therefore, all you dearest of friends, extend now your hands and hearts to God and ask Him to help you together with His angels." And when the king had spoken this, a great light came down from heaven upon him and out of this light he heard the voice of the Lord, saying thus: "Oswald, you will live eternally with me.")

---

[150] Bayart, "Les Offices de Saint Winnoc et de Saint Oswald," 62.

The scene is in the best tradition of martyr *vitae* and constitutes an amplification of Bede's account of how Oswald had exhorted his men before the battle of Hefenfeld. Oswald's prayer before battle and his words of encouragement to his men are also reminiscent of a corresponding scene in *Hendreks saga ok Kunegundis*, when Henry addresses his men prior to a battle with the heathen Wends:

> "Kærasti vinir, upphefjið þér yðrar hendur og hjörtu til guðs almáttugs, þvíað hann vill gefa oss sigur á sínum óvinum og vorum, og biður ég yður að hver dugi eftir sínu megni og hugsum eftir því að eilíf laun og sæla er þeim vís sem í hans nafni arbeiða, hvort sem heldur lifa menn eður deyja fyrir hans skuld." (*Rhb.*, 1.38:4–9)

> ("Dearest friends, lift up your hands and hearts to almighty God, for He will give us victory against His enemies and ours, and I ask you that each put himself forward in accordance with his might and main, for let us remember that an eternal reward and bliss is assured those who labor in His name, whether men live or die for His sake.")

In *Ósvalds saga*, unlike *Hendreks saga*, the battle is to end in death for not only the king but also many of his men. When Oswald sees

> að hans fólk varð niður slegið sem annar hráviði, þá leit hann upp til himna og mælti: "Herra Jesus Christus, þú almektugur guð, tak til þín þeirra manna sálir sem hér í dag láta sitt líf fyrir þíns helga nafns skuld." Og þegar í stað fékk hann að sjá hvar sem englar guðs komu ofan af himnum og tóku sálir hans manna jafnótt sem þeir urðu drepnir af þeirra óvinum og færðu þá aftur upp með sér með miklum fagnaði og lofsöngum til eilífrar dýrðar.

> (that his men were being mowed down like tender plants, he raised his eyes to heaven and spoke: "Lord Jesus Christ, you Almighty God, take to yourself the souls of those men who lose their lives here today for the sake of your holy name." And at once he got to see how God's angels came down from heaven and took the souls of his men the moment they were killed by their enemies and carried them back up with them to eternal glory with much rejoicing and hymns of praise.)

The nature of the death blow to Oswald is reported neither in the Latin nor the vernacular accounts, but the saga transmits his prayer of thanksgiving and dying words:

> "Lof sé þér utan enda, drottinn minn, þvíað nú hefur ég mikinn fögnuð séð að sálir minna manna eru nú undan mér farnar til dýrðar þinnar og fyrir því er ég nú glaður til að deyja með þeim og fara úr þessum heimi og til þeirra." Síðan mælti hann: "Drottinn Jesus Christus, faðir himneskur, í þínar hendur fel ég anda minn," og gaf jafnskjótt sinn anda upp.

("Praise be to you without end, my Lord, for now I have experienced great joy that the souls of my men have now left me for your glory, and for this reason I am now happy to die with them and to leave this earth and join them." Then he spoke: "Lord Jesus Christ, Heavenly Father, into your hands I commend my spirit," and at once he gave up his spirit.)

The prose legend thus has lifted the report of Oswald's final prayer (complete with its quotation of Christ's last words in Luke 23:46) from Bede's miracle tale and placed it in its proper chronological context. Oswald's soul is carried off the field of battle by the angels.

The saga's predilection—and thus also that of its German source—for dramatizing Bede's terse accountreflects a similar tendency in later Latin texts, for example, the *Gesta Regum Britannie*, a metrical paraphrase of Geoffrey of Monmouth's *Historia Regum Britanniae*, written in the mid-thirteenth century, which depicts Oswald's death as follows:

Osualdus, regum sanctissimus, arma Peande
Dum fugeret, sociis secum fugientibus inquit:
'O deuota Deo Christique domestica turba,
Submissis manibus et supplice uoce precemur
Auctorem nostre fidei regemque polorum
Ut nos de manibus Britonum seuique Peande
Liberet.' Effusis lacrimis genibusque reflexis
Turba precatur idem. Deus audit iusta precantes.
Nam Phebo retegente diem capit arma Peanda
Et capit Osualdus. In primo marte Britanni
Deuicti fugiunt. Quod rex Caduallo relatu
Addiscens, mouet arma ferox ferturque superbus
In sanctum regem. Sanctus rex ense peremptus
Sanguine sacrat humum; melior pars transuolat astra.[151]

(Oswald, the holiest of kings, fleeing before the weapons of Penda, says to his comrades in flight: 'O company devoted to God, dwellers in the house of Christ, let us with humble hands and suppliant voices beg the Originator of our faith and the King of Heaven to free us from the grasp of the Britons and of cruel Penda.' With flowing tears and bended knee the troops repeat his prayer. God hears their just entreaty. When the sun renews the daylight, both Penda and Oswald take up arms. In the first clash the Britons are defeated and put to flight. When King Cadvallo hears report of this, he fiercely sets his army in motion and arrogantly attacks the saintly Oswald.

---

[151] *The Historia Regum Britannie of Geoffrey of Monmouth. V. Gesta Regum Britannie*, ed. and trans. Neil Wright (Cambridge: D.S. Brewer, 1991), 10:173–186 (268–69).

The holy king is cut down by the sword and consecrates the ground with his blood, while his better part soars up above the stars.) [152]

In the saga Oswald's soul is carried off the field of battle by the angels. The martyrdom of Oswald concludes with the dismemberment of the saint's body by Penda, as reported by Bede, and the impalement of his head and arms. Robert Folz comments on the clash between Oswald's offering the souls of his warriors to God—Folz bases this on Bede because he does not know the saga—and the pagan treatment of Oswald's remains by Penda: "selon la coutume ancestrale, le roi de Mercie immolait son adversaire à Wodan."[153] It should be recalled that Oswald himself was a convert and that the very name 'Oswald' is pagan, deriving as it does from *áss* '(heathen) god' and *vald* 'power, might'. Indeed, Oswald's pagan ancestry is recalled by Drogo when he writes: "Sicut ergo rosa de spinis, sic idem Oswaldus de paganis parentibus ortus est" (94: 'Therefore like a rose among thorns, Oswald issued forth from pagan parents'). And in the responsory of the First Nocturn of Matins for the Vigil of St. Oswald, Drogo repeats the simile: "Ut rosa de spinis pulcherrima surgit acutis" ('As a most beautiful rose he arose from the sharp thorns').[154]

The portrayal of the saint in *Ósvalds saga* (and in the condensed version in *Der Heiligen Leben/Dat Passionael*) as the proselytizer and martyr king derives from Bede's account, but it underwent considerable expansion as it was dramatized. The narrativization of the facts of Oswald's battles against pagan forces parallels that found in the legend of Henry II, and it may in fact have been inspired by and modeled after this contemporary legend. The correspondences between *Hendreks saga* and *Ósvalds saga* in the construction of similar scenes are so striking that derivation of some of the material in the latter German legend from the former is not out of the question. This would explain the great similarity of the two legends in their Icelandic translations.

---

[152] *Gesta Regum Britannie*, 268–69.

[153] Folz, "Saint Oswald roi de Northumbrie," 51. It should be remembered that "with the exception of Essex all the genealogies of the English royal families which have been preserved go back to Woden": Colgrave and Mynors, *Bede's Ecclesiastical History*, 51, n. 2.

[154] Bayart, "Les Offices de Saint Winnoc et de Saint Oswald," 60. The image, a variant of "a lily among brambles" in the Song of Songs 2:2, is a popular Marian simile. See Anselm Salzer, *Die Sinnbilder und Beiworte Mariens in der deutschen Literatur und lateinischen Hymnenpoesie des Mittelalters. Mit Berücksichtigung der patristischen Literatur. Eine literar-historische Studie* (Seitenstetten: Programm des k. k. Ober-Gymnasiums zu Seitenstetten, 1886–1894; repr. Darmstadt: Wissenschaftliche Buchgesellschaft, 1967), 14.34, 15.29, 68.28, 146.31, 167.24, 183.9f., 186.9f.

# VII.
## THE MIRACLES

*Ósvalds saga* concludes with four additional chapters (chaps. 13–16) containing accounts of miracles that occurred after Oswald's death. As Wallace-Hadrill has noted: "For Bede the significance of Oswald's death is that a Christian warrior-king may not be victorious in battle but there will be rich compensations. The king is active for good after his death."[55] The many miracles attest Oswald's post-humous intervention on earth. It is noteworthy that the miracle section transmits with but minor deviations what we read in the *Historia Ecclesiastica*. This is not the case in the *vita* and *passio*, which underwent significant development in the vernacular prose version as a result of the incorporation of the coronation legend and the expansion of already existing text through the addition of new characters, most notably the raven, and the incorporation of extensive dialogue.

*Ósvalds saga* contains the following miracles:

1) A knight's horse falls ill and is cured at the spot where Oswald was slain (Bede, *HE* 3.9)
2) A young girl is cured when she sleeps on the spot where Oswald was slain (Bede, *HE* 3.9)
3) Oswald's relics, which were found at the place where he was buried, remain safe in a house that is otherwise burned to the ground (Bede, *HE* 3.10)
4) A man retrieves Oswald's relics and gives them to the queen of Austria, who subsequently donates them to a monastery in Lindsey, where a man possessed of the devil is cured (Bede, *HE* 3.11)
5) A blind man is cured by rubbing soil from Oswald's grave on his eyes (Bede, *HE* 3.9)
6) Water containing chips from a cross on the spot where St. Oswald was slain cures people and animals (Bede, *HE* 3.2)

The third miracle, of Oswald's unscathed relics after a fire, has undergone some development in its transmission in the vernacular versions. In the saga, as in the *Passionael*, some people come to a place where there are many strange plants not found elsewhere and they surmise that a holy person has been slain or buried there. They begin to dig and find bones that emit an extraordinary fragrance. They take the relics along with them for the express purpose of curing others. They come to a place where a great feast is in progress and are invited to join. A

---

[55] Wallace-Hadrill, *Bede's Ecclesiastical History of the English People, 102.*

fire breaks out and the entire place burns down, but the relics come to no harm. They inquire as to the nature of the place where the remains were found and are told that St. Oswald was slain and buried there.

Bede's account of this miracle (*HE* 3.10) has been somewhat altered in transmission. The *Historia Ecclesiastica* tells of a Briton who comes to the place where Oswald's final battle took place. When he notices that some grass is greener in one spot than elsewhere, he surmises that someone holier than the rest of the army must have been slain there. He then removes some soil, not Oswald's relics, and it is this, wrapped in a cloth, which does not burn during the fire. Bede reports: "Consumta ergo domu flammis, posta solummodo, in qua puluis ille inclusus pendebat, tuta ab ignibus et intacta remansit" (*HE* 3.10: 'So the whole house was burnt down with the single exception that the post on which the soil hung, enclosed in its bag, remained whole and untouched by the fire').

The reason for the corruption in the vernacular versions may be that the immediately following chapter in Bede (*HE* 3.11) tells of miracles wrought by means of Oswald's bones after they were discovered and translated to the monastery of Bardney in Lindsey. Bede reports that this came about through the efforts of Oswald's niece Osthryth, queen of Mercia. She had the relics transported on a carriage to the monastery, wishing to donate them to the monks, but they were slow to realize the treasure they were receiving. Bede tells us that even though they knew that Oswald was a saint, "tamen quia de alia prouincia ortus fuerat et super eos regnum acceperat, ueteranis eum odiis etiam mortuum insequebantur" (*HE* 3.11: 'but, nevertheless, because he belonged to another kingdom and had once conquered them, they pursued him even when dead with their former hatred'). Hatred born of politics is vanquished, however, when the bones, which were left outside all night, are illuminated by a column of light stretching all the way from heaven and seen throughout the entire kingdom of Lindsey: "Nam tota ea nocte columna lucis a carro illo ad caelum usque porrecta omnibus pene eiusdem Lindissae prouinciae locis conspicua stabat" (*HE* 3.11). The miracle tale concludes with the relics being washed and placed in a shrine especially constructed for them. When the water is subsequently poured out, the soil "ad abigendos ex obsessis corporibus daemones gratiae salutaris haberet effectum" (*HE* 3.11: 'had the power and saving grace of driving devils from the bodies of people possessed').

This last sentence generated a minor miracle tale in the vernacular legend, though the relics themselves are the cause of the miracle. The saga relates:

Í þessu var einn fátækur maður þar kominn til þess ef hann mætti fá nokkura líkn síns meinlætis er hann hafði. En það var að óvinurinn bjó með honum og hafði hann af tilvísan guðs almáttugs dregist þangað er bein Osvaldus voru. En er hann hafði legið þar litla hríð varð hann frelstur af þessum óvin so að hann gjörði honum aldregi upp frá því og fór í burtu aftur alheill og þakkaði guði og sankti Ósvald. Samaleiðis gjörði og bræðurnar allir í klaustrinu er þessa sýn og jarteikn bæði sáu og heyrðu.

(At this moment a poor man came there to see whether he might get some relief for the affliction he had. And this was that he was possessed by the devil, and guided by almighty God he was drawn to the spot where Oswald's bones were. And when he had lain there for a little while, he was freed of this devil so that he never again plagued him from this day on, and he went away completely cured and thanked God and St. Oswald. All the brothers in the monastery, who saw and heard about this vision and miracle, did the same.)

The additional miracle at the time of the translation is presumably the work of the vernacular author. Nonetheless, the narrativization of the simple sentence in Bede into an exemplum—"the soil which had received that holy water had the power and saving grace of driving devils from the bodies of people possessed"—presumably was inspired by Bede himself, for he reports that after the translation of St. Oswald, Queen Osthryth stayed on in the monastery and was visited by an abbess named Æthelhild. She asked for some of the miracle-working soil and after her return to her own monastery, she received a visit from a man "who used very often to be greatly troubled in the night, without warning, by an unclean spirit" (*HE* 3.11). When exorcism fails to drive the devil from the man, the abbess remembers the soil, and the tale now proceeds very much as in the vernacular version above:

Et cum illa adferens, quae iussa est, intraret atrium domus, in cuius interioribus daemoniosus torquebatur, conticuit ille subito, et quasi in somnum laxatus deposuit caput, membra in quietem omnia conposuit. . . . Et post aliquantum horae spatium resedit qui uexabatur, et grauiter suspirans 'Modo' inquit 'sanum sapio; recipi enim sensum animi mei.' (*HE* 3.11)

(No sooner had the servant brought the soil as ordered, and entered the porch of the house in which the demoniac was lying in his contortions, than he was suddenly silent and laid his head down as if he were in a relaxed sleep, while his limbs became quiet and composed. . . . After about an hour the man who had been afflicted sat up and said with a deep sigh, 'Now I feel that I am well and have been restored to my senses.')

The author of the vernacular version chose not to include the account of the meeting of Queen Osthryth and Abbess Æthelhild in the legend—this would not have been appropriate in any case, since the last section of *Ósvalds saga* relates the miracles seriatim—at the same time that he realized the advantage of linking the cure of the possessed man to the translation of St. Oswald's relics.

The account of the translation of Oswald's relics became both corrupt and enriched in the process of vernacularization. Presumably a German copyist is to blame for the identification of Oswald's niece Osthryth with the name of a country. In the saga we learn that the man who discovered St. Oswald's relics "flutti síðan með sér í Austurríki og gaf þau drottningunni þar. En hún var bróðurdóttir Ósvalds konungs" ('then took them with him to Austria and gave them there to the queen. And she was the daughter of King Oswald's brother'). How the relics were to end up in Austria before they were given to Lindsey in the German legend is not difficult to understand, given the similarity between the name of Oswald's niece, *Osthryth*, and the German name for Austria, MHG *Ôsterrîche*, MLG *Osterîke*. The error most likely occurred through a misreading of the second syllable of her name—Osthryda/Ostrida —and the resulting corruption then called forth an explanation as to how the relics came back to England. The saga attests that the corrupt text was already found in the German source of *Der Heiligen Leben/ Dat Passionael*. In the latter we read that the man who had found the relics

> gaff id der konninginnen van Osterike de was sunte Oswaldes broder dochter. de nam dat myt groten vrouden. vnde voerde dat to husz. vnde leet eyn schonen sark dar to maken dar in lede se dat hyllychdoem myt groter werdicheyt. vnde voerde dat in dat lant Lindissino. (C.v.a)

> (gave them to the queen of Austria; she was the daughter of St. Oswald's brother. She accepted them with great joy and took them home and had a beautiful shrine made for them and laid the relics in it with great ceremony. And she took it to the country called Lindsey.)

*Ósvalds saga* contains an additional bit of information not found in Bede, a second minor miracle that precedes the miracle of the column of light. The saga has the relics arrive in the monastery in the evening, just as in Bede, but unlike the monks' frosty reception in his account, they were implicitly welcomed by them in the saga. The queen and her retinue decide to get up early the next morning to visit the relics, "fyrir afláts skyld" ('in order to gain an indulgence'), we are told,

> En þegar birti guð henni fagra sýn, og þeim er henni fylgdu, so að þeir sáu eina hvíta dúfu. Hún gjörði ýmist að hún settist niður á bein sankti Ósvalds ellegar fló hún í burtu aftur. Af þessari sýn gladdist mjög drottningin og lofaði guð fyrir. Um morguninn eftir sagði drottningin og menn hennar bræðrunum í klaustrinu hvað þeir höfðu séð. Þá fögnuðu bræðurnir þessari sýn og slíkum helgum dómi er guð hafði þeim og þeirra klaustri gefið.

> (And at once God granted her a beautiful vision as also to those who accompanied her, for they saw a white dove. Now and then it alighted on the bones of St. Oswald and then flew away again. The queen rejoiced greatly at this vision and praised God for it. The next morning the queen and her people told the brothers in the monastery what they had seen. The brothers rejoiced at this vision and the relics that God had given them and their monastery.)

While the tale of the dove is not related by Bede, nor by Drogo, the miracle of the dove is recounted, as one would expect, in the *Heiligen Leben/Passionael* prose legend. In the latter we read:

vnde in der suluen nacht do de konnynghynne vnde eer ghesinde to deme sarcke ghingen. do seghen se ene schone witte duuen van deme hyllichdom upvaren vnde wedder aff. Des tekens worden se ghans vro. (C.v.b)

(And during the same night when the queen and her retinue went to the shrine, they saw a beautiful white dove fly up from the relics and back down. They rejoiced greatly at this miracle.)

The miraculous dove must have been incorporated fairly early into the account of the translation of Oswald's relics. Drogo's Office of St. Oswald, as transmitted in MS. 14 of the Bibliothèque de Bergues, dating from the twelfth century,[156] does not know the miracle of the dove but mentions the column of light. The five antiphons at Lauds are dedicated to the miracles associated with St. Oswald, and in the fourth antiphon Bede's *columna lucis* is referred to as *clara columna*. In a thirteenth-century copy of this Office of St. Oswald, a manuscript from Weingarten, the same antiphon has a striking discrepancy, for now we read: "Suscipitur clara meritum testante columba"[157] ('He was raised up, a bright dove attesting his merits'). The antiphon in the Weingarten manuscript provides the explanation as to how the miracle of the dove came to be interpolated into the vernacular legend of St. Oswald. The *columba* in the Weingarten manuscript is a corruption of *columna* in Drogo's antiphon: "Suscipitur, clara meritum testante columna" ('He was raised up, a bright column [of light] attesting his merits').[158] Therefore it is most likely that the miracle of the white dove in the vernacular legend of St. Oswald had a liturgical origin and was occasioned by a scribal error. The author of the German Oswald legend knew not only the *columna lucis* from Bede but also the *columba clara* from the liturgy and related both miracles in the account of Oswald's translation.

The last two miracle stories in *Ósvalds saga* and the *Heiligen Leben/Passionael* redaction tell of cures effected at the grave of St. Oswald. These miracle

---

[156] Bayart, "Les Offices de Saint Winnoc et de Saint Oswald," 6. In the period 1181–1224, the relics of several saints were translated at Bergues-St. Winnoc, Oswald's in 1221, and it may be possible that a copy of the Offices of Sts. Winnoc and Oswald was made on one of these occasions (6, n. 1).

[157] *Analecta Hymnica Medii Aevi, 13. Historiae Rhythmicae. Liturgische Reimofficien.* Zweite Folge, ed. Guido Maria Dreves (Leipzig: Reisland, 1892; repr. New York: Johnson Reprint Co., 1961), 211.

[158] Bayart, "Les Offices de Saint Winnoc et de Saint Oswald," 63. See also n. 2, with the comment that in the fourth antiphon "*suscipitur* s'entend de l'élévation du corps du Saint."

tales are mentioned only in a general way by Bede and in a different context. A remark by Bede about the curative power of a material object associated with St. Oswald generated in the vernacular legend a specific miracle tale, as was the case with the story of the man possessed by demons in the account of the translation of Oswald's relics. In *Ósvalds saga* the place where Oswald was slain and the site of his grave are considered to be one and the same, and the saga reports that a large cross had been raised up here. According to Bede, this is actually the cross that Oswald himself had raised, but this did not occur before his final battle (cf. *Ósvalds saga*, chap. 11). Bede reports:

> In cuius loco orationis innumerae uirtutes sanitatum noscuntur esse patra-
> tae, ad indicium uidelicet ac memoriam fidei regis. Nam et usque hodie
> multi de ipso ligno sacrosanctae crucis astulas excidere solent, quas cum
> in aquas miserint, eisque languentes homines aut pecudes potauerint siue
> asperserint, mox sanitati restituuntur. (*HE* 3.2)

> (Innumerable miracles of healing are known to have been wrought in the
> place where they prayed, doubtless as a token and memorial of the king's
> faith. And even to this day many people are in the habit of cutting splinters
> from the wood of this holy cross and putting them in water which they then
> give to sick men or beasts to drink or else they sprinkle them with it; and
> they are quickly restored to health.)

In the vernacular legend, that is, in the Icelandic and German versions, the above is individualized and becomes a particular miracle—"En þá sem nokkurir fátækir komu þangað til grafarinnar, þá fóru þeir til og tálguðu sér spónu af krossinum þessum. . ." ('And when some poor people came there to the grave, they went and cut chips off this cross. . .')—and the saga reports that this place was subsequent-ly called in Latin *"caelestis locus*, en á engelsku *himneskur staður"* (*'caelestis lo-cus*, but in English *Heavenly Stead'*). This agrees with Bede, except that the place name, like the miracle above, is associated with the place where Oswald himself had raised a cross before battle (*HE* 3.2).

The case is similar with the miracle of the blind man who takes some soil from Oswald's grave and rubs it over his eyes. Bede has no report of such a mir-acle, but he does relate that

> in loco ubi pro patria dimicans a paganis interfectus est, usque hodie sanitates
> infirmorum et hominum et pecorum celebrari non desinunt. Vnde contigit
> ut puluerem ipsum, ubi corpus eius in terram conruit, multi auferentes et in
> aquam mittentes suis per haec infirmis multum commodi adferrent. (*HE* 3.9)

> (in that place where he was slain by the heathens fighting for his fatherland,
> sick men and beasts are healed to this day. It has happened that people have

(often taken soil from the place where his body fell to the ground, have put it in water, and by its use have brought great relief to their sick.)

Bede's general observation about the curative effects of soil from the spot where Oswald was slain becomes in the vernacular legend the individualized miracle story of how a blind man regains his vision at Oswald's grave. In Bede, the soil, just like the chips of wood taken from St. Oswald's cross, is first placed in water, but the blind man in the vernacular legend applies it directly to his eyes. In this tale, as in the one concerning the chips of wood from Oswald's cross, the miraculous healing occurs at Oswald's grave.

The last four chapters in *Ósvalds saga* attest that the miracle tales, like the account of Oswald's life and death, underwent further narrativization, albeit comparatively modest, in the vernacular legend. In the stories attesting Oswald's sanctity, just as in the account of incidents in Oswald's life, whether his marriage to Cynegisl's daughter or his habit of praying before battle, general remarks by Bede or the most fleeting of observations came to generate specific incidents and dramatically constructed scenes.

A final element in the vernacular legend of St. Oswald needs to be addressed, which, while not a miracle tale like those discussed above, nonetheless falls into the category of the miraculous, by virtue not only of its fantastic character but even more so of its role in indirectly furthering the bridal quest and hence the conversion of the heathens. Just as the raven is a messenger from God who plays an extraordinarily important and useful role in bringing about Oswald's engagement with pagan peoples, so also a stag accompanying the king on his bridal quest is indispensable for Oswald's escape with the princess. Thus the animal is also indirectly linked to Oswald's conversion of Gaudon's pagan forces.

Oswald arrives in pagan territory accompanied by a superb-looking stag, "en í sumlegum bókum greinir so að það væri engill" ('and in some books it says that it was an angel'). The *Passionael* conveys the same information in a slightly more authoritative manner: "vnde men vind bescreuen. dat id ein engel was" (C.iii.d: 'and one reads that it was an angel'). *Ósvalds saga* presumably transmits the original text. While the statement might be interpreted to suggest that the author had more than one version of the legend at hand, which is possible, it might also merely convey the author's interpretation of this aspect of the legend with recourse to the authority of books. Whatever the case may be, the very existence of the statement suggests a popular understanding of the episode that follows, at the same time that it may also be a key as to how the story of the stag came to be incorporated into the life of St. Oswald.

The story of the stag is the story of a hunt for a wondrous animal. According to *Ósvalds saga*, King Gaudon visits Oswald, whom he takes to be a merchant, in his tent, and suddenly a large stag runs past the opening to Oswald's tent. The saga reports that when Gaudon sees the animal, "dynur þegar ágirndaröngu í brjóst kónginum so að hann segist ekki annað mega en eignast dýrið" ('the king's heart at once pounds wildly with the anguish of greed and he says that he wants nothing other than to possess the animal'). Oswald tells him that the animal belongs to him but that it has escaped and is quite skittish. The king and his men pursue the stag and, oddly enough, "gjörir dýrið stundum að það staldrar við líkt sem það vilji þá og þá láta taka sig, en stundum hefur það sig undan so að varla komast þeir í augsýn við það" ('now and then the animal stops as though just then it wanted to let itself be taken, but now and then it darts off so that they hardly keep sight of it'). Many days pass in this manner: by evening they have lost the animal, but the next morning they meet up with it again. And the narrator reports that the king and his men think this rather strange. With the hunt undecided, the scene shifts in the saga to the princess who sees the stag and decides to go watch the hunt. It is at this point that she and her maidens make their escape with the help of God.

The incident with the stag is strange. Neither the saga nor the German prose legend provides any other information as to the animal's origin than that cited earlier. In any case, the legend interprets this animal as out of the ordinary, as supernatural. It is not unlikely that the stag in the legend of St. Oswald, despite appearing to be a stag and nothing else, has biblical or hagiographic antecedents. The Psalmist uses the image of the stag to comment on the soul's yearning for God: "As a hart longs for flowing streams, so longs my soul for thee, O God. My soul thirsts for God, for the living God. When shall I come and behold the face of God?" (Ps. 42:1-2). The stag in *Ósvalds saga* may have evoked these familiar verses, given the fact that Oswald is intent on leading Gaudon to Christ and especially since deer play a prominent role as a messenger of God or Christ Himself in other conversion narratives. Conversion is, after all, the reason why Oswald undertook the journey into pagan territory in the first place.

Deer frequently have the function of showing the way, as happens, for example, in Gregory of Tours's *Historia Francorum*, where a hind is sent by God to show Clovis how he can ford the river Vienne in his campaign against the Arians. We read:

> Cumque illa nocte Dominum depraecatus fuisset, ut ei vadum quo transire possit dignaretur ostendere, mane facto cerva mirae magnitudinis ante eos nuto Dei flumine ingreditur, illaque vadante, populus quo transire possit agnovit. (2.37)

> (That night he prayed that God might deign to indicate a ford by which he might make the crossing. As day dawned an enormous doe entered the water, as if to lead them at God's command. The soldiers knew that where the doe had crossed they could follow. [trans. Thorpe, 152])

In this incident the animal is indirectly connected to Clovis's proselytization efforts, but the link between the stag and conversion is more direct and, in fact, quite similar to the incident in *Ósvalds saga*, in the legends of Eustace and Hubert.

The stag plays an important role in the legend of St. Eustace, and this may have been the inspiration for the incorporation of the episode in the legend of St. Oswald. In the account "De sancto Eustachio" in the *Legenda aurea* we read that Placidus, as the saint was called before his conversion, and his companions went to the mountains one day in order to hunt. There they come upon some deer,

> inter quos unum caeteris speciosiorem et majorem conspexit, qui ab aliorum societate discedens in silvam vastiorem prosiliit. Verum aliis militibus circa cervos reliquos occupatis Placidus hunc toto nisu insequitur et ipsum capere nitebatur. Quem cum totis viribus insequeretur, cervus tandem super quandam rupis altitudinem conscendit et Placidus appropians, qualiter capi posset, animo sedulus revolvebat. Qui cum cervum diligenter consideraret, vidit inter cornua ejus formam sacrae crucis supra solis claritatem fulgentem et imaginem Jesu Christi.[159]

> (among which one stag stood out by his size and beauty, and this deer broke away from the others and bounded into a deeper part of the forest. Leaving his soldiers to follow the rest of the herd, Placidus gave his full effort to pursuing the stag and did his best to catch it. The deer kept well ahead of him, however, and finally stopped at the edge of a high peak. Placidus, coming near, pondered how he might capture the animal. As he studied it, he saw between its antlers what looked like the holy cross, shining more brightly than the sun. Upon the cross was the image of Jesus Christ.)[160]

Christ addresses Placidus through the stag's mouth and asks why he has been pursuing Him and concludes by saying: "I have come, that through this deer which you have hunted, I myself might hunt you!" (2:267). Placidus is converted to Christianity and receives the name Eustace in baptism.

A similar incident occurs in the legend of St. Hubert (d. 727), bishop of Maastricht and Liège and patron of huntsmen. While he is trying to hunt down a stag, a voice issuing from the animal addresses him: "Huberte, ut quid in vanum agens pretiosum tempus deperdis? Tu bestias seu animalia silvestria insequeris, cum ego de te decreverim aliud: non enim ex hoc bestias, sed homines eris capiens"[161] ('Hubert, why are you wasting your precious time in vain? You are pursuing the beasts and animals in the woods, while I have determined another [task]

---

[159] *Jacobi a Voragine Legenda aurea*, ed. Graesse, 712.
[160] Jacobus de Voragine, *The Golden Legend*, trans. Ryan, 2:266.
[161] *AA SS* Novembris, I:839.

for you: for you are not to capture these beasts but rather men'). In another redaction of the legend, the voice is reported to have said: "Tempus est jam ut et me veneris. Ego enim sum Dominus Deus tuus, qui hodie pro te et omnibus hominibus crucifixus sum" ('It is now time for you to come to me. For I am the Lord, your God, who today was crucified for you and all men' [*AA SS* Novembris, I:834]). In both legends, Christ, in the form of a stag, exhorts Placidus/Hubert to come to Him, that is, to accept Christianity.

Hippolyte Delehaye, remarking on the ability of certain motifs to become attached to any number of saints, included that of the crucifix between the antlers of a stag:

> Many striking episodes . . . are mere reminiscences or floating traditions which cling sometimes to one saint, sometimes to another. The miraculous crucifix which appeared to St. Hubert between the antlers of a stag, is in no sense the exclusive property of this saint. It may be found equally in the legend of St. Meinulf and that of St. Eustace, as well as in those many others in which variations of detail render the theme less easily recognisable.[162]

That is the case in the legend of St. Oswald, in which there is no explicit connection between the pursuit of the stag and the search for Christ, that is, Gaudon's eventual conversion to Christianity. Yet it is clear that Gaudon's pursuit of the stag is the reason why Oswald and the princess can escape and why Gaudon is ultimately converted. The stag in *Ósvalds saga* behaves very much like the stag in the legends of Eustace and Hubert, without, however, being in any way identified with Christ. Noteworthy is the fact that Gaudon's immediate reaction to the stag is quite similar to that of the Roman general Placidus in the legend of Eustace. Gaudon, like Placidus, "wants nothing other than to possess the animal."

Delehaye's observation that variations of detail in narratives containing the motif of the hunt for a wondrous stag can render it less recognizable applies to the legend of St. Oswald. As was shown above, the *Münchner Oswald* has lost the original hagiographic features of the Oswald legend and transformed the martyr king into a confessor. While the motif of conversion is transmitted, it does not play the important role it does in *Ósvalds saga* and the German prose legend. What happens to the stag in the German metrical version is instructive: the mysterious creature that presumably is a reflex of the Christ-as-stag motif in the Oswald legend becomes in the hagiographic romance a piece of art. When Oswald sets out upon his bridal quest, he is to bring along—thus the princess's instructions—"ainen ubergulten hirsch" ('a gilded stag': vv. 1180, 1408). A stag, it

---

[162] H[ippolyte] Delehaye, *The Legends of the Saints: An Introduction to Hagiography,* with an introduction by Richard J. Schoeck, trans. V. M. Crawford (1907; South Bend: University of Notre Dame Press, 1961), 28; idem, *Les Légendes hagiographiques,* 27.

turns out, has been raised by Oswald and been at his court for eighteen years, and this stag "der het so vil schons gezind, / daz wundert daz fremt hofgesind" (vv. 1601–1602 'there were so many fine prongs to its antlers that servants from other courts were amazed' [99]). We are told that they prepare the stag for the journey (v. 1603), but no details are given. When Oswald subsequently takes the stag with him, but forgets the raven, the latter, with its extraordinary anthropomorphic features, quips in a pique of *schadenfreude*: "nun hat er ainen hirsch an mein stat genomen, / des ist er in not chomen" (vv. 1823–1824 'but he took a stag instead of me; that's why he is in distress' [101]).

The role the stag is to play is not revealed in the *Münchner Oswald* until the king has been in pagan territory for some time, unable to see the princess. He awakens one morning with an idea and tells his goldsmiths to make golden hoofs and antlers for the stag and to place on his back a golden cloth reaching all the way to the ground (vv. 2344–54). This stag Oswald intends to let loose, so that the pagan king will pursue it while he enters the castle and thus gains access to the princess. When King Aron hears the news of the stag, he guesses that the goldsmiths whom Oswald has brought along have hollowed out the stag and that it moves about by the force of the wind (vv. 2400–2403). In other words, Aron sees this as an opportunity to obtain a very clever and extraordinarily precious mechanical device. The stag is, however, a stag, and the author of the *Münchner Oswald* depicts, from the perspective of the stag (vv. 2446–2450), its fright when it suddenly sees the men and dogs giving chase. It takes off, over the mountains, and ends up in the camp of Oswald's army (vv. 2445–2468). Only once is there a hint of the divine, when the narrator remarks that the stag escapes to Oswald's encampment, "als ez got selber wolt" (v. 2466 'as God had willed' [107]).

The teasingly elusive stag in *Ósvalds saga* that for several days plays endless games of tag with the pagans has become, despite its surrealistic golden trappings, a frightened, fleeing animal in the *Münchner Oswald*. In all likelihood the motif of the hunted stag was introduced into the Oswald legend because of its certain association with conversion. Yet the saga, which presumably represents the earliest German Oswald legend, contains but a titillating echo of the hagiographic stag motif.[163]

---

[163] In his edition of the *Münchner Oswald*, Baesecke expresses the contrary belief that the wondrous stag was originally a mechanical stag (309). This is in keeping with his general thesis that certain motifs in the *Münchner Oswald*, such as the talking raven, derive from German romance (see 292–294).

# VIII.
## CONCLUSION

In the 1492 imprint of *Dat Passionael* the legend "Van sunte Oswaldo deme ko-
nunghe" is accompanied by a woodcut the iconography of which embraces every
salient event of Oswald's life and death (fig. 1). A crowned and haloed Oswald
is seated on a throne, a scepter in his left hand[164] and a palm in his right, thus
identifying him as both king and martyr. On his left, that is, left of the hand carrying the scepter, a raven flies toward the saint; it has a phial in its beak, and a
letter to which seals are attached hangs around its neck. Flying away from the
king above the palm on the right is the same raven, this time bearing a ring in its
beak. The location of the chrism-bearing raven next to the royal scepter clearly
denotes the introductory coronation narrative with its divine intervention through
the heavenly chrism and St. Peter's letter. The position of the ring-bearing raven
above the palm of martyrdom connects the bridal-quest/conversion narrative to
Oswald's martyrdom. The phial in this woodcut has been understood by some as
a reinterpretation of the silver dish that Oswald had distributed in pieces to beggars one Easter Sunday, as related by Bede.[165] A miniature in the Berthold Missal
relates the incident, depicting Oswald and Aidan and two beggars. In his hand
Oswald does not hold a dish, but rather a vessel that resembles a ciborium (fig.
2). It is most unlikely, however, that this container was reinterpreted in the German Oswald legend as the chrismatory, since the delivery of the heavenly chrism
and the distribution of Oswald's dish to the poor occur in two quite different episodes. Moreover, the vernacular tale clearly identifies the dish as "de sulueren
schottelen dar he vth ath" (*Pass.* C.iiii.b: 'the silver bowl from which he ate'),[166]
and the Icelandic version uses the noun *diskur*, that is, 'dish' or 'plate'. The High
and Low German redactions of *Oswald* call the vessel holding the chrism a *pueh-
sen/bussen*, a term designating a container for holding a salve or ointment, and
this is replicated in the saga by the word *buðkur*. The woodcut in the *Passionael*
unequivocally depicts the chrismatory as a phial or flask. It should be noted that
the raven approaching Oswald with the vessel in its beak bears no little resem-
blance to the dove delivering a phial in a fourteenth-century miniature depicting
the baptism of Clovis (fig. 3).

---

[164] The object in Oswald's left hand resembles a pilgrim's stave rather than a sceptre.
Whatever the artist's intent may have been, the legend itself demands that this be interpreted as a sceptre.

[165] See Baker, "St. Oswald and his Church at Zug," 116–117.

[166] In the High German version, the king takes "di guldein schusseln" (*HL* 364 "the
golden bowl").

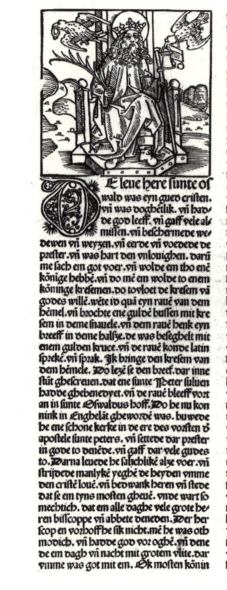

ghe.hertoghen.greuen.vñ eddelmäne bor
ghe vñ lande vä em entfangē. Do he nu so
doghentlyken vñ salichlikē leuede to gode
vñ den minschē.do menede de herē he scol
de ene iuncfrouwe nemē.wēte stozie he ane
erue.so scolde eyn ander syn gued vñ syn ri
ke besitten.deme yd nee sure were ghewoz/
den.Do quaz alzo dzade eyn old man van
deme wylle godes.de hadde enen grawen
langen baert. vñ dzoech enen palm vñ staff
in synre hant Jn etlikē bokē steyt ghescreuē
dat id eyn engel was. vñ stellede syk yst he
eyn pelegrim were.Den entfenk sunte Os/
waldus ghans guetliken vñ bzochte em in
syn pallas. Do spzak de olde man:yck byn
eyn pzophete.vñ my sint.lxxij.lande bekant
vñ do dy kundich vä gode.dat du ene tüc/
frouwe scalt nemē. de is enes heydens kon
nynges dochter.de heet Saudon.vñ de
iuncfrouwe heet Pbia.vñ is tomale schone
vñde ys de wylle godes.dat du darumme
strijdest.vñde bringest se to deme cristen lo
uen.dar to hest se god vtherkozē.Do spzak
sunte Oswaldus. Hu hebbe yk nenen den
re de mi de bodeschop werue.de sik in dat
lant kan vntrichten.Do spzack de gude ol/
de man. Sendestu dar dusent mäne.de do
det der iuncfrouwē vader alle. wente do se
waert ghebozē.do nam he se vp den schoet
vñde lede dze vinghere vp ere houed.vñ
swoez dze eede na der heydescken ee.dat he
eer nummermeer enen man wolde gheuen
he enwunne se denne mit dem sweerde. dat
was sunte Oswald ghans leed.vñde wiste
nicht wo he doen scolde.Do spzak de olde
man.Du hefst enen rauen in dyneme houe
wol twelff iar ghetoghē.de krycht dy voz
waer de iuncfrouwen.Do heet syk Oswal
dus den rauen bzingen.do wolde he nicht
to em vleghē.do wart em ghäs lede Do se
de de olde man. Wes quedes modes.god
schykket dy ene dzade wedder.vñd darna
vloech de rauen voz den olden man vp de
tafelē.vñ spzak to em dat he synem herē wil
lekame were. Do spzack sunte Oswaldus.
Jk hebbe dy.xij.iaer ghehat.vñ hebbe dy
nee so mynschlykē bozē spzeken.daer mede
vozswand de olde man.Do screeff de leue
sūte Oswald' de.xij.stukke des hylgē louē

p ij

E leue here sunte os
wald was eyn gued cristen.
vñ was doghētlik. vñ had/
de god leeff. vñ gaff vele al/
missen. vñ beschermede we/
dewen vñ weyzen.vñ eerde vñ voedede de
pzester. vñ was hart den vnlouighen. darū
me sach em got voer.vñ wolde em tho enē
könige hebbē.vñ do mē em wolde to enem
köninge kresemen.do tovloet de kresem vä
godes wille.wēte id quä eyn raue van dem
hēmel.vñ bzochte ene guldē bussen mit kre
sem in deme snauele.vñ dem rauē henk eyn
bzeeff in deme halsze.de was beseghelt mit
enem gulden kruce.vñ de rauē konde latin
spzekē.vñ spzak. Jk bringe den kresem van
dem hēmele. Do lezē se den bzeef.dar inne
stūt ghescreuen.dat ene sunte Peter sulten
hadde ghebenedyet.vñ de rauē bleeff vozt
an in sunte Oswaldus hoff.Do he nu kon
nink in Enghelät ghewordē was. buwede
he ene schone kerke in de ere des vozsten d
apostele sunte peters. vñ settede dar pzester
in gode to denēde.vñ gaff dar vele gudes
to.Darna leuede he salichlikē alze voer.vñ
strijdede manlykē yeghē de beyden vmme
den cristē louē.vñ bedwank heren vñ stede
dat se em tyns mosten gheuē. vñde wart so
mechtich. dat em alle daghe vele grote he
ren bisscoppe vñ abbete deneden. Der her
scop en vozhoffhe sik nicht.mē he was oth
modich. vñ hadde god voz oghē.vñ dene
de em dagh vñ nacht mit grotem vlite.dar
vmme was got mit em. Ok mosten könin

---

FIGURE 1.
*Dat Passionael* (Lübeck: Steffen Arndes, 1492), fol. C.ii. c. Photograph courtesy of
the Royal Library, Copenhagen, Denmark.

FIGURE 2.
Photograph courtesy of The Pierpont Morgan Library, New York. MS M. 710, fol.
101 v.

FIGURE 3
Photograph courtesy of the Bibliothèque nationale de France, Paris, Grandes Chroniques de France, FR 2813, fol. 12v.

The *Passionael* woodcut is emblematic for the vernacular legend of Oswald that was composed in the German-language area. This legend was not the crudely abbreviated version in *Der Heiligen Leben/Dat Passionael* but rather the German text from which *Ósvalds saga* derives. The Icelandic version has until now been ignored, however, in discussions of the development of the German Oswald legend. More than a century ago, Charles Plummer, who edited Bede's *Historia Ecclesiastica,* dismissed the Icelandic text as "a perfectly fabulous and worthless saga."[167] He could not have known the text. *Ósvalds saga* has not merited the attention of scholars because of a general belief that it derived from the German prose legend in *Der Heiligen Leben/Dat Passionael,* and that this prose legend in turn derived from the metrical version in the *Münchner Oswald,* thought to represent the original German Oswald legend. Far from being a sixteenth-century derivative of a prose text from the turn of the fourteenth to the fifteenth century, *Ósvalds saga* is the Icelandic translation of one of many German texts available to the anonymous compiler of *Der Heiligen Leben,* and like the other legends in the anthology that of Oswald was condensed and pared down so as to render it suitable for the needs of a monastic community. The saga is the sole witness to the original German legend of St. Oswald and represents a text, presumably metrical,[168] that antedates the production of the German legendary. Whether the composition of this German text goes back as far as the twelfth century cannot be ascertained,[169] but the developing cult of the Northumbrian saint in the German-language area makes this likely. A liturgy that revered King Oswald as "martyr et regum piissime" and lavished its praise on the "regi martyrum,"[170] as an eleventh-century sequence from St. Gallen

---

[167] Charles Plummer, ed., *Venerabilis Baedae Historia Ecclesiastica gentis Anglorum, Historia abbatum, Epistola ad Ecgbertum una cum Historia abbatum auctore anonymo* (Oxford: Clarendon Press, 1896; repr. 1969), 2:161.

[168] Analysis of the Oswald legend in *Der Heiligen Leben* actually reveals a few instances of what appear to be traces of rhymed couplets, several corresponding to text in the metrical *Münchner/Wiener Oswald,* but others that do not, such as the following: "Vnd schraib im ain prief hin wider / vnd net dem raben den prief vnter sein gefider" (360:21); "vnd schuelt got piten, was dor an ste, / daz das schier zwischen ev peden gescheh" (361:16); "vnd wer ihtes von im begert, / dez waz er gewert" (366:32). More than a century and a quarter ago ago Edzardi noted traces of rhyme in the prose legend; he even went so far as to claim that entire stanzas can be reconstructed (*Untersuchungen,* 9–18).

[169] Edzardi strongly believed that some aspects of the oldest form of the German Oswald legend can be reconstructed on the basis of the prose legend and *Ósvalds saga* and that this Ur-Oswald was a metrical work composed in the second half of the twelfth century *(Untersuchungen,* 18*)*. In respect to plot, however, he thought that the original legend conformed to what we read in the *Münchner Oswald,* to judge by his summary on p. 53.

[170] *Analecta Hymnica Medii Aevi,* ed. Clemens Blume, vol. 53, *Thesauri Hymnologici Prosarium. Die Sequenzen des Thesaurus Hymnologicus H. A. Daniels und anderer Sequenzenausgaben.* Erster Teil (Leipzig: Reisland, 1911), 324.

puts it, would have been accompanied not only by a Latin *vita* but also within a reasonable time by a vernacular legend celebrating the martyr king.

An early sixteenth-century translation of a no longer extant German Oswald legend, *Ósvalds saga*, permits us to claim that a vernacular legend of St. Oswald was transmitted in the German-language area, a text that faithfully transmitted the legend as first told by Bede at the same time that it enlarged upon it by including a prefatory coronation legend and developing the fact of Oswald's marriage to a heathen king's daughter into a bridal-quest narrative. The additions were presumably inspired by and composed under the influence of Clovis's baptismal legend and the bridal-quest legend of Henry and Cunegund. Despite the fictionalization of the Oswald legend, produced through the addition of this new material and the dramatization of events throughout the narrative—but to a lesser degree in the miracle sequence—the German Oswald legend that was the source of *Ósvalds saga* related the facts of Oswald's life, as told by Bede, and, most importantly, the facts of his death. Oswald died on the battlefield, a martyr for his faith.

This martyr legend, it has here been argued, was the oldest vernacular legend to accompany the cult of the Northumbrian king in the German-language area. Once the entertaining bridal-quest narrative had been introduced into the legend, it was an easy matter for this part of the narrative to be severed from the rest of the legend and to develop into an independent romance, as happened, I argue, in the *Münchner Oswald*. Whatever may have motivated the decision—possibly the example provided by Henry and Cunegund—the author chose to transform the martyr saint into a confessor saint. The demoted martyr could retain his status as saint only if he was shown to have practiced heroic virtue. Therefore the motif of conjugal chastity, which surfaced in Reginald of Durham's Latin Oswald *vita* but already flourished on the continent in the legend of Henry and Cunegund, was introduced into the *Münchner Oswald* and generated the new conclusion in this hagiographic romance. Thus the historical martyr became the fictionalized confessor saint.

*Ósvalds saga* provides more than ample evidence that the bridal quest and conversion of the heathens are inextricably linked to one another; that a vernacular Oswald legend that derived ultimately from Bede circulated in the German-language area; and that this was a conversion legend which culminated in the proselytizing king's martyrdom. The German source of *Ósvalds saga* antedates the prose narrative in the High and Low German legendaries, that is, it existed before the end of the fourteenth century when the Oswald legend was condensed for inclusion in *Der Heiligen Leben*. Considering that the *Münchner* and *Wiener Oswald* are known to us only in fifteenth-century manuscripts, the extant prose version indisputably antedates the extant texts of the metrical version. While absolute proof of the seniority of the *Ósvalds saga* version—that is, its German source—vis-à-vis the metrical *Münchner/Wiener Oswald* is lacking, common sense suggests that it is more likely that the cult of St. Oswald was introduced on the continent with a vernacular legend corresponding to the extant Latin *vita* in respect to the salient biographical facts and accounts of miracles, and that this legend should have been expanded with fictional material similar to that found in other Latin and vernacular legends. The incorporation of folk tales and fantastic material into the lives of saints was a given in medieval hagiography. One need only recall the dragon-slayer episode in the legend of St. George, the grateful-lion tale in the legend of St. Jerome, the Christ-bearer narrative in the legend of St. Christopher, or the hairy-anchorite story that came to be part of the legend of St. John Chrysostom. Even the lives of medieval saints quickly became fictionalized, an egregious example of which is the bridal-quest narrative culminating in a chastity test that found its way into the legend of Henry and Cunegund. This was not a case of a legend being fictionalized in the process of vernacularization, for the extended bridal-quest narrative antedated Ebernand von Erfurt's German legend. It already existed in the *Additamentum* to Adalbert's *Vita Heinrici*, which was composed around 1200. The fictional elements in the vernacular legend of St. Oswald, that is, those elements not found in Bede's *Historia* and Drogo's *vita*, presumably derive from the legends of two continental royal personalities known for their ecclesiastical politics, namely Clovis and Henry II. The ultimate source of *Ósvalds saga* was most likely not only composed in the wake of the canonization of Henry II in 1146 but also inspired by and modeled in part after his legend.

*Ósvalds saga* attests that a fairly long vernacular legend of St. Oswald existed in the German-language area, a version that transmitted the material known from Latin hagiography but which interpolated the coronation and bridal-quest narratives. The saga permits one to argue that the metrical bridal-quest romance derives from the sacred legend rather than vice versa. Indeed, it is most likely that the German source of *Ósvalds saga*—and thereby also *Ósvalds saga* itself—actually represents the earliest version of the Oswald legend on the continent.

# IX.
## THE EDITION OF *ÓSVALDS SAGA*

The text of *Ósvalds saga* is based on Agnete Loth's edition in *Reykjahólabók: Islandske helgenlegender* (Copenhagen: Munksgaard, 1969), though photocopies of the manuscript have been consulted, and occasionally the text of Loth's edition has been corrected. Here and there the manuscript is damaged and illegible. Agnete Loth's emendations or suggested readings have in most instances been silently accepted, but where this has not been the case, it has been noted. For a description of the abbreviations in *Reykjahólabók*, see Loth's edition, 1:liv.

The language of *Reykjahólabók* is a strange amalgam of Early Modern Icelandic and late Middle Low German in respect to lexicon and syntax. The text is here presented in normalized modern Icelandic orthography, but where Low German, and also Latin, loans occur, their origin is left transparent, as is the case, for example, with *platz* 'place', which is not normalized to modern Icelandic *pláss*, or the word *eðel* in *eðel bornir*, which has not been normalized to the indeclinable modern form *eðal*. Similarly, the Latin loan *propheta*, written thus in the manuscript, is not normalized to modern Icelandic *prófeti*. Orthographic variants and variant forms have not been leveled. The edition thus follows the manuscript and transmits both *konungr* and *kóngr*, *jungfrú* and *jómfrú*, *maður* and *mann*, *yðart* and *yðvart*, *aldri* and *aldregi* (once *aldrei*), *eða* and *eður*, *orðlof* and *orlof*, *skuld* and *skyld*. The decision to transmit these variants was guided largely by usage in *Hið nýja Testament* of Oddur Gottskálksson of 1540[171] and the *Guðbrandsbiblía* of 1584.[172] Not a few loan and foreign words in *Ósvalds saga* also occur in *Saga heilagrar Önnu*, a sixteenth-century translation of the so-called *St. Annen-Büchlein* (Braunschweig: Hans Dorn, 1507), and reference is made to this text in the edition where appropriate.[173]

Some of Björn Þorleifsson's idiosyncratic vacillations in the nominal and verbal systems are also transmitted in this edition. As happens in the *Guðbrandsbiblía*, *Reykjahólabók* writes both *móðir* and *móður* throughout the singular, and *dóttir*

---

[171] Jón Helgason, *Málið á Nýja Testamenti Odds Gottskálkssonar*, Safn Fræðafjelagsins 7 (Copenhagen: Hið íslenska Fræðafjelag, 1929; repr. [Reykjavík]: Málvísindastofnun Háskóla Íslands, 1999).

[172] Oskar Bandle, *Die Sprache der Guðbrandsbiblía*.

[173] See Kirsten Wolf, ed., *Saga heilagrar Önnu*, Stofnun Árna Magnússonar á Íslandi 52 (Reykjavík: Stofnun Árna Magnússonar á Íslandi, 2001). I am grateful to Kirsten Wolf for making the edition available to me while it was still in proof.

and *dóttur* in the nom. sg. In the present tense singular the verb *hafa* ends now in *-ir*, now in *-ur*. The 1st pers. sg. present tense of strong verbs, with two exceptions—*ég geng* and *ég fel*—carries the ending *-ur*: *ég biður, heldur, kemur, lætur, verður*. The pronoun *nokkur* vacillates between syncopated and unsyncopated forms, and, as happens at times in the *Guðbrandsbiblía*, the pret. subj. of *þurfa* occurs without umlaut. *Ósvalds saga*, like the *Guðbrandsbiblía*, also vacillates between the two forms of the word for 'faith', namely *trú*, gen. *trúar*, and *trúa*, gen. *trú*. Throughout, notes refer the reader to corresponding usage in Oddur Gottskálksson's translation of the New Testament and to the *Guðbrandsbiblía*.

*Reykjahólabók* consistently writes *himiríki* (written *himeʀike* in the manuscript) instead of *himinríki*, *herranir* instead of *herrarnir*, and *vær* for the 1st pers. pl. pronoun. These orthographic conventions, which, except for the plural of *herra*, conform to those in the sixteenth-century Bible translations, are retained in the edition. While the name *Jesus Christus* consistently occurs in its Latin form and is integrated into the Icelandic syntax with the corresponding Latin inflectional ending, the name of St. Oswald occurs in the Latin form *Osvaldus*, the German *Osvald*, and the Icelandic *Ósvaldur*. The modifying adjective has either the Latin form (*sanctus*)—occasionally in the vocative *sancte Osvalde*—or Icelandic (*sankti*); at times the indeclinable Icelandic *sankti* modifies a Latin *Osvaldus*. In some instances the Latin form of the name is inappropriate, given the Icelandic syntax; notes are provided to that effect.

Such editorial intervention as the addition of a missing ending or the introduction of a conjectured word is indicated within angle brackets ( < > ). Punctuation in the manuscript as well as capitalization after periods is arbitrary at best. Consequently, these have been silently inserted by the editor in the interest of facilitating reading. Any other modifications of the text are explained in the footnotes.

# X.
## THE TRANSLATION

*Ósvalds saga* is a difficult text because of its idiosyncratic lexicon and syntax. The source of the translation is a no longer extant Low German legend, related, however, to the legend in *Dat Passionael*, a severely abridged version of the no longer extant High German legend that is the ultimate source of our text. While Björn Þorleifsson was a good translator as far as accuracy is concerned, he was not an elegant translator, for all too frequently he translates word-for-word rather than idiomatically. On the whole his language reflects that of the sixteenth-century biblical translations and other Icelandic imprints, but some of the lexicon in *Reykjahólabók*, while also occurring in printed sources, retains a distinctly Low German meaning which does not conform to that in other Icelandic texts of the time (to judge by the studies of Jón Helgason, Oskar Bandle, and Christian Westergård-Nielsen). Hence, German loans have here been translated in accordance with their meaning in German—if so called for by the context and as far as this is ascertainable—rather than contemporary Icelandic usage. One example of this is the word *útlesa*, which, to judge by the examples given by Jón Helgason and Christian Westergård-Nielsen, only had the meaning 'to weed out', 'to pick out' in sixteenth-century Icelandic. *Ósvalds saga* shows, however, that Björn Þorleifsson transferred the word directly from his Low German source, so that it is to be construed as a compound, consisting of the perfective prefix *út-* and the verb *-lesa* 'to read', with the meaning 'to finish reading'. A similar case is the loan *aflát*, which existed in older Icelandic with the meaning of 'remission of sins'. In *Ósvalds saga* the word occurs in the tale of the translation of Oswald's relics (chap. 15), where the queen and her entourage get up early in order to venerate the relics of the saint "fyrir afláts skyld" 'to gain an indulgence', that is, remission of punishment for sin. The noun *reisa* is repeatedly used in *Ósvalds saga*; it is found throughout sixteenth-century sources with two meanings: either as the noun 'journey', 'trip' or as the numerative adverb indicating 'times', 'point of time'. The word occurs in both of these meanings in *Ósvalds saga*, but also in the more limited meaning it can have in Low German, that is, 'military expedition', either by land or sea, and this is how the word is translated, if demanded by the context. Finally, *Ósvalds saga* has also introduced Low German words and meanings that are otherwise not attested in Icelandic, such as *mak* (see p. 19) and *verðugheit*. The latter replicates MLG *werdicheit* 'in a worthy, reverent manner', 'festivity', 'pomp', 'ceremony'. While *verðugliga* 'worthily' occurs in the 1540 translation of the New Testament (*NT*, 397), the nominal form does not.

Since the beginning of narrative in Iceland, shifts of tense within a scene or even a sentence have been the norm. This can be problematic in translation. Where acceptable, that is, where a tense shift does not grate too much on one's ears, this has been transmitted in translation, so that phrases like "she answers and said" ('hún svarar og sagði') "Gaudon answers and said" ('Gaudon svarar og sagðist'), "he gets angry and spoke" ('verður hann . . . reiður og mælti') are found alongside "he got angry and spoke" ('varð hann . . . reiður og mælti'), "the hermit answers and says" ('einsetumaðr svarar og segir').

Oswald's feathered emissary and proxy wooer is referred to in Icelandic as both *hrafn* and *krummi*, the latter a nickname. To reflect this usage, the Scottish word for raven, 'corbie', has been used to translate *krummi*.

The notes provide information and references to semantic and syntactic problems.

# THE TEXTS

# ÓSVALDS SAGA

So finnst skrifað í heilagri skrift að í Englandi var einn ágætur herra er Ós-valdur[1] hét og var vel kristinn herra, þvíað hann var dygðugur og góðgjarn við alla þá er þurftugir voru og til hans hjálpar leituðu með orðum og verkum. Ekkjur fátækar og föðurlaus börn tók hann undir sína vernd og varðveislu til allra réttra mála. Hann heiðraði og fæddi alla kennimenn er til hans vildu sækja, en harður og stríður var hann ómildum vantrúöndum og öðrum óráðvöndum mönnum þar sem hann átti yfir að stýra. Hann var og iðjufullur til að fremja góð verk með föstum og vökum so og með guðligu bænahaldi og mildum ölmusugjörðum, so að hann hafði guðs vináttu og góðra manna, og hans góð verk er jafnan framdi hann fóru víða eigi aðeins um England nema heldur[2] líka um mörg lönd önnur.

Í þenna tíma var enginn kóngur í Englandi sem að réttum erfðum átti ríkinu stýra. Þá með guðs fyrirætlan og samþykki hinna mektugustu[3] og so vísustu[4] herra í landinu, þá kjöru þeir Osvaldum fyrir einn einvaldsherra yfir sig. Þetta vildi hann ekki og sagðist þar óverðugur til vera í öllum hlutum. En það var ekki so: þó að hann væri og ekki sérlega kóngborinn, þá var hann þó kominn af göfugri ætt bæði að föðurkyni og móður, og so var það ekki á móti guðs vilja þó hann yrði kóngur, sem brátt má heyrast. En er Ósvaldur heyrir að þetta er þeirra fullur vilji til þess að hefja sig til ríkisstjórnar, þá tók hann sig í burtu[5] á laun frá þeim og ætlaði að koma sér með því undan þessari tign, en það hjálpaði ekki, þvíað þegar sem þeir vissu af hans burtför sendu þeir eftir honum og báðu hann með allri alúð að[6] koma aftur og vera þeim samþykkur. Þá um síðir mæðir huggæði og kemur inn í staðinn aftur með sendimönnum er til hans voru sendir. Verða allir við það glaðir í staðnum bæði ríkir og fátækir. Þá sem sá dagur kom að hann átti að krýnast til konungs[7] og smyrja hann eftir venju með krisma, þá eftir guðs tilskikkan fannst hvergi krismi að smyrja hann með.

---

[1] Throughout, the text vacillates between the Icelandic form of the name, *Ósvaldur*, and the Latin, *Osvaldus*—and even the German form *Osvald* without an ending—and the respective Icelandic and Latin endings in the oblique cases. I follow the manuscript and also distinguish between *sankti Ósvaldur* and *sanctus Osvaldus*. Occasionally, the inde-clinable Icelandic adjective *sankti* occurs with the Latin form of the name.

[2] *eigi—nema heldur* is not idiomatic Icelandic, but variations of this construction oc-cur subsequently; it may possibly have been formed in analogy to MLG *sunder nemelik*. The phrase may be analogous to *at heldur*, translating German *sondern*, in the 1540 trans-lation of the New Testament. See *NT*, 218.

[3] The word *mektugur*, which W–N lists as a loan from Middle Low German (222), al-ready occurs in Old Icelandic, but mostly in saints' lives and romances. Cf. Wolf, cxxvi.

[4] This is not the Icelandic word *viss/víss*, the cognate of MLG *wis, wisse* 'certain', 'sure', but rather a loan of MLG *wîs* 'wise'. Cf. *MNW*, 5:738: "*ein wîs man.*"

[5] *tók sig í burtu* is unidiomatic Icelandic and was presumably formed in analogy to MLG *sik wechnemen*.

[6] Corrected from the manuscript, which writes *og*.

[7] The text uses both *konungr* and *kóngr* for 'king'. I follow suit.

# OSWALD'S SAGA

1. It is written in a sacred text that there was a noble lord in England whose name was Oswald and he was a good Christian lord, for he was virtuous and kind to all who were needy and who sought his help by word or deed. He took poor widows and fatherless children under his protection and in his safekeeping in all just cases. He honored and fed all priests who wanted to appeal to him, but he was harsh and severe toward all unrighteous unbelievers and other wicked men whom he had to rule. He was also diligent in carrying out good works along with fasts and vigils as well as pious devotions and generous alsmgiving, so that he had God's friendship and that of good men, and report of the good works that he always performed spread far and wide not only throughout England but also many other lands.

At this time there was no king in England who was properly in line of succession to rule the kingdom. Then in keeping with God's providence and the consent of the mightiest and also wisest lords in the land, they chose Oswald to be their ruler. This he did not want and said that he was unworthy of it in every respect. But that was not the case: even though he was not of particularly royal birth, he was still descended from an illustrious family both on his father's and his mother's side,[1] and thus it was not against God's will that he become king, as you will soon hear. And when Oswald hears that it is their definite will to exalt him as their ruler, he secretly stole away from them and thought that in this way he could avoid this honor, but that did not help, for as soon as they found out about his flight, they sent men after him and asked him in all humility to come back and give his consent. Then at last his resolve weakens and he comes back into the town with the messengers who were sent to him. Everyone in the town, both rich and poor, becomes glad at this. Then when the day came on which he was to be crowned king and anointed with chrism, as was customary, then in keeping with God's design no chrism could be found to anoint him with.

---

[1] Oswald was the son of Ethelfrid, who was the son of Ethelric, king of the Bernicians.

Þá mælti Osvaldus: "Sjáið nú, góðir vinir, að drottinn guð minn birtir nú fyrir öllum að ég er óverðugur til slíks."

Þá þögðu allir þvíað þeir þóttust[8] ekki vita hvað þeir skyldu til gjöra eða hvað guðs vilji mundi vera um þetta. En í þessu kom einn hrafn fljúgandi ofan af himnum og hafði einn buðk fullan af krisma er sankti Pétur hafði sjálfur vígt. Þennan buðkinn hafði hann í nefinu á sér og var gjörður af skíru gulli, en á hálsinum á hrafninum var hengt eitt bréf og innsiglað með einum gulllegum krossi.

Þessi hrafn kunni og að tala latínu og mælti: "Sé hérna krismann þann er þér eigið að smyrja Osvaldum með. Hann hefur ég flutt ofan af himni."

Síðan taka þeir bréfið og lesa. Stóð þar inni[9] eins og fyrr segir að sankti Pétur hafði bæði vígt krismann og blessað hann.

Og þessi hrafn var eftir á allt jafnt í palacio[10] Ósvalds konungs.

En þá sem Ósvaldur hafði nokkura stund kóngur verið í Englandi, þá lét hann byggja eina kostulega kirkju guði til heiðurs og sankti Pétri postula. Og lagði þar til mikla rentu[11] til uppheldis. Þar með fékk hann þangað kennimenn er þar skyldu þjóna guði og heilagri kirkju. So hélt hann og allri sinni venju um alla nytsamlega breytni sem hann gjörði fyrr nema heldur lætur hann vaxa stór örlög[12] við heiðnar þjóðir fyrir skuld heilagrar trúar og þvingaði bæði mektuga herra og stóra staði undir heilaga kristni og sig, so að þeir urðu að gjalda honum stóra skatta og þar <til>[13] þjónkan nær hann vildi þá kalla. Og innan fárra ára varð hann so

---

[8] The manuscript incorrectly writes *pottezt*.

[9] *þar inni* is a loan translation from MLG *darinne*. The corresponding passage in the *Pass.* reads: "dar inne stunt ghescreuen" (C.ii.c).

[10] The word *palacio* is a loan from Latin *palatium* and not from Low German, where the word is *pallas* (*MNW*, 3:294). The manuscript writes *pallacio* here, declining the word as in Latin; when the word recurs later in this chapter, it is written with one -*l*-. The loan is otherwise not attested in Icelandic; W–N does not list the word in *Låneordene*. The corresponding passages in *Der Heiligen Leben* and *Dat Passionael* have the German *hof/hoff* rather than the Latin loan.

[11] The word *renta* is borrowed from MLG *rente*, but it is already found in some older texts, mostly Norwegian law texts and Norwegian and Icelandic diplomata. Cf. VÓ, 308; Wolf, cxxviii. The word also occurs in *Hendreks saga og Kunegundis*, indeed in a rather similar passage: "gaf hann stórar eignir og rentu til uppheldis þeim er þar þjónuðu" (*Rhb.*, 1:49.5–6: 'he gave great possessions and income to those who served there').

[12] The word *örlög* means 'fate' in Icelandic, but here it is cognate with Low German *orloge*, *orloch* and means 'battle' (*MNW*, 3:235). The word *örlög* recurs several times in *Ósvalds saga*, each time in its Low German meaning. It does not occur in the corresponding passages in the *Passionael*, but must have been found in the saga's Low German source.

[13] The word is missing; in her edition Agnete Loth suggests adding *með* rather than *til*, but it is more likely that the MLG source had the phrase *dar tô*, which would have generated *þar til*.

Then Oswald spoke: "See now, good friends, that the Lord my God now manifests to all that I am unworthy of this."

All then remained silent, since they did not think they knew what they should do or what might be God's will in this matter. But at this moment a raven came flying down from heaven and had a vessel full of chrism which St. Peter himself had consecrated. He had this vessel in his beak and it was made of pure gold. And around the raven's neck there hung a letter sealed with a golden cross.

This raven could also speak Latin and he said:[2] "See here the chrism with which you are to anoint Oswald. I have brought it down from heaven."

They then take the letter and read it. It said in it, as was told before, that St. Peter had consecrated the chrism and blessed it.

And this raven stayed from then on in King Oswald's palace.

And when Oswald had been king of England for some time, he had a precious church built in honor of God and St. Peter the Apostle. And he provided much income toward its upkeep. In addition he obtained priests for it who were to serve God there and Holy Church.[3] And he continued, as was his custom, his meritorious conduct as he had done before, except that he also waged great battles against heathen peoples for the sake of the holy faith, and he subjected both mighty lords and large towns to Christianity and to his rule, so that they came to pay him large sums of tribute and in addition render him service whenever he

---

[2] Considering the raven's ability to speak Latin and, as we shall see, his other anthropomorphic characteristics, the use of the masculine pronoun for the bird seems justified.

[3] According to Bede, King Edwin began to build the church of St. Peter at York, but Oswald completed it after Edwin was killed in battle against Cædwalla in 633 (*HE*, 2:14; 2.20). This corresponds to what Drogo tells us: "Construxit namque templum honorabile beati Petri Apostoli, quod mirificè decoravit, & dignos ministros, qui ibidem Deo deservirent, regio usu deliberavit" (95).

mektugur að herrar og höfðingjar, biskupar og ábótar stóðu fyrir hans borðum og þjónuðu þar dags daglega.

Af þessari mekt og stórri herlegheit[14] upphóf[15] hann sig ekki til neins metnaðar eða drambsemi nema að heldur var hann því lítillátari og góðgjarnari í öllu og hafði guð jafnan fyrir augum sér. Og þjónaði honum með allri ástúð bæði nætur og daga og guð var ætíð með honum. So veitti hann út af sér hertogum og greifum, jörlum og barúnum og eðelbornum[16] lönd, heil og ríki en sumlegum borgir, þorp og kastala hverjum eftir sinni stétt og verðugri tign. Og þá sem hann hafði nú so prýðilega eflt sitt ríki og sett sína göfuga herra í hvern stað sem hann vildi og öllum þótti so mega fara, þvíað hann var hugljúfi allra manna, þá eitt sinni tóku sig til samans nokkurir hans trúlegir vinir og gjörðu ráð sín á meðal að þeir skyldi fara á fund kóngsins og ráðleggja honum að fá sér eitthvert sæmilegt kvonfang, so að ríkið stæði ekki so lengur erfingjalaust.

2. Þá sem nokkrir[17] dagar voru liðnir frá þessu sem nú var sagt, þá komu þeir til samans aftur herranir[18] með það erindi er fyrr greinir og gengu síðan fyrir Ósvald

---

[14] The word *herlegheit* is a loan from Middle Low German *herlicheit* 'rule', 'power', 'authority'. See W-N, *Låneordene*, 154. The corresponding passage in the *Pass.* uses the word *herscop* (C.ii.c).

[15] While *hefja upp* ('to raise up') exists in Icelandic, the compound form *upphefja*, meaning 'to assume a lofty bearing', does not (Bandle lists the verb only in the meaning of 'to raise up' [404–5]) and must be a loan translation from Middle Low German. While MLG *upheven* can be used metaphorically in the sense of 'exalt', 'aggrandize', it is more likely that the source contained a form of the verb *sik vorheven* 'to become arrogant', 'to become proud' (*MNW*, 5:366), as in the corresponding passage in the *Pass.*: "Der herscop en vorhoff he sik nicht" (C.ii.c). A nearly identical sentence occurs in *Hendreks saga og Kunegundis*, which immediately precedes *Ósvalds saga*: "Af þessari tign og verdugheit upphóf hann sig ekki í neinu drambi eður ofmetnaði" (*Rhb.*, 1:35.12–14). Here too the corresponding passage in the *Pass.* has the verb *vorhoef*: "vnde vorhoef syck nycht in synen eren" (lviii.a). The entire statement in *Ósvalds saga* derives ultimately from Bede who writes: "Quo regni culmine sublimatur, nihilominus (quod mirum dictu est) pauperibus et peregrinis semper humilis benignus et largus fuit" (*HE* 3.6: 'Though he wielded supreme power over the whole land, he was always wonderfully humble, kind, and generous to the poor and to strangers').

[16] The manuscript writes *edel bornvm*, which transmits MLG *edel geboren*. The uninflected form *eðla* occurs regularly in the *Guðbrandsbiblía* (see Bandle, 319); there it apparently occurs only as *edla*, not the direct MLG loan *edel*, as is the case here. Cf. Wolf, cxviii.

[17] Concerning syncopated and unsyncopated forms of *nokkur*, see Bandle, 368–69.

[18] Since the manuscript consistently writes *herraner* rather than *herrarner*, as one would expect, we accept this practice.

wanted to demand these.[4] And within a few years he became so mighty that lords and chieftains, bishops and abbots attended his tables and served there daily.

For all of this power and great authority he did not become puffed up with pride or arrogance but rather was all the more humble and benevolent in everything and set his eyes ever upon God (Psalm 25:15). And he served him with great love both night and day and God was ever with him. On dukes and counts, earls and barons and those nobly born he bestowed lands, wealth, and power, and on some he bestowed towns, villages, and castles, to each according to his station and noble rank. And now when he had so nobly endowed his realm and set his noble lords in every place he wanted, and everyone thought things would go on in this way, for he was beloved by all men, then on one occasion some of his faithful friends got together and decided among themselves to go see the king and advise him to find for himself a suitable wife, so that the kingdom would no longer be without an heir.

2. When some days had passed after what has just been told, the lords came together again concerning the matter mentioned before, and they then went to

---

[4] This accords with Drogo's *vita*: "Non solùm autem Oswaldus rex gloriosissimus suæ gentis sollicitus fuit; verum etiam aliarum gentium, quæ sub extero jure regum erant constitutæ, volens omnes ad cultum unius veri Dei, veræque religionis tramitem adducere. . . . Nonnumquam per se, suique præsentiam eos monebat, uti religionem suam pio quidem animo amplecterentur, Deoque omnipotenti colla submitterent" (98.b).

kóng og biðja hann orðlofs[19] að þeir mega bera sitt erindi fram fyrir hann. Hann biður þá skila því er þeir vilja.

Síðan mælti einn þeirra fyrir þá alla, so segjandi: "Verðugi herra, nú frá því að þér hafið sett og samið yðvart ríki með góðri stjórn og nytsemdar verkum so að allir lifa nú með friði og farsæld er undir yðvart vald eru gefnir, þá vonum vær[20] so til að guði muni so líka um yðvart efni sem oss. En þó er eftir einn sjá hlutur er oss þykir á vanta og hans virðist oss með öngu móti mega án vera."

Kóngurinn spyr þá mjög vandlega eftir hvað það væri og sagðist að þeirra ráðum vilja gjöra það mögulegt væri.

Þeir þakka kónginum og segja: "Með yðru orlofi, verðugi herra, þá þykir oss það helst á vanta að þér eigið öngva drottningu þá er þér megið láta sitja og stjórna yðru ríki eftir yðvarn dag, þvíað vær vildum ekki gjarnan eiga gefast lengur undir þá herra er ekki eru réttilega komnir til ríkisins; og þeir hlutir margir sem þér hafið bæði eflt og bætt vort ríki þá skulu aðrir eyða því og spilla í staðinn sem hvorki eiga né so nokkuð ómak hafa fyrir haft. Og viljum vær ekki ef vær skulum ráða."

En er kóngur hefur gjörla skilið þeirra erindi, þá svarar hann og segist vilja hugsa hér eftir[21] og gefa þeim svar aftur nær sem hann hefir <hugsað>[22] til þeirrar er sig girnti eftir að eiga. En þetta svar gaf hann til þess að hann vildi so með því koma þeim af sér enn með hreinni samvitsku. Var honum í hug að kvongast ekki heldur að halda hreinlífi. Og sem herranir þenktu sér í burtu að ganga, þá var klappað á dyrnar og sá sem klappaði sagðist eiga erindi við kónginn. Þetta er kónginum sagt. Biður hann dyrasvein að láta hann inn[23] og so biður hann herrana að biðleika við og heyra hvað sá vill sem kominn var og so gjöra þeir.

Síðan gekk þessi maður inn fyrir kónginn og sýndist að vilja guðs sem hann væri allur grár af hærum, bæði hár og skegg og var það mjög langt; og hafði í hendinni annarri einn pálmkvist en í annarri staf og gjörði sig líkan einum pílagrími.[24] En í sumlegum bókum stendur so skrifað að það væri engill guðs.

---

[19] The manuscript writes both *orðlof* (*ordlof*) and *orlof*. The former is attested throughout the *Guðbrandsbiblía*; see Bandle, 119.

[20] Björn Þorleifsson consistently writes *vær*—rather than *vér*—for the first person plural pronoun. See Bandle, 345–46, for examples from the *Guðbrandsbiblía*, where both *vær* and *vér* occur.

[21] *hugsa . . . eftir* is not an Icelandic construction. There is no corresponding passage in the *Pass.*, but see *NT*, 285, where "hugxit þat epter" literally translates "dem dencket nach."

[22] In her edition, Agnete Loth suggests that the word *spurt* follow *hefir*, but *hugsað* seems a more appropriate emendation.

[23] *Láta . . . inn* with the meaning here of 'to let in' is not Icelandic; the phrase was presumably generated by analogy to MLG *inlaten, innelaten* (*MNW*, 2:367).

[24] While the word *pílagrímr* exists in Old Icelandic, here it happens to replicate *pelegrim* in *Pass.* (C.ii.d).

King Oswald and ask leave to convey their mission to him. He tells them to state what they want.

One of them then spoke for all, saying: "Worthy Lord, now that you have established and secured your realm with good government and useful works, so that all who are subject to you now live in peace and happiness, we expect that God is as pleased by your rule as we are. Yet there is the one thing that to us seems lacking and which we deem to be impossible to be without."

The king then asks very carefully what that might be and he said that he would act on their advice if it were possible.

They thank the king and say: "With your leave, worthy Lord, we think what is most wanting is that you have no queen whom you might have preside over and rule your kingdom after your day, for we would rather not want to have to submit any longer to those lords who have not rightfully obtained the kingdom; and the many things with which you have strengthened and improved our kingdom, others will then spoil and destroy instead, others who neither have a right to it nor for which they have earlier gone to such pains. And we do not want this if we have a say."

And when the king has fully heard their story, he then answers and says that he wants to think this over and give them an answer when he has thought about her whom he might like to marry. He gave them this answer, however, because he wanted to get rid of them with his conscience still clear. He had in mind not to get married but to preserve his virginity instead. And when the lords intended to leave, there was a knock on the door and the one who knocked said that he had a message for the king. The king was told this. He asks the doorkeeper to let him in and asks the lords to stay behind to hear what the newcomer wanted, and they do so.

Then this man went in before the king and through God's will he appeared to be completely grey, both his hair and beard, and that was very long; and in one hand he had a palm branch but in the other a staff, and he presented himself as a pilgrim. But in some books it says that he was an angel of God. And as soon as

Og þegar að hann kemur fyrir kónginn fellur hann á hné og heilsar honum kurteislega. Kóngur tekur honum vel og bað hann ganga með sér í sína palacia.²⁵ Það gjörir hann. Og er kóngur var kominn í sitt sæti kallar hann á komumann og fréttir hvað manna²⁶ hann væri.

Hinn svarar og segist vera einn propheta²⁷ "og eru mér kunnig tvö og sjötíu þjóðlönd, og er ég einn sendiboði af guði sendur að kunngjöra²⁸ þér að þú skalt taka þér til drottningar eina jungfrú²⁹ og er eins heiðins konungs dóttir³⁰ og heitir hann Gaudonus³¹ en þessi jungfrúin dóttir hans heitir Pia og er harla mjög væn og hyggin. Og guð býður þér að þú skalt halda mikið örlög³² fyrir hennar skuld³³ og koma henni til heilagrar trúar, og guð drottinn hefir hana út valið til þessa."

En sem herranir heyra þetta, verða þeir í þeirra hjörtum mjög glaðir og lofa guð, og þó eigi síður kóngurinn og mælti: "Kæri vin," segir hann, "hversu skal ég mega þessu af stað koma³⁴ þar ég hefur öngvan þann mann að minn boðskap flytji hér til og sig getur rétt leitt bæði til máls og útvegar."

---

²⁵ The word *palacia* is here incorrectly construed as a fem. sg., but see n. 10, where the form corresponds to the Latin neuter noun. The *Pass.* writes: "in syn pallas" (C.ii.d).

²⁶ The manuscript is damaged here and the word *manna* is not legible; I follow Agnete Loth's suggested emendation.

²⁷ In Icelandic texts of this period, the word is Icelandicized to m. *própheti* while transmitting the *-ph-* of the loan (cf. W-N, 269–70; Bandle, 120–21). Here, however, the masc. Latin ending *–a* is retained. Note that the *Pass.* writes: "yck byn eyn prophete" (C.ii.d).

²⁸ The verb is a loan translation of MLG. There is no corresponding passage in the *Pass.*, but the same verb occurs in *Jóhannes saga gullmunns* (*Rhb.* 2:168.30) and in the corresponding passage in the *Pass.*, where we read: "My is huden wes kundich gedaen" (CCC.xlvii.b). Cf. *NT*, 300.

²⁹ The text uses both *jungfrú* and *jómfrú*, the older and younger variants of the word. I follow the text. Cf. Wolf, cxxiii.

³⁰ On the genitive before—rather than after—the governing word in the sixteenth century, see *NT*, 171–72.

³¹ The name here has a Latin ending, but later in the text it is treated as an Icelandic name with the respective endings, e.g., *til Gaudons*. The *Pass.* writes *Gaudon* (C.ii.d).

³² Here again the word *örlög* occurs in its Low German meaning, that is, 'battle'. The corresponding passage in the *Passionael*, however, writes: "vnde ys de wylle godes. dat du darumme strijdest" (C.ii.d).

³³ The manuscript uses both *skuld* and *skyld*, and we follow suit. On the double forms, see Bandle, 67.

³⁴ *af stað koma* is not idiomatic Icelandic; the phrase may have been generated by a MLG phrase such as *in steden stân* 'to come about' or *tokomen* 'to happen', 'to occur'; cf. Sw. *åstadkomma* 'to achieve', 'to bring about'.

he comes before the king, he falls on his knees and greets him courteously. The king welcomes him and asked him to go with him into his palace. He does so. And when the king had sat down in his seat, he calls on the newcomer and asks who he might be.

He answers and says that he is a prophet, "and seventy-two countries are known to me, and I am a messenger sent from God to make known to you that you are to take as your queen a maiden who is the daughter of a heathen king, and his name is Gaudon, but this maiden, his daughter, is called Pia and she is exceedingly beautiful and wise. And God commands you to wage a great battle for her sake and to convert her to the holy faith, and the Lord God has chosen her for this."

And when the lords hear this, they rejoice greatly in their hearts and praise God, and no less the king, and he spoke: "Dear friend," he says, "how shall I be able to accomplish this when I have no one who might undertake my errand and who would be able to carry this out properly both in respect to the message and the route to be followed?"

Hinn gamli manninn[35] svarar: "Þó að þú sendir þangað sextíu sveina, þá lætur hennar faðir deyða þá alla og er það til einskis. Þvíað þá sem hún kom til, þá tók hann hana upp eitt sinni í fang sér og lagði þrjá fingur í höfuðið á henni og <sór>[36] þrjá eiða eftir heiðinsku lögmáli so látanda að hann skyldi aldregi gefa hana nokkurum[37] manni, nema[38] sá er hennar bæði skyldi vinna hana af sér með herskildi."

Þetta þótti sankti Ósvaldi mikið vera að hann vissi ekki hvernin þessu skyldi af stað koma.

Þetta fornam[39] hinn gamli manninn að kónginum féll þetta so þungt og sá hans hug og mælti: "Góði herra, verið ekki hryggvir um þetta, þvíað ég veit hér ráð til. Þér hafið einn hrafn í yðru herbergi þann sem þér hafið fætt í tólf ár. Hann fær þessa jungfrú fyrir yður án allan efa."

Þá gladdist kóngurinn og bað láta hafa hrafninn til sín, en hann varðist og vildi ekki fljúga til kóngsins sem hann var vanur. Það þótti kónginum mikið mein á sig leggja.

Þá mælti hinn gamli manninn: "Verið vel til friða,[40] herra, þvíað guð mun láta hann snart koma aftur til yðar eftir lítin tíma."

Þaðan í frá kom hrafninn aftur og fló inn í höllina og inn á borðið fyrir gamla manninn, þar er hann sat, og mælti: "Þu ert[41] mínum herra velkominn."

Þá mælti sankti Ósvaldur: "Ég hefir nú haft þig í minni hjávist nær í tólf ár og hefir ég enn aldregi fyrr heyrt þig mæla so skýrt nema í fyrstunni er ég sá þig og nú í annað sinn."

---

[35] The manuscript has both *maður* and *mann* as the nom. sg. form; cf. Bandle, 256–57; *NT*, 59–60.

[36] *höfuðið . . . sór*: The manuscript is illegible here; I follow AL's suggested reading, except for *sorv*, that is, *sóru*, which is syntactically incorrect.

[37] The manuscript has the syncopated form *nokkrum*.

[38] This is not idiomatic Icelandic and may be a loan translation generated by MLG *utgenomen, utenomen* 'with the exception of', 'except for'.

[39] The verb *fornema, fornam* is a loan from MLG *vornemen* 'to comprehend', 'to realize', 'to understand'. Cf. W-N, 109–10; *NT*, 252; Wolf, cxxii.

[40] The expression *til friðar* 'for the sake of peace' does exist in Old Icelandic, but this is not the meaning in our text; *til friða* appears to be a gen. pl. The expression is a loan of Low German *tovrede wesen*, meaning something like 'be at ease', 'calm down', 'don't worry' (*MNW*, 5:520–21). The expression is found in a number of sixteenth-century texts, but usually in the singular *til friðs*. See W-N, 134–35; Bandle, 319. The expression recurs in chap. 3 and here the *Pass.* has the corresponding *wes to vreden* (C.iii.a).

[41] The word is illegible in the manuscript, but can be reconstructed from the Low German, which corresponds to the Icelandic except that the utterance is given in indirect discourse: "vnde sprak to em dat he synem here willekame were" (C.ii.d).

The old man answers: "Even if you send sixty young men there, her father will have all of them killed and it will be for naught. For when she came into the world, he took her into his arms one time and laid three fingers on her head and swore three oaths according to heathen law, saying that he would never give her to any man, unless the one who asked for her hand in marriage were to win her from him with arms."

This was very troubling to St. Oswald for he did not know how this should be accomplished.

The old man realized that this disturbed the king greatly and he read his mind and spoke: "Good lord, don't be distressed about this, because I know of a plan. You have a raven in your chambers whom you have nurtured for twelve years. He will without any doubt obtain this maiden for you."

Then the king became glad and asked to have the raven brought to him, but he resisted and did not want to fly to the king as he was wont. The king thought this was a great affront to him.

Then the old man said: "Be at ease, lord, for God will soon have him come back to you after a little while."

Thence the raven came back and flew into the hall and onto the table before the old man where he was sitting, and he spoke: "My lord welcomes you."

Then St. Oswald spoke: "I have now had you with me for close to twelve years, yet I have never before heard you speak so clearly as when I first saw you and now for a second time."

En í þessu þá hvarf í burtu hinn gamli maður. Síðan spyr[42] kóngurinn hrafninn að hvort hann vildi fara með sitt erindi út í heiðindóminn til Gaudons kóngs "og fá dóttur hans mér til handa." Hrafninn sagðist þangað vilja fara er hann vildi sig senda. Síðan skrifaði sankti Ósvaldur eitt bréf og setti þar inn þá tólf parta heilagrar trúar. Og lét sauma eftir á bréfið undir vænginn á honum, en einn gull hring undir annan vænginn og bauð honum að færa þetta jungfrúnni Pia, dóttur kóngsins, og þar með skyldi hann segja þau sín orð, að hann hefði hana út valið fyrir allar meyjar í heiminum sér til unnustu og hún væri sér kærri en nokkur önnur í veröldinni síðan hann heyrði hennar getið. Eftir það tók krummi[43] orlof. En sankti Osvald[44] bífalar[45] hann guði í vald og jómfrú Maríu og bað þau að sjá fyrir honum. Síðan hóf krummi sig upp til flugs og fór leiðar sinnar.

3. Eftir það að sanctus Osvaldus hafði skilið[46] við hrafninn sem hann vildi og fyrr segir, þá fló hann eftir guðs tilvísun í tuttugu daga áður en hann kom þangað er Gaudon kóngur átti fyrir að ráða og hans höfuðborg var. Og þá er hrafninn kom á borgina var þar so háttað að kóngurinn var nýkominn undir borð og voru sumlegir glergluggar látnir upp[47] so að sólin mætti[48] að betur lýsa um höllina og so gusturinn blása af ódauninn ef nokkur væri og líka sakir ofurhita sólar er í þeim löndum er meir[49] en í öðrum stöðum.

Þetta sér krummi og lætur sér það að ráði verða og flýgur inn í gegnum einn gluggann á höllinni og setur sig niður á borðið fyrir kónginn og drottninguna og so dóttur þeirra Pia og hneigði sig og mælti: "Góði herra, Gaudon kóngur, gefið

---

[42] This word is illegible in the text. The king's inquiry and the raven's answer are not found in *HL* and *Pass*.

[43] *krummi* is an Icelandic nickname for the raven. The word derives from *krumma*, *krymma* 'to bend', 'to make crooked'. This is a cognate of Middle High German *krimme*n 'to bend the claws for the catch'.

[44] In the *Passionael*, the saint's name occurs both in the Latin (*Oswaldus*) and German (*Oswald*) forms. In this instance the Icelandic text uses the German form, written *Osvalld* in the manuscript. The corresponding passage in the *Pass.* has the Latin form *Oswaldus* (C.iii.a).

[45] The word is a loan from Middle Low German *bevelen, bevalen*, which already occurs in the Old Norse *Tristrams saga*, but is not widely attested until the sixteenth century (see W-N, 22–23). The corresponding passage in the *Pass.* reads: "Do beuoel ene sunte Oswaldus vnseme leuen heren vnde vnser leuen vrouwen" (C.iii.a). Cf. Wolf, cxvi–cxvii.

[46] Corrected from the manuscript, which writes *skilað* (*skilat*).

[47] See *NT*, 388, for a similar use of *upplāta*: "bækrnar vrdu vpplatnar."

[48] Corrected from the manuscript which writes *mátti* (*matte*), the past indicative.

[49] One would expect here the comparative adjectival form *meiri*; the adverbial form *meir* is attested, however, e.g., in the *Guðbrandsbiblía*, where elision possibly accounts for the form before a word beginning with a vowel, as happens here. See Bandle, 322–23.

And at this moment the old man disappeared. The king then asks the raven whether he wanted to go as his messenger into heathendom to King Gaudon, "and fetch his daughter for me." The raven said that he wanted to go where he wanted to send him. St. Oswald then wrote a letter and put in it the twelve articles of the holy faith.[5] And then he had the letter sewed under his wing, and under the other wing a golden ring, and he told him to take this to the maiden Pia, the king's daughter, and he should also give her this message: that he had chosen her above all maidens on earth to be his beloved and that she was dearer to him than any other on earth ever since he heard of her. After that the corbie[6] took leave. But St. Oswald commends him to God and to the Virgin Mary and asked them to look after him. Then the corbie took wing and flew on his way.

3. After St. Oswald had instructed the raven as he wanted and as was told above, he flew with God's guidance for twenty days before he came to the place where King Gaudon ruled and his principal castle was. And when the raven arrived at the castle it so happened that the king had just come to table and some glass windows had been opened so that the sun could better light up the hall and the breezes could waft out any unpleasant odors there might be and also on account of the excessive heat of the sun which is greater in those lands than in other places.

The corbie sees this and takes the opportunity to fly through a window into the hall and he alights on the table before the king and queen and their daughter Pia, and he bowed down and spoke: "Good lord, King Gaudon, give me leave to

---

[5] The reference is to the twelve "articuli fidei" of the Apostles' Creed that originated in the baptismal liturgy, which required an expression of belief. See J. N. D. Kelly, "Apostolisches Glaubensbekenntnis," in *LTK* 1:760–62; H. Bacht, "Glaubensartikel," in *LTK*, 4:934–35; A. Stenzel, "Glaubensbekenntnis," in *LTK*, 4:935–39.

[6] The bird is initially identified as a *hrafn*, cognate with 'raven', but subsequently *hrafn* alternates with *krummi*, an Icelandic nickname for the raven. The word derives from *krumma*, *krymma* 'to bend', 'make crooked', and refers to the bent claws readied for the catch. Here the Scottish word *corbie* is used for the raven whenever the word *krummi* occurs.

mér orlof að tala við yður þvíað ég á að skila nokkuru erindi við yður. Og so biður ég yður fyrir guð lifandi og fyrir allra jómfrúa skuld að þér reiðist mér ekki, so að ég megi ekki hafa frjálst leyfi í burtu aftur nær sem ég hefur út skilað mínu erindi, hvort sem það er yður með eða á móti."

Sem kóngurinn heyrir að hrafninn talaði mannlegt mál og þó vel skilið, horfir hann lengi þegjandi á fuglinn og undrast stórlega hverju þetta muni gegna og þó undrast kóngurinn ekki <einn> að[50] þetta nema jafnvel allir er í höllinni voru og til hans heyrðu.

Síðan mælti kóngurinn: "Nú þá so að þú hefur þér so vel orlofs beðið og so þar með frítt leiði,[51] þá má ég með öngu móti neita þér, og seg nú fram það þú vilt."

Hrafninn hneigði sig þá fyrir kónginum og mælti: "Mig hefur minn herra Osvald kóngur af Englandi hingað sent til yðar, og lætur biðja yður góðfúslega að þér viljið gefa honum yðra dóttur Pia til eiginnar kvinnu, þvíað það er guðs vilji og hans signuðu móður jungfrú María. Og ef þér gjörið so þá verðið þér guði kærir og loflegir."

En þegar að kóngurinn heyrði að hrafninn nefndi guð og hans móður Maríu, þá varð hann mjög reiður og mælti: "Takið hann og fangið fyrir guðs hans skyld og Maríu og deyðið hann snart án dvöl og skal so reyna hvað hans guð formá."[52]

En jómfrúin vildi það ekki fyrir því þegar að hún heyrði þann boðskap[53] er Ósvaldur kóngur hafði til hennar gjört, þá fékk hún mikla elsku til hans so hún hafði að sjá mikinn hryggleika á sér ef hrafninum væri nokkuð gjört til meins, og mælti til kóngsins:

"Faðir, gjörið eigi so sem þér hafið sett yður að gjöra, þvíað ef þér látið deyða þennan fuglinn þá má ég nálega aldregi vera glöð upp frá því, þó mest fyrir það að þér hafið sjálfir gefið honum orlof að tala það er hann vildi og so átti hann að hafa frjálst leyfi til að fara hvert er hann vildi, og væri það óherralega gjört að brigða sinni trú og lofun fyrir eins fugl<s> skuld eða annars hégóma."

---

[50] The following word is illegible and Loth inserts *eins* after *að,* suggesting that the word is *aðeins*, as in the similar construction at the end of chap. 11, but is is more likely that *að* is the complement to the verb *undrast*. *einn* has been inserted after *ekki* in conformity with other such constructions in the text.

[51] The manuscript writes *fritt leide*, and the adjective can be rendered either *fritt*, 'peaceful', that is, 'safe' or 'secure', or *frítt* 'free.' Since the earlier reference to safe conduct uses the common Icelandic expression *frjálst leyfi*, literally 'free leave,' I have chosen to normalize *fritt* as *frítt*. The corresponding passage in the *Passionael* reads: "Du hefft so wol orloff ghebeden vnde gheleyde. Dat yk dy nicht weygheren enmach" (Ciii.a). MLG *geleide* means 'safe passage', 'salvus conductus' (*MNW*, 2:41).

[52] The verb *formega*, 3rd pers. sg. pres. ind. *formá*, is a loan from MLG *vermogen*, *formagha*. See W-N, 104.

[53] The manuscript writes *badskap*; the *Pass.* has the corresponding: "Do de iuncfrouwe de bodeschop hoerde . . . " (C.iii.a).

speak with you for I have a message to deliver to you. And so I ask you by the Living God and for the sake of all maidens that you do not get angry at me so as not to grant me safe-conduct after I have finished my message, whether that pleases you or not."

When the king hears that the raven spoke with human speech and very distinctly, he looks for a long time in silence at the bird and wonders greatly how this might be, and not only the king wonders at this but just as much all who were in the hall and heard him.

Then the king spoke: "Now since you have asked so well for leave to speak and also for safe-conduct, I cannot in any way deny you this, and say now whatever you want."

The raven then bowed down before the king and spoke: "My lord Oswald, king of England, has sent me here to you and he has me ask you kindly to give him your daughter Pia in marriage, for that is the will of God and His blessed mother, the Virgin Mary. And if you do this, then you will be dear to God and praiseworthy."

But as soon as the king heard the raven name God and His mother Mary, he became very angry and spoke: "Take him and seize him for the sake of his God and Mary and kill him quickly without delay, and thus will be proved what his God can do."

But the maiden did not want that, for as soon as she heard the message that King Oswald had sent regarding her, she was seized by great love for him so that she would experience great distress if any harm were done to the raven, and she spoke to the king:

"Father, don't do what you are intent on doing, for if you have this bird killed, I shall never really be happy again from now on, but most of all since you yourself have given him leave to say whatever he wanted and he was to have safe-conduct to go wherever he wanted, and it would be unbecoming to a lord to break one's pledge and promise on account of a bird or other nonsense."

Kóngurinn svarar: "Kæra[54] dóttir, vertu vel til friða,[55] þvíað ég vil gefa þér í vald þennan fuglinn og gjör með hann hvað sem þú vilt."

Þá gladdist jómfrúin og þakkaði föður sínum. Kallaði hún þá á hrafninn, en hann fló þegar til hennar og settist á höndina á henni. Síðan gengur hún út úr höllinni og hafði fugl sinn með sér og bar hann í sitt herbergi og tók hann og lagði við brjóstið á sér og þrýsti honum að sér.

Þar með klappaði hún honum og mælti: "Kæri fugl, seg þú mér enn nokkuð meira af þínum herra Osvaldo."[56]

Hrafninn svarar: "Þú eðla[57] jómfrú, takið þér yðvarri hendi undir mína vængi og munið þér finna þar eitt bréf og einn gull hring. Þetta hefur minn herra hvorttveggja sent yður. Og það mig það segja yður með að hann hafði yður í sínu hjarta kærri en neinni jómfrú eður kvinnu annarri í veröldinni."

Síðan tekur hún bréfið og les. Og finnur þar eins sem hrafninn hafði sagt henni og það með hversu að hún skyldi frjálsast frá eilífri pínu og dauða ef hún vildi snúast frá heiðni og villu en trúa á sannan guð og halda þessa tólf parta heilagrar trúar. En þegar að hún hafði útlesið[58] bréfið, þá af miskunn heilags anda uppkveikist hennar hjarta með þeirri logandi ást til guðs so að hún sagðist gjarnan öllu því trúa er hann vildi sér til þeirra hluta kenna, og lyfti sínum augum upp til himna samaleiðis sínum höndum so mælandi:

"Faðir á himnum, þér gjör ég þakkir fyrir þína mildi er þú mér virðist að veita," og féll á sín hné með tárum og lá so nokkra[59] stund. Eftir það lætur hún skrifa annað bréf eftir því sem hún vildi og lét búa um það virkulega og þar með eitt fingur handsal.

4. Annan daginn eftir finnur krummi jómfrúna aftur. Tekur hún þá bréfið og saumar undir vænginn á honum líka og fyrr var og so líka býr hún um gull hringinn.

Síðan tekur hún so til orðs og segir: "Far nú og fær þetta þínum herra og seg honum það með að ég veit öngvan þann í veröldinni nokkurn mann að ég hafi

---

[54] Corrected from the manuscript, which writes *kæri*. Bandle notes, however, the similar occurrence of the nom. sg. fem. form *kæri* in the *Guðsbrandsbiblía* (313).

[55] The manuscript writes *til fridar*. Concerning this expression, see n. 40.

[56] The corresponding passage in the *Pass.* similarly has the dative of the Latin form of the name: "Leue rauen segge my meer van dyneme heren Oswaldo" (C.iii.a: 'Dear raven, tell me more about your lord Oswald').

[57] The manuscript writes *edle*, that is, with a German ending; this is a loan from Low German *ed(d)el*, 'noble', 'illustrious'. Cf. n. 16.

[58] *útlesa* is a loan from MLG *útlesen* 'to finish or complete reading'. The word is otherwise not attested in Icelandic with this meaning, in which *út* has a perfective character; the word occurs only in the sense of 'to pick out'. See *NT*, 391; W-N, 369.

[59] On the syncopation of *nokkur* in the gen., dat., and acc. sg. fem., see Bandle, 368–69.

The king answers: "Dear daughter, be at ease, for I shall entrust this bird to you and do with him what you want."

Then the maiden became glad and thanked her father. She then called to the raven, and he flew to her at once and sat down on her hand. She then goes out of the hall and took her bird along and brought him into her room and took him and rested him against her breast and pressed him close to her.

She also stroked him gently and spoke: "Dear bird, tell me a little more about your lord Oswald."

The raven answers: "Noble maiden, put your hand under my wings and you will find there a letter and a golden ring. My lord has sent you these two things. And he asked me to tell you also that he holds you dearer in his heart than any other maiden or woman on earth."

She then takes the letter and reads. And she finds there what the raven had told her and in addition how she would be saved from eternal punishment and death if she converted from paganism and error and believed in the true God and accepted these twelve articles of the holy faith. And as soon as she has finished reading the letter, then by the mercy of the Holy Spirit her heart is kindled with a burning love for God so that she said that she would gladly believe everything that he wanted to teach her about these things, and she lifted up her eyes and hands to heaven, speaking thus:

"Father in heaven, I give you thanks for your kindness which You have vouchsafed to grant me," and she fell on her knees in tears and lay thus for a time. After that she has another letter written just as she wanted and had it readied properly and with it a finger ring.

4. The next day the corbie meets the maiden again. She then takes the letter and sews it under his wing just as had been done before and she also does this with the golden ring.

She then starts speaking and says: "Go now and take this to your lord and tell him also that I know of no other man on earth whom I hold so dear as him and bid

so kæran sem hann, og bið hann að hann þiggi það af guði að allt það verði sem hann vill honum og mér á milli og hann finnur skrifað í bréfinu, og það að hann komi eftir mér á næsta ári hér eftir með tveimur og sjötíu skipum og hafi þúsund manns á hverju skipi og hugsi so fyrir að hann hafi kost og drykk fyrir sitt lið so að þeim dugi þrjú ár í samt og láti þetta fólk vera að öllu vel til reitt hvað sem til þarf að taka. So vil ég og að hann láti þig fara með sér, annars mega þeir aldregi ná mér héðan úr heiðindóminum. En mig grunar þó að þetta verði seinna en ég vilda, þvíað ef sá guð er himnum ræður vill[60] að þetta verði þá ske það sem fyrst í hans nafni."

Eftir þetta hóf krummi sig upp til flugs, en hún bífalaði[61] hann guði í vald og hans kærustu móður jungfrú Maríu. En er hrafninn hafði flogið vart í níu daga yfir um hafið, þá fékk hann á seinasta deginum mikinn storm so að hann gat varla stýrt sér og slitnuðu böndin um gullhringinn og so líka um bréfið og féll hvorttveggja ofan í sjóinn. En þegar kom að einn fiskur og svalg bæði bréfið og so hringinn. Af þessu varð krummi hryggur og fló til lands. Þar fann hann einn einsetumann fyrir sér og sat á einum steini. Þetta lét og krummi sér að kenningu verða og setur sig niður á annan stein er þar var nærri einsetumanni og ber sig mjög lítillega.

Síðan mælti einsetumaður til hrafnsins: "Seg mér þú hinn fríði fugl nokkuð af þínum herra, sankti Osvaldo."[62]

Hrafninn svarar: "Hvað kunnu þér af mínum herra segja eða hver hefur þér sagt frá honum?"

Einsetumaður svarar og segir: "Það hefur gjört vor herra Jesus Christus[63] nú á þessu árinu til þess að ég skyldi biðja fyrir honum."

Þá mælti hrafninn: "So vil ég þér þá kunngjöra að ég var og sendur af mínum herra Osvaldo inn í heiðindóminn til einnar kóngsdóttur sem heitir Pia, og hún hafði skrifað honum eitt bréf til aftur um þeirra erindi beggja og þar með sendi hún honum eitt kostulegt handsal af skíru gulli. Og báðir þessir hlutir eru frá mér fallnir í sjóinn."[64]

---

[60] Corrected from the manuscript, which writes *vile*.

[61] The *Pass.* has a corresponding passage: "vnde beuoel em vnseme leuen heren" (C.iii.c). Cf. n. 45.

[62] The manuscript conjoins here the Icelandic form of the uninflected adjective *sankti* (written in the manuscript *sancte*) and the Latin dat. form *Osvaldo*. Consistency would demand *sancto Osvaldo*. Cf. "af mínum herra Osvaldo" below.

[63] Throughout *Ósvalds saga* the name appears in the Latin form and is declined in Latin as the Icelandic syntax demands.

[64] The phrase *eru frá mér fallnir í sjóinn* is syntactically un-Icelandic; it corresponds to the reading in the *Pass.*: "dat is my in dat meer gheuallen" (C.iii.b).

him ask God that everything turn out between him and me as he wants and finds written in the letter, and that he come after me next year with seventy-two ships and that he have a thousand men on each ship and that he remember to take along food and drink for his army to last for three years in all, and have his people properly outfitted with all that is necessary. And I also want him to let you go along, otherwise they will never be able to get me out of heathendom. Yet I suspect that this will happen more slowly than I would want; but if the God who rules heaven wants this to come to pass, then it will happen as soon as possible in His name."

Thereupon the corbie rose up in flight, and she entrusted him into the care of God and His dearest mother, the Virgin Mary. But when the raven had flown not quite nine days across the sea, he got into such a great storm on the last day that he could hardly fly on and the laces around the golden ring broke as did those around the letter and each fell down into the sea. And at once a fish came along and swallowed both the letter and the ring. The corbie was upset about this and flew to land. There he saw a hermit and he was sitting on a rock. The corbie let this be a sign for him and he alights on another rock, which was near the hermit, and he bears himself very humbly.

The hermit then spoke to the raven: "Tell me, you handsome bird, something about your lord, St. Oswald."

The raven answers: "What can you tell me about my lord, but who has told you about him?"

The hermit answers and says: "Our Lord Jesus Christ did so this year, so that I would pray for him."

Then the raven spoke: "Then I will make known to you that I was sent by my lord Oswald into heathendom to a princess called Pia, and she had written him a letter in reply about their situation, and she sent along a precious ring of pure gold. And both of these things have dropped off me into the sea."

Þá svarar einsetumaður: "Það sé fyrir guði klagað[65] og hans kærri móðir[66] Maríu," og féll til jarðar mjög grátandi og bað til guðs af klökku hjarta og barði hnefunum fyrir brjóstið á sér og var harðla mjög harmandi þessu. En guð heyrði ákall hans og sá hans góðgirndarfullt hjarta og bauð einum engli að finna þann fiskinn er bæði hafði gullhringinn og bréfið "og bjóð honum," sagði hann, "í mínu nafni að leggja hvorttveggja aftur." Það gjörir hann og færir hrafninum þessa hlutina aftur.

Þetta sér einsetumaður og mælti: "Lofaður sé guð allra guða," og mælti síðan við hrafninn að hann skyldi vera þar hjá sér um nóttina, og so gjörir hann og var heldur kátur.

5. Um morguninn eftir tekur einsetumaður bæði bréfið og so hringinn og býr um sem best kann hann. Síðan flýgur hann aftur til sjós og so lætur hann fara jafnt í átta daga, en á hinum níunda deginum kom hann heim aftur til Ósvalds kóngs. En þegar að kóngurinn sér að hans hrafn er aftur kominn verður hann harðla glaður við það og tekur hann að sér góðmótlega og gengur eftir á í sitt heimuglegt mak[67] og skipar síðan öllum út að ganga nema krumma einum. Síðan fréttir hann eftir hvað góðra tíðinda hann kunni[68] að segja sér af kóngsdóttur.

Hinn svarar: "Takið þér hér eitt bréf og einn gull hring í fiðri mínu er hún sendi yður og lét það vera með í sínu boði að hún hefði öngvan kærri á jarðríki en yður, og þér skylduð biðja guð að það mætti ske sem fyrst ykkar á vegna á milli[69] og eftir því sem þér sjálfir megið vel finna í bréfinu. So hefur og þessi jungfrú gjört yður boð að þér skulið koma eftir sér að næstu sumri með tveimur skipum og sjötíu og skulið hafa mig með yður, annars náið þér henni aldregi þaðan sem nú er hún."

Síðan las Ósvaldur kóngur bréfið og mælti: "Lofaður sé guð fyrir alla hluti mér veitta," og þakkaði hrafninum mikillega fyrir sína reisu.[70]

---

[65] *klaga* is a loan from MLG and in this case corresponds to *dat sy gode gheclaghet* in *Pass.* (C.iii.b).

[66] See Bandle, 265–67, for the vacillating declension in this period of *faðir, móðir,* and *dóttir*; we find both *móðir* and *móður* throughout the singular.

[67] Both *heimuglegt* and *mak* are Low German loans, *heimuglegt* deriving from MLG *heimelik, hemelik* 'private', 'secret' (*MNW*, 2:237), and *mak* from *mak* 'private chambers', 'a comfortable room' (*MNW*, 3:7). Here, however, the noun *mak* has a meaning other than the one occurring in other sixteenth-century Icelandic texts, where the word has the sense of 'peace', 'quiet'. See W-N, 212; Bandle, 273.

[68] Corrected from the manuscript, which writes *kynna.*

[69] The pronoun *ykkar* does double duty, as the object of both *á vegna* and *á milli.* The *Pass.* reads: "dat dat drade ghesche twisscken iuw beyden" (C.iii.c). See Bandle, 448, for the derivation of *á vegna* from German *van ênes wegene*; on *á milli,* see *NT*, 175; Bandle, 449.

[70] The noun *reisa* is a loan from MHG *reise* (W-N, 274–75), which means not only 'trip', 'journey' but also 'military expedition by land or sea'.

The hermit then answers: "This cries out to God and His dear mother Mary," and he fell to the ground weeping profusely and prayed to God with a humble heart and struck his breast with his fists and lamented this very much. And God heard his prayer and saw his fervent heart and bade an angel find the fish that had the golden ring and the letter, "and command him," He said, "in my name to return both." The angel does this and gets these things back for the raven.

The hermit sees this and spoke: "Praised be the God of all gods," and then he said to the raven that he should stay with him for the night, and he does so and was in high spirits.

5. The next morning the hermit takes both the letter and the ring and readies them as best he can. After this he flies back out to sea and thus he proceeds for eight days straight, and on the ninth day he came back home to King Oswald. And as soon as the king sees that his raven has returned, he becomes very glad and receives him kindly and then goes into his private chamber and tells everyone to leave except for the corbie. Then he asks him what good news he can tell him about the princess.

The raven answers: "Take out of my feathers a letter and a golden ring which she sent you along with her message that she holds no one dearer on earth than you; and you are to ask God that things in respect to the two of you might happen as soon as possible and in accordance with what you yourself will find in the letter. This maiden has also instructed you to come for her next summer with seventy-two ships and you are to bring me along; otherwise you will never get her away from where she is now."

King Oswald then read the letter and spoke: "Praised be God for everything He has granted me," and he thanked the raven greatly for his journey.

Eftir það sendir kóngur eftir smiðum og gjörir ráð fyrir í öllum stöðum um England að hans vinir skulu láta gjöra so stór skip er hann megi hafa þúsund manns á hverju skipi og þar til þriggja ára[71] kost til áts og drykkjar og búa þau til með bestum föngum er þeir gæti. Kom nú fram er kóngsdóttir sagði sig gruna að seinna mundi þeirra fundur verða en hún vildi og hún hafði gjört ráð fyrir, þvíað skipin er kóngur lét gjöra urðu ekki reiðubúin so snart.

En þegar að skipin voru búin og hlaðin eftir hans vild, þá sendi hann eftir mektugum herrum, hertogum og greifum, so og eftir tólf biskupum og níu ábótum, þar með marga riddara og eðelborna[72] menn so að hann hafði alls sjö þúsundir og tveim betur. Síðan lét hann gjöra marga krossa og gaf hverjum sinn og þá skyldi hver sem einn bera á sínum klæðum og styrkti sinn her með ljúfum og góðum fyrirheitum so segjandi:

"Kærustu vinir og dýrlegir herrar, allir sem hér eru nú í guðs augliti til samans komnir eftir minni bón og boði, hafið þér yður vel hvað sem fram kann koma fyrir oss í þessari vorri reisu og stríðið mannlega fyrir trú heilagrar kristni ef þess kann við að þurfa þvíað guð vill vera með oss. Og hver sem síðan deyr af oss í réttu stríði og í þessari reisu, þá hefur sá eilíft líf og ríki með honum og hans útvöldum vinum í himiríki[73] utan enda."

En allir þökkuðu kóngi og kváðust með honum gjarnan vilja bæði lifa og deyja.

6. Þegar að Ósvaldur kóngur var til reiðu og hans föruneyti láta þeir í haf og fá góða byri og koma við land Gaudons kóngs er þeir höfðu úti verið eigi fullar átján vikur. Síðan siglir hann inn eftir ríkinu allt þar til er hann var kominn í nánd við þá borg er kóngurinn sjálfur sat á.

Þá mælti Ósvaldur: "Það þyki mér ráð," segir hann, "að senda boð undan oss, so að einhverjir viti til vor."

Öllum þótti það gott ráð. Þá var kóngi sagt að hrafninn hafði orðið eftir er hann sendi áður. Þá hrygðist kóngur mjög og kom í hug hvað kóngsdóttir hafði sagt, að hans reisa og stórlegt ómak mundi sér til lítils koma ef hann væri ekki með, og féll allur til jarðar og bað guð að sýna sér sína milda náð og láta hrafn sinn komast til sín so að hann færi eigi erindislaust aftur. Samaleiðis bað hann og jungfrú að hún skyldi vera og í fulltingi með sér bæði hér um og annars er hann við þyrfti.[74] Og guð heyrði hans ákall og sá hans nauðsýn og sendi einn

---

The manuscript incorrectly writes *ars*.

[72] The manuscript writes *edel borna*; cf. n. 16. The MLG origin is clear, but the *Pass.* does not have a corresponding phrase here.

[73] See W-N, 156–57, on this form—rather than *himinríki*, as in Old Icelandic—which Björn Þorleifsson uses consistently. Cf. Wolf, cxxii.

[74] The manuscript writes *þvrftte*. The pret. subj. without umlaut also occurs sporadically in the *Guðsbrandsbiblía*; cf. Bandle, 424.

After that the king sends for smiths and everywhere in England he sees to it that his friends have such large ships built that he can have a thousand men on each ship and in addition three years' provision in food and drink, and that they outfit them with the best equipment they can get. Now it happens as the princess said she suspected, that they would meet later than she wanted and she had intended, since the ships that the king ordered built could not be readied in such haste.

But as soon as the ships were ready and loaded according to his will, he sent after mighty lords, dukes and counts, as well as after twelve bishops and nine abbots, and in addition many knights and nobly born men so that he had in all seven thousand and two hundred to boot. After this he had many crosses made and gave one to each, and everyone was to wear one on his clothes, and he encouraged his army with gentle and good promises, saying thus:

"Dearest friends and noble lords, all who have now assembled in God's sight in accordance with my request and command, behave well no matter what may befall us on our expedition[7] and fight manfully for the faith of holy Christianity if this becomes necessary, for God will be with us. And whoever among us later dies in the just fight and on this expedition, that one will have eternal life and rule with Him and His chosen friends in the heavenly kingdom without end."

And all thanked the king and said they gladly wanted both to live and die with him.

6. As soon as King Oswald and his companions were ready, they put out to sea and they have a fair wind and come to King Gaudon's shores after they had been not quite eighteen weeks at sea. Then he sails along the coast of the kingdom all the way until he had come into the vicinity of the castle where the king himself resided.

Oswald then spoke: "I think it advisable," he says, "to send word ahead of us so that some of the people are aware of us."[8]

Everyone thought this was a good idea. Then the king was told that the raven whom he had earlier sent here had been left behind. The king was then very upset and he remembered what the princess had said, that his journey and great effort would have little result if the raven were not along, and he prostrated himself on the ground and asked God to show His gentle mercy and have his raven come to him so that he would not go back with his mission left unaccomplished. At the same time he also asked the Virgin that she be of asisstance to him both in this

---

[7] The Icelandic word used here is *reisa*, loaned from MLG where it means not only 'journey', 'trip', but also 'military expedition by land or sea'. Hence our translation.

[8] The Icelandic form of the pronoun is the *pluralis majestatis*; Oswald is thus referring only to himself.

engil til að færa honum aftur hrafninn. Þegar að kóngur sér hann, lofar hann guð og verður nú glaður og tekur að sér hrafninn blíðlega og biður fara á fund kóngsdóttur og bera henni sína kveðju og það með að hann lætur biðja hana að leggja til með sér nokkuð ráð so hann mætti ná henni og so hvort að hann skyldi fara þá strax með örlögi[75] eða eigi að föður hennar. Hrafninn kveðst gjöra skyldu hans boð hvað hann vildi.

Síðan flýgur hann upp á borgina til kóngsdóttur að einum glerglugga er opinn var, en hún var þá að klæða sig í herberginu er krummi kom að glugganum. Flýgur hann jafnsnart inn til hennar er sér hana. En hún þekkti hann strax[76] og tók hann upp í fang sér og frétti hann eftir hvar hans herra væri. Krummi segir henni og so allan boðskap er Ósvaldur kóngur hafði gjört henni boð til.

Hún svarar og sagði: "Farðu þegar aftur áður en nokkur verður var við þína kvámu eða hans og seg honum að hann láti gjöra sér eina örn forgyllta af nobil gulli,[77] en sjálf skal hún vera af silfri og láti so um búa sem hún væri lifandi, og eina tólf gullsmiði skal hann hafa með sér. Síðan sigli hann hingað allt undir borgina er faðir minn er á og skal hann gjöra sig að kaupmanni og þegar að hann kemur hér við land, þá slái hann sínum landtjöldum upp og beiðast leyfi af föður mínum að selja sinn varning og kostulegt kramverk[78] er hann hefir[79] flutt. Og ef so ber til að faðir minn eða aðrir fréttir hann eftir því hann er þar kominn eða hvað hann vill, þá skal hann segja að sér væri sagt að Gaudon kóngur hafði so gott sem[80] gift dóttur sína Pia einum stórmektugum herra eða konungi, og því væri þeir þar komnir, ef það væri nokkur hlutur sem jungfrúna[81] og föður hennar girntust að eiga hvort það væri heldur kostuleg fingurhandsöl eða aðrir hlutir, þá vildi hann fyrst að bjóða þeim að kaupa. Væri og so að kóngurinn vildi láta smíða nokkura gripi þá[82] sem fásénir væri í þeim löndum, þá væri í hans skipi frábærir

---

[75] Once again the word *örlög* is used here in its Low German meaning of 'battle.' See n. 12.

[76] The manuscript writes *straktt*.

[77] The first element of the phrase is a loan from Low German, deriving from the name of an originally English gold coin, the *nobele* (*MNW*, 3:190).

[78] The compound *kramverk* is a loan from *MLG krâmwerk*, 'merchandise', 'wares'. The coupling with the Icelandic synonym *varning* suggests that the German loan may here be used to distinguish *varning* 'cargo' from small merchandise, later referred to, again with a loan word, as *handsala* and *klenódía*, that is, jewelry. There is no exact corresponding passage in the *Pass.*, but the princess says that Oswald "scal dar enen groten kraem vpslaen" (C.iii.d).

[79] See Bandle, 377, for the vacillation between *hefir* and *hefur* in the 3rd pers. sg. pres. of *hafa*.

[80] *So gott sem* appears to be a loan translation of MLG *so gût/gôt we* 'nearly', 'all but'.

[81] Corrected from the manuscript, which writes *jvngfrvne*.

[82] Corrected from the manuscript, which writes *þeir*.

and whatever else he needed. And God heard his prayer and saw his need and sent
an angel to fetch his raven for him. As soon as the king sees him, he praises God
and he now becomes glad and picks up the raven gently and asks him to go to the
princess and give her his greeting and also to ask her for some advice as to how
he might get her and whether he should immediately engage her father in battle or
not. The raven says that he would do his bidding as he asked him.

He then flies up onto the castle and to the princess through a glass window
which was open, and she was just dressing in her chamber when the corbie came to
the window. He flies straight in to her when he sees her. And she recognized him
immediately and took him in her arms and asked him where his lord was. And the
corbie tells her and also the entire message that King Oswald had sent her.

She answers and said: "Go back at once before someone becomes aware
of your arrival or his, and tell him that he is to have an eagle made, gilded with
golden noble coins, but the eagle itself shall be of silver, and have it made so as
to seem alive, and he is to bring some twelve goldsmiths along with him. Then
he is to sail here all the way to the foot of the castle where my father is and he
is to pretend to be a merchant, and as soon as he comes on land, he is to set up
his tents and ask for permission from my father to sell his cargo and the precious
merchandise he has brought. And should it happen that my father or others ask
him why he has come there or what he wants, then he is to say that he has been
told that King Gaudon has as much as married his daughter Pia to a very powerful lord or king, and that is why they have come there, in case there should be an
item that the maiden or her father wanted to have, be it precious finger rings or
other objects, in which case he wanted to offer it to them first for purchase. And
should it be that the king wanted to have some precious objects made that were
rare in these regions, then there were on his ship excellent men for such skilled

menn til hagleiks. En um örnina, er ég sagða þér, skaltu honum segja, hann setji hana upp yfir tjaldið fyrir framan og láti so búa um, hvaðan sem vindurinn blæs þá skuli hún æ sýnast vera á flug og fljúga til sjóvar burtu af landinu."

Og þegar að jungfrúin hafði þau ráð út gefið sem hún vildi, fló krummi í burtu aftur og til síns herra Osvaldo.[83]

7. Nú sem hrafninn hafði fengið sitt erindi af jungfrúnni, þá beiðist hann orlofs og fór aftur til síns herra og segir honum alla hluti er jungfrúin hafði sagt. Kóngur verður þessu glaður og fór í einn stóran kaupstað og fékk sér þar tólf gullsmiði og sigldi síðan inn fyrir borgina er Gaudon kóngur sat í og gjörði allt eftir því sem Pia kóngsdóttir sendi honum boðin til.

Þetta fékk að sjá einn heiðingi sem var á borginni[84] og hljóp sem hann mátti inn fyrir kónginn og segir honum að fjöldi skipa hafi lagt inn fyrir borgina og reistu þegar sín tjöld er þeir komu á land, "og gjöreg því so ráð fyrir að þetta sé heldur friðmenn en öðruvís."

En í öðrum stað er af því að segja að jafnsnart sem Ósvaldur kóngur hefur búið um sín skip, gjörir hann boð Gaudoni kóngi að hann vilji gefa þeim orlof að liggja þar á meðan að þeir selja sitt kram[85] og annan varning er þeir höfðu þangað flutt, og væri það so að þeir hefði nokkurn gáning kóngsins er hann vildi á girnast, þá byði þeir honum fyrstum að kaupa. En þá Gaudon fær þessi boð, segir hann so að kaupmenn allir mega vel friðland hafa sem með friði vilja fara. Þetta svar lætur Ósvaldur kóngur sér vel ánægja.

Einn dag gengur kóngur og drottning hans ofan til tjaldbúðar Ósvalds kóngs og vill skoða hvað kram[86] að þessir kaupmenn hafa flutt. Og er Ósvaldur kóngur sér Gaudon vera að næsta kominn, gengur hann með allan sinn her á móti honum og vill bjóða Gaudoni inn í tjöldin sem hann og gjörði. En er Gaudon hefur setið og litist um það sem <í> búðunum var, þá skoðar <hann> og vandlega eigi síður að[87]

---

[83] The dat. sg. of the Latin form of the name is used here rather than the gen., which one would expect in agreement with *síns herra*, the obj. of the preposition *til*.

[84] The distinction is made between being in the castle, as in the previous sentence *fyrir borgina er Gaudon kóngur sat í*, and being outside, on top of the castle—*á borginni*—presumably on the battlements, as in this sentence.

[85] *kram*, like the compound *kramverk* above, is a loan from MLG *kram, kraem* 'merchandise', 'wares'. Once again the loan word is coupled with Icelandic *varning*.

[86] The corresponding passage in the *Pass.* reads: "Do gink he myt synre vrouwen vnde alle syn ghesinde to deme krame vnde beseghen den arne vnde den kraem ghans wol" (C.iii.d).

[87] *skoðar . . . að:* This is not idiomatic Icelandic and may be a loan translation of MLG *anschouwen*. Two sentences previously, the verb *skoða* occurs intransitively while the *Pass.* uses *beseghen* transitively (C.iii.d; see the previous note); here the verb *skoða* is used transitively, however, and may be a loan translation transmitting MLG *beseghen* or *anschouwen* 'to look at'.

work. But concerning the eagle that I told you about, you are to tell him to set it on the top of the front of his tent and it should be so arranged that no matter from where the wind blows, it should always seem to be in flight and flying out to sea away from land."

And when the maiden had given him whatever advice she wanted, the corbie flew back to his lord Oswald.

7. Now when the raven had received his message from the maiden, he asks for leave and flew back to his lord and tells him all the things the maiden had said. The king becomes glad at this and went to a large marketplace and got himself there twelve goldsmiths and then sailed up to the castle where King Gaudon resided, and he did everything that Princess Pia had told him to do in her message.

A heathen who was up on the castle caught sight of this and ran in to the king as quickly as he could, and he tells him that a multitude of ships had anchored off the castle and immediately raised their tents when they landed, "and it is my opinion that they are men of peace rather than not."

On the other hand it is told that as soon as King Oswald had readied his ships, he sent a message to King Gaudon asking permission for them to lie there at anchor while they sell their merchandise and the other cargo that they have brought along, and should it be that any item caught the king's attention and he wanted to have it, they would offer it to him first for purchase. And when Gaudon gets this message, he says that all the merchants who behave peaceably will have safe-conduct. King Oswald is quite pleased at this answer.

One day the king and his queen go down to King Oswald's tents and the king wants to see what wares these merchants have brought. And when King Oswald sees that Gaudon is approaching, he goes to meet him with his entire army and he wants to invite Gaudon into his tent. And so he entered. And when Gaudon has sat down and looks around at what is in the booths, he looks no less carefully at selskap[88] Ósvalds en öðru, þvíað alla þá er sá þá höfðu þeir heilagt krossmark á klæðunum.

Af þessu verður hann ákaflega reiður og mælti: "Eigi mun so vera sem mér sýnist að þér berið krossmark á yðrum klæðum allir, og veit ég þá víst að það merkir að þér eruð kristnir allir. Og fyrir hvað eruð þér so djarfir að þér hafið siglt hingað í mitt land, þar sem ég lætur öngva kristna menn lifa þá sem ég kann yfirkoma?"

Ósvaldur svarar: "Þér gjörið betur herra kóngur en þér talið til, þvíað vær erum komnir upp á[89] yðra náð og höfum vær heldur þenkt að fá sæmd af yður en nokkur harðindi,[90] hvað manna sem vær vorum, af því að oss var sagt að þér hefðið gift yðra dóttur einum ofur ríkum kóngi og fyrir því fórum vær hingað, ef þér eður yðar dóttir þurfti[91] nokkurra þeirra handsala eða annarra klenódía[92] sem höfum, eða þurfið þér og láta gjöra nokkura fáséna hluti sem ekki eru iðulega með yður hér, þá höfum vær flutt þá menn hingað með oss að stórhagir menn eru. En þurfið þér og vor vit,[93] þá munu þér fyrir yðvars heiðurs[94] skuld að láta oss fara á burtu aftur með friði."

En Gaudon þagnaði er hann heyrði þetta og kvaðst mundu finna þá að morgni.

8. So er og sagt að Ósvaldur kóngur hafi haft hjá sér einn hjört mjög ágætan stundum að sjá bæði að stærð og fegurð. En í sumlegum bókum greinir so að það væri engill og so var að hvað nær er hann var hjá kóngi, þá var hann so fagur að líta að allir þeir er hann sáu þá vildu þeir eiga hann. Og so mun enn verða. Snemma

---

[88] *selskapur*, m., is borrowed from MLG *selschap, -schop*. In MLG the word functions both as a collective noun 'company' and to refer to individuals, 'companions'. See W-N, 289; *NT*, 347; *MNW*, 4:184; Wolf, cxxix.

[89] Bandle notes that the use of *upp á* instead of simply *á* already occurs in later Old Icelandic (451), while Jón Helgason regards this usage in Oddur Gottskálksson's translation of the New Testament as having roots in the common Icelandic of the period (*NT*, 173: "ætla má að hafi átt rót í venjulegri íslenzku þessarar aldar").

[90] Corrected from the manuscript which writes *hardinda*. The noun is a pl. n. noun, but the manuscript presumably construes it as weak masculine.

[91] Here, as above, the manuscript does not show umlaut in the pret. subj.; cf. Bandle, 424.

[92] In the phrase *handsala eða annarra klenódía*, the latter noun is a loan from Low German *klênode, kleinode*, indicating precious artwork, especially that of goldsmiths; see *klênode, kleinode* in *MNW*, 2:479. The corresponding phrase in *Pass.* reads: "vingerlinge edder clenode" (C.iii.d).

[93] To judge by the corresponding text in *Pass.*—"behoue gy vnser nicht" 'if you do not need us' (C.iii.d)—the Icelandic should read: "En þurfið þér og vor eigi"; yet in the manuscript the last word is quite clearly *vith*. It is tempting to explain the error as a careless misreading of *n* for *u* (*v*) in MLG *nit*, the alternate spelling of the negative.

[94] Corrected from the manuscript, which writes *yðarn heiður* (*ydarn heidr*).

Oswald's companions than at the other things, for all the men he saw had the holy sign of the cross on their clothes.

At this he becomes exceedingly angry and spoke: "It can't really be as it seems, that you are all wearing the sign of the cross on your clothes, and I know for sure that this means that you are all Christians. And how dare you be so bold as to have sailed into my land, when I permit no Christians to live whom I can overcome?"

Oswald answers: "You are bound to do better, lord king, than what you have been saying, for we have placed ourselves at your mercy and we rather thought we would receive honor from you, not abuse, no matter who we are, for we were told that you have promised your daughter in marriage[9] to an exceedingly rich king and for this reason we have come here, should you or your daughter need some of the rings or other precious jewels we have; or should you need to have some rare items made that are not common here among you, we have brought those men along with us who are very skilled artisans. And should you not need us,[10] then for the sake of your reputation you should let us depart in peace."

But Gaudon fell silent when he heard this and said that he would meet with them the next morning.

8. It is also told that King Oswald had brought along a quite splendid stag both in respect to size and beauty. And in some books it says that it was an angel. And so it was that when it was near the king it was so beautiful to see that all who saw it wanted to own it. And thus it still happens. Early in the morning Gaudon

---

[9] Strictly speaking, Oswald says that he has heard that King Gaudon has married his daughter to someone, but this does not fit the context. The corresponding passage in the *Pass.* has the verb *ghelauet* (C.iii.d) 'to promise in marriage'.

[10] The corresponding Icelandic clause— "En þurfið þér og vor vit"—is corrupt and makes no sense (see n. 93 of the edition). The translation corresponds to the reading in the *Pass.* (C.iii.d).

um morguninn stendur Gaudon upp og gengur til ráðs við sína spekinga, hvað hann skuli gjöra við þá kaupmenn er þar voru komnir og kristinna manna teikn bæri á sér. Taldi þó það til að sér þætti illt að drepa sakalausa er hann sjálfur hafði gefið þeim frið og frelsi áður. En væri það að þeir fengu honum nokkurar góðar gersimar, þær sem honum girntist til að eiga, þá mundi hann það þiggja og láta þá eftir á fara hvert þeir vilja. Þetta þótti öllum hans ráðunautum vera ið besta ráð. Síðan lætur hann blása til saman mikinn fjölda manns og gengur ofan til sjóvar að finna Ósvald kóng. Og þegar að þeir finnast býður Ósvaldur kóngi í tjöld en kóngur lætur dræmt við. En í þessu þá hleypur einn mikill hjörtur fyrir dyrnar á tjaldinu. Og þegar Gaudon kóngur lítur hjörtinn, dynur þegar ágirndaröngu[95] í brjóst kónginum so að hann segist ekki annað mega en eignast dýrið, og fréttir Ósvald hvort hann hefur þetta ið mikla dýr haft þangað. Hann segir að so sé.

"Þetta ið fagra dýr verður ég at eiga," segir kóngur.

"Það má vel," segir Ósvaldur, "og er hann sloppinn fyrir oss óforsynju,[96] þvíað ég þenkir að hann sé styggur að taka."

Gaudon kveðst ekki því skeyta. En allt á meðan[97] að þeir ræðast við, þá hleypur hjörturinn aftur og fram þar hjá þeim og leikur sér. En kónginum[98] líst æ því betur á dýrið og býður að taka hest sinn og skeyti. Hér með kallar Gaudon á alla sína menn og býður þeim að fara með sér og taka dýrið so það komist eigi undan. En þegar dýrið sér ok skilur kóngsins vilja og hans manna, hefur það sig á rás undan en kóngur og hans fylgjarar eftir. Gjörir dýrið stundum að það staldrar við líkt sem það vilji þá og þá láta taka sig, en stundum hefur það sig undan so

---

[95] The manuscript has *agirndaravgv*, but the second part of the composite *-avgv* does not make grammatical sense. In his edition, Jón Sigurðsson wrote *ágirndaraugn*, but there is no doubt that the manuscript writes *-avgv*. If we accept the manuscript reading, then the word would have to be emended to *-avgvm*, and the text would mean something like: "the eyes of greed thunder in the king's breast," a strange mixed metaphor at best. The emendation proposed above posits omission of a nasal stroke over the *-av-* of *-avgv*; the final *-v* is to be interpreted as a sg. fem. dat. ending (cf. Bandle, 231–32, on the fem. dat. sg. ending *-u*).

[96] The manuscript writes *ofrsyniv*; *óforsyniu* is the archaic form of *ófyrirsyniu* (cf. ÁBM, 686). Given the fact that Björn Þorleifsson occasionally uses an existing Icelandic word but in the meaning of a similar word in MLG, it is possible that his source had *unvorsêndes* 'unintentionally', 'accidentally', 'suddenly', and that this is the meaning he meant to transmit with the word *oforsyniu* 'out of the blue', 'for no reason at all'. The MLG word *unvorsêndes* makes more sense here; there is, however, no corresponding passage in the *Pass.*

[97] *allt á meðan* is not idiomatic Icelandic; *allt* is used here presumably just as *al-/all-* in MLG, that is, as an intensifier; see *NT*, 145, for the use of *á meðan* to convey German *sintemal* and *dieweil*.

[98] The manuscript writes *því* following *kónginum*, but this makes no sense and the word has been deleted.

gets up and seeks advice from his counselors as to what he should do with the merchants who had come there and were wearing Christian emblems on their clothes. He did remark, though, that he thought it evil to kill them without cause when he himself had earlier granted them peace and safety. And should it be that they obtained for him some precious treasures that he yearned to have, then he would accept that and then let them go wherever they wanted. All of his counselors thought this was the best plan. Thereupon he has a large entourage called together and he goes down to the sea to meet King Oswald. And as soon as they meet, Oswald invites the king into his tent, but the king is slow to accept. At this moment a large stag runs past the opening of the tent. And as soon as King Gaudon sees the stag, the king's heart at once pounds wildly with the anguish of greed and he says that he wants nothing other than to possess the animal, and he asks Oswald whether he has brought this large animal along. He says that this is so.

"I must have this beautiful animal," says the king.

"That may well be," says Oswald, "but it has escaped us accidentally, and I think that it will be skittish if we try to take it."

Gaudon says that he does not care. But suddenly while they are speaking, the stag leaps back and forth before them and frolics. And the king likes the animal all the more and he asks for his horse and javelin. Moreover, Gaudon calls upon all his men and tells them to accompany him and to catch the animal so that it won't get away. But when the animal sees this and senses the king's intent and that of his men, it rapidly takes off, with the king and his companions in pursuit. Now and then the animal stops as though just then it wanted to let itself be taken,

að komast varla þeir í augsýn við það. En kóngur og hans menn keppast því meir að elta það og vilja komast yfir það því heldur, og líður so marga daga í samt að þar sem þeir skiljast við dýrið um kveldið, þar finna þeir það aftur um morgnana. Þetta þykir kóngi og hans fylgjörum undrum gegna en gá þó aldri sín til þess að snúa aftur.

9. Nú er og nokkuð frá því að segja hvað sem kóngsdóttur[99] hefst að,[100] að hún er í herbergjum sínum heima að borginni. Og áður en kóngur faðir hennar fór heiman, þá hafði hann látið læsa aftur dyrnar er hún var fyrir innan með sterkum járnfestum, so að enginn skyldi mega komast inn til hennar á meðan hann væri í burtu og so hún samaleiðis eigi heldur út komast. Og þar hjá henni voru fjórar meyjar er henni skyldi skemmta og stytta fyrir tíma meðan faðir hennar væri úti. En þegar að hún vissi að faðir hennar var heiman farinn, þá gengur hún og meyjar hennar upp í hæstu vígskörð á múrnum og fær að sjá hvar sem einn mikill hjörtur leikur sér niður á grundinni hjá kóngunum er þeir talast við.

Þá kallar hún á meyjarnar og segir til þeirra: "Kærar[101] systur, sjáið þetta ið fagra dýrið, hversu það skemmtir sér. Viljum vær búa oss út og sjá gjör þenna hlut, þvíað mig fýsir til þess mjög."

Þær svara: "Vær viljum gjarnan gjöra það þér viljið oss bjóða, og þess viljum vær yður biðja, hvað sem viljið fremja, þá látið þér oss ekki við yður skilja."

Hún kvað so vera skyldu. Síðan klæða þær sig <í> karlmanns klæði allar og þar með býður hún þeim að taka með sér sína kórónu, er faðir hennar hafði gefið henni, og so þeirra klæði og aðrar dýrlegar klénodía[102] er í hennar varðveislu voru geymdar, so miklar sem þær mætti bera. Þær gjöra nú so. Eftir það gjörir hún so ráð fyrir að þær skulu fara annan veg en vant er að ganga. Þær segja so gjöra skulu og fara af stað. En þá sem þær komu að dyrunum, er þá allt annars[103] en þær vildu og ætluðu, þvíað dyrnar voru læstar fyrir utan með sterkum járnviðjum.

Þetta þótti kóngsdóttur mikið og mælti fyrir munn<i> sér: "Þú guð allra guða, sem kristnir trúa á og skapað hefur himin og jörð, sýn þú mér nú þína miskunn og gef mér og mínum systrum er hér standa að vær mættum fá heilaga

---

[99] Thus the manuscript. On the vacillating declension of *dóttir* (*faðir, móðir*) in the singular at this time, see Bandle (263–70), who writes: "Einerseits endet der Nom oft auf -*ur*, andererseits ist -*ir* aus dem Nom in den GenDatAkk eingedrungen" (265).

[100] *hvað—hefst að*: This is not idiomatic Icelandic and was probably generated by MLG *sik hebben* 'behave', 'comport', or 'conduct oneself', which also has the form *heffen*, e.g., *heft zik, zyk . . . hefft* (*MNW*, 2:263).

[101] Corrected from *kæri* (Ms.: *kære*). Bandle notes a similar occurrence of the ending -*i* in the nom. sg. fem. and the nom. pl. in the *Guðsbrandsbiblía*; see 313.

[102] The corresponding passage in the *Pass.* reads: "ok andere clenode" (C.iiii.a).

[103] This is a Germanism, presumably generated by MLG *anders* 'different' 'otherwise'; cf. *vel anderst* (*MNW*, 1:82).

but now and then it darts off so that they hardly keep sight of it. And the king and his men vie all the more in chasing it and want to catch it all the more. And many days pass in this manner: where they lose the animal in the evening, there they meet up with it again the next morning. The king and his companions think this is strange, but they do not at all care to turn back.

9. Now it is time to say something about what the princess was doing in her chamber back at the castle. Just before the king, her father, left the castle, he had the door to her rooms locked with strong iron locks so that no one might be able to get in to her while he was away and similarly so that she would not be able to get out either. There were four maidens with her who were to entertain and amuse her while her father was gone. But as soon as she found out that her father had left, she goes with her maidens onto the highest ramparts on the wall and catches sight of a large stag frolicking down below near the kings as they are talking.

She then calls to the maidens and says to them: "Dear sisters, look at this handsome animal, how it is enjoying itself. Let's get ready to go out and take a good look at this, for I very much want to do this."

They answer: "We'll gladly do what you want to bid us, but we want to ask this of you: no matter what happens, do not let us be parted from you."

She said that this would be so. All of them then dress in men's clothing, and she tells them to take along her crown which her father had given her and also their clothes and other precious objects which were in her keeping, as many as they could carry. They now do so. After that she decides that they should go a different way than they are wont to go. They say that they would do this and they leave. But when they came to the door things turn out to be very different from what they wanted and had intended, for the door was locked from the outside with strong iron bands.

The princess was upset at this and spoke to herself: "You God of all gods, in whom Christians believe and who has created heaven and earth, show me your mercy now and grant me and my sisters who are standing here that we will be

skírn í þínu nafni og að ég óhindruð megi komast á vald Ósvalds kóngs, þíns þénara og míns unnasta."

Og slóg[104] með hendinni á hurðina. En af guðs krafti spratt hurðin upp á gátt en járnfestirnar allar í sundur.

Þær urðu yfirmáta glaðar og sögðu sem með einum munni: "Lofaður sé guð himnanna og kristinna manna, þvíað það sjáum vær nú að hann er bæði mikill og máttugur, og þetta mætti[105] aldregi Mahomet vor guð gjöra."

Síðan gengu þær að öllu óhindraðar allt þar til að þær komu til tjaldbúðar Ósvalds kóngs. Stóð hann upp í móti kóngsdóttur og fagnaði henni með allri blíðu. Verður nú bæði kóngur og allt hans föruneyti glaðir við þetta og lofa guð og hans blessaða móður jungfrú Maríu.

Og er kóngur hafði setið nokkra[106] stund, kallar hann og segir: "Góðir herrar, ef þér viljið sem ég, þá vil ég héðan fara, þvíað það er nú mér hér í hendi er ég gjörða mína reisu til hingað til landa."

Allir segjast vilja so gjöra sem hans vilji sé helst til.

"Flytjum þá til skipa," segir kóngur, "nema tjöldin. Þau skulu kyr standa og lengst bíða." Og so er gjört. En þegar að kóngur og hans föruneyti eru reiðubúnir, þá vinda þeir upp akkeri sín og segl og sigla til hafs og gaf þeim vel í nokkura daga.

10. Nú er þar enn fyrst til að taka er fyrri var í frá horfið, að Gaudon kóngur hefur farið um skóga og merkur stórar til að veiða hjörtinn sem fyrr var frá sagt, en var hirtinum og hans fylgjarar eftir á að jafnnærri og áður. Af þessu angraði Gaudon og sneri þá aftur með so búið. En sem hann kom heim, batnaði honum ekki að heldur fyrir brjósti, nema nú lá honum við nálega að hamast og ganga af vitinu er hann fékk vita að dóttir hans var í burtu. Eftir það lætur hann boða til sín öllum sínum vinum og mektarhöfðingjum og lætur so vera með þeim orðum að þeir sé komnir innan fimmtar með so mikla mekt sem hver gæti af stað komið.[107] Og sem þessir eru til samans komnir allir, fóru þeir þá eftir Ósvaldi kóngi og fundu hann undir einni ey. Gaudon kóngur gengur á land upp með allt sitt fólk, en það var so margt að hann hafði þrjá fyrir einn er Ósvaldur kóngur hafði. En þegar að Gaudon kemur nokkuð langt upp á eyna, sér hann hvar Ósvaldur situr og dóttir sín[108] hjá honum.

---

[104] On the addition of -g after -ó- in the preterite, 3rd sg., which also occurs in the *Guðbrandsbiblía*, see Bandle, 135.

[105] Corrected from the manuscript, which uses the indicative form *mátti* (*matte*).

[106] The syncopated form of *nokkur* in the sg. fem. is consistent with usage in the *Guðbrandsbiblía*; see Bandle, 369.

[107] *af stað komið*: this is not idiomatic Icelandic. See n. 34.

[108] *sín*: the reference is not to Oswald but to Gaudon.

able to receive holy baptism in your name and that I can reach unhindered the protection of King Oswald, your servant and my beloved."

And she struck the door with her hand. And by God's power the door sprang open and the iron locks asunder.

They became exceedingly glad and said as with one voice: "Praised be the God of heaven and of Christians, for we now see that he is both great and mighty, and Mohammed our god would never be able to do this."

Then they walked totally unhindered all the way until they came to the tent of King Oswald. He stood up to meet the princess and greeted her with great amiability. Both the king and his companions now rejoice at this and praise God and His blessed mother, the Virgin Mary.

And when the king had tarried for a while, he speaks out and says: "Good lords, if you agree with me, then I want to set sail, for I have now obtained here what I undertook my expedition abroad for."

All say that they want to do whatever he wants to do most.

"Let's board the ships then," says the king, "but without the tents. They are to stay and remain for a long time." And so it was done. And as soon as the king and his companions are ready, they weigh anchor and hoist the sails and head out to sea, and they had a good wind for a number of days.

10. Now it's time to return again to where we left off before, when King Gaudon went into the woods and great forests to hunt the stag, as was told before, and the stag and its pursuers were still as close to each other as before. Gaudon was annoyed at this and turned back at this point. And when he got home his spirits did not improve, for now he nearly went berserk and lost his mind when he found out that his daughter was gone. Thereupon he orders all his friends and mighty chieftains to come to him and says in so many words that they should arrive within five days with as great a force as each could assemble. And when all of them have come together, they pursued King Oswald and came upon him anchored off an island. King Gaudon goes on land with all his people and this was such a large force that he had three for every man King Oswald had. And as soon as Gaudon comes some way up on the island, he sees Oswald sitting there and his daughter beside him.

Verður hann ákaflega reiður og kallar sem hann má á Ósvald kóng með þessum orðum: "Þú hinn ótrúasti óvinur! Þú og þínir fylgjarar hafa tekið mína dóttir í burtu með flærð og undirhyggju, og fyrir þann skuld verði þér að þola dauða."

Þá svarar Ósvaldur: "Ef ekki á betra í efni[109] <að> verða, þá er mér það ekki á móti þó að láti líf mitt fyrir minn skapara og heilag<r>a<r> trú[110] skyld[111] og er þér það ið besta ráð, Gaudon, að þú takir heilaga trú og trúir á sannan guð."

Þá reiddist Gaudon og tókst þá með þeim mikil orrusta og mannfall á beggja síður, og með það síðasta þá missti Gaudon sitt lið so mjög að hann varð yfirunninn og Ósvaldur mátti láta við hann gjöra sem hann vildi, og mælti síðan til Gaudons:

"Nú er so komið fyrir þér, Gaudon, að ég vil að þú látir þig skíra í nafni Jesu Christi ellegar skaltu deyja."

Gaudon svarar og sagðist aldri skyldi sig láta skíra nema Ósvaldur kóngur þiggi það af sínum guði so hann megi sjálfur sjá hans magt, að hann gæfi öllu sínu fólki aftur líf.

Þá svarar Ósvaldur: "Sannlega er mínum guði þetta engin þraut," og féll síðan til jarðar og bað guð af öllu hjarta að hann skyldi sýna þeim sína miskunn og gefa þeim hvorttveggjum aftur þeirra líf, bæði sínum mönnum og so þeim er fallið hafði fyrir þeirra vopnum so að hans dýrð yrði að meiri. En því bað sankti Ósvaldur um sína menn að honum kom í hug að Gaudon mundi ekki vera so trúr sem vera skyldi og fram kom sem brátt má heyra.

Þvíað jafnsnart sem guð hafði heyrt ákall Ósvalds kóngs og fólkið reis upp aftur af dauða sem fallið hafði, þá varð Gaudon þegar að öngu betri en fyrri og slóg[112] þá enn í bardaga bæði so mikinn og ákaflegan að með guðs fulltingi þá á lítilli stundu hrundi so mjög niður gjörsamlega allt fólk það sem farið hafði með Gaudoni kóngi so að fátt eitt var eftir.

Þá mælti Ósvaldur kóngur til Gaudons: "Tak þú enn Gaudon við heilagri trú, og trú á sannan guð ellegar skal ég láta deyða þig."

Þá svarar Gaudon: "Það máttu nú gjöra ef þú vilt, en af trú minni geng ég ekki nema guð þinn sé so kraftauðigur að hann láti þann harða steininn er þar liggur gefa[113] vatn af sér so að ég sjái það."

---

[109] Corrected from the manuscript which has *aa betre efne*.

[110] Björn Þorleifsson uses both *trú* (gen. *trúar*) and *trúa* (gen. *trú*); previously he wrote "fyrir skuld heilagrar trúar," that is, with the gen. of *trú*, but here, and once subsequently, he uses the gen. of *trúa*, that is, *trú*. See Bandle, 251–52, on the use of the two forms of the noun in the *Guðbrandsbiblía*.

[111] *fyrir. . . skyld* is not idiomatic Icelandic, but a Germanism; see *skuld, NT*, 357, and *skyld, NT*, 358, with an example of the latter: "fyrer truarinnar skylld." Cf. MLG syntax in "von enes mannes sculden" or "dit is dusser wive schult" (*MNW*, 4:149).

[112] On the addition of *-g* after *-ó-* in the preterite, 3rd sg., see n. 104.

[113] The manuscript has *giefi*.

He gets extremely angry and shouts at King Oswald as loudly as he can with these words: "You most untrustworthy fiend! You and your followers have abducted my daughter with deception and trickery, and for that reason you will have to suffer death."

Then Oswald answers: "If things are not going to turn out better, then I am not against losing my life for my Creator and for the sake of the holy faith, and it would be best for you, Gaudon, to decide to accept the holy faith and to believe in the true God."

Gaudon then got angry and a great battle between them began and men fell on both sides and in the end Gaudon lost so many of his men that he was overcome and Oswald could do with him whatever he wanted, and he then spoke to Gaudon: ·

"It has now come to this, Gaudon, that I want you to let yourself be baptized in the name of Jesus Christ or else you are going to die."

Gaudon answers and said that he would never let himself be baptized unless King Oswald obtains from his God that Gaudon himself is able to see His power by restoring all his people to life.

Then Oswald answers: "Truly this is no great feat for my God," and he then fell to the ground and asked God with all his heart to show them His mercy and to restore each of them to life, both his own men and also those who had fallen before their weapons, so that His glory might be all the greater. But St. Oswald asked this for his own men, since it occurred to him that Gaudon probably would not be as trustworthy as he should be, and this happened, as you will soon hear.

For as soon as God had heard King Oswald's prayer and the folk who had been slain rose again from the dead, Gaudon became no better than before and once again engaged in such a great and fierce battle that with God's assistance within a short time so many of those men who had accompanied King Gaudon were struck down altogether that but few were left.

Then King Oswald spoke to Gaudon: "Once again, Gaudon, accept the holy faith and believe in the true God or else I will have you killed."

Then Gaudon answers: "You can do that now if you want, but I am not going to abandon my faith unless your God is so powerful that he has water gush out of this hard rock that is lying there as I watch."

Ósvaldur segir: "Sannlega er mínum guði þetta ekki meira en það fyrra er hann hefur tvisvar sýnt þér, og meiri er dýrð hans og góðsemi ef hann vill sér sóma láta og birta þér slíka hluti[114] og aðra þvílíka heldur en þú ert verður til. En til þess að hans guðleg mekt verði að ljósari fyrir þeim sem áður eru blindir, þá biður ég hans háleita mildi að reiðast mér ekki þó að ég freista enn þessa." Og gekk að einum miklum steini og sté á með fæti sínum og mælti síðan: "Þú steinn," sagði hann, "gef þú vatn af þér so að allir þeir er hér standa megi sjá guðs dýrð."

En jafnsnart heyrði guð hans ákall so að steinninn varð so blautur sem leir og spratt þar út skírt vatn.

Þá svarar Gaudon: "Sannlega og án allan efa er þinn guð bæði mikill og máttugur og fyrir víst mætti[115] Mahomet[116] slíka hluti aldregi gjöra og vil ég nú að þínum ráðum fara."

Ósvaldur kóngur gladdist nú og hélt höndum til himna og lofaði guð. Síðan skírdist Gaudon og það lið sem hann hafði haft með sér og guð hafði tvisvar af dauða reist og var Gaudoni gefið annað nafn í skírninni og skyldi upp frá því heita Símon. En á þriðja degi upp frá því lét Ósvaldur kóngur skíra drottningarefni sitt og fjöldi manna er faðir hennar fékk henni til fylgdar. Eftir það fór Símon kóngur heim aftur í ríki sitt með sinn her og skildust með miklum kærleika. Gaf Símon kóngur Ósvaldi allt það hann vildi beiðast[117] og í hans ferð var.

Þegar að Símon kóngur var heim kominn segir hann drottningu sinni allt hvernin farið hafði og talaði þá fyrir henni so mikið að hún lét skírast og so síðan hverjir af öðrum so að innan átján daga varð allt fólk þar í landinu snúið til heilagrar trúar.

En Ósvaldur kóngur sigldi heim í England aftur með fögrum sigri, og hélt þegar sitt bruðhlaup er hann var heim kominn, og stóð jafnt í fjörutíu daga með

---

[114] Corrected from the manuscript, which writes *hlvta*.

[115] Corrected from the manuscript, which writes *mátti* (*matte*).

[116] The manuscript writes *Machameth*. In the *Guðbrandsbiblía* this name appears as *Machometh*; see Bandle, 286.

[117] The manuscript writes *beidizt*.

Oswald says: "Truly this is no greater thing for my God than what He has already twice shown you,[11] and His glory and goodness are greater if He deigns to manifest to you such things and others like them of which you are not worthy. But so that His divine power might become all the more manifest to those who otherwise would be blind, I ask of His great mercy not to be angry with me though I make a further test." And he went to a large rock and placed his foot on it and then spoke: "You rock," he said, "let water gush out so that all those who are standing here may see God's glory."

And God heard his prayer at once, for the rock became as soft as loam and out of it spurted pure water.

Gaudon then answers: "Truly and without a doubt your God is both great and powerful and Mohammed certainly could never do such things, and I now want to do as you say."

King Oswald rejoiced now and raised his arms to heaven and praised God. Then Gaudon was baptized[12] and all the people he had brought along and whom God had raised twice from the dead; and Gaudon was given a different name in baptism, and henceforth he was to be called Simon. And on the third day after this, King Oswald had his future queen baptized and all the people her father had given her as an entourage. After that King Simon went back to his own kingdom with his army, and they parted with great fondness. King Simon gave Oswald everything he wanted and which was appropriate.

As soon as King Simon had come home, he tells his queen all about how things had gone and he talked to her so much about it that she had herself baptized and then one after the other so that within eighteen days all the people in the country had been converted to the holy faith.

But King Oswald sailed back to England, having won this fair victory, and he celebrated his wedding when he came home, and it lasted for forty days with

---

[11] This and the subsequent reference to two miracles suggest that the text is corrupt. While one might here interpret the statement to God's manifesting his power twice as indicating that Oswald considers the resurrection of Gaudon's and his own men as two separate miracles, this is not the case, since the text subsequently clearly indicates that Gaudon's men were raised from the dead on two occasions. It is likely that the original legend had three miracles—a twofold resurrection of Gaudon's men and the miracle of the rock giving off water—but that the second resurrection got lost in transmission. Such a second miracle, however, occurs neither in the *HL/Pass.* nor the *Münchner Oswald*. (See introduction, pp. 75–77.)

[12] In *HL* and *Pass.* (C.iiii.b) we read that Oswald baptized Gaudon with the water that flowed from the stone. This may have been an original feature of the legend. In the *MO* Gaudon declares that if God lets water flow from the rock, he will let himself be baptized: "und birt dein got rain, / daz er aus dem herten stain / ainen prun lat erspringen, / do tauf ich mich innen" (vv. 3055–3058).

allri vegsemd og heimsins blíðu. Og lifðu vel, guðrækilega og hreinlega og
uppfylltu sína lífdaga með guðs kærleika.

So greinist og af Ósvaldi kóngi að hann settist aldri fyrr til síns borðs en
hann hafði áður látið mat búa fyrir mörgum hundruðum fátækum mönnum og
gaf þeim úr sínum eiginum höndum þessa ölmusu á hverjum degi.

11. So bar til á einum páskadegi er kóngur sat undir borðum og hann hafði
gjört eftir sínum vana að borða[118] fyrir mörgum þurftugum, þá komu enn aðrir
fátækir til hans og báðu hann ölmusu í guðs nafni. Þá tók kóngur diskinn er fyrir
honum stóð sjálfum og át af og bauð að brjóta hann í sundur og gefa hann eftir á
pílagrímunum sem komnir voru.

Og sagði: "Það væri ekki vel, ef minn herra Jesus Christus kæmi til mín og
léti ég hann[119] fara í burtu aftur frá mér synjandi, þó heldur komi hann til mín í
pílagríms mynd heldur en öðruvís; þvíað þá sem ég kemur til hans, þá léti hann
mig fara frá sér erindislaust og segir so: 'Ég þekki þig ekki fyrir því að þú þekktir
mig ekki á meðan að þú lifðir í heiminum.'"

En þá sem kóngur sagði þetta, þá sat undir borðinu nærri kónginum einn
heilagur biskup er Aidanus hét. Þessi biskup tók höndina á kónginum og mælti:
"Sé," sagði hann, "þessi hægri höndin er ég heldur á mun aldregi rotna, þvíað
margir menn munu bæði verða fæddir og styrktir af henni." Og so hefur það
og haldið síðan, þvíað hans hönd er enn í dag so fersk sem hún væri á lifanda
manni og er sett í eina silfurþró og búið um mjög ágætlega í sankti Péturs kirkju
á Englandi og er þar dýrkuð og margir gjöra þangað pílagríms reisur með stórum
gjöfum.

Sankti Ósvaldur hafði og látið steypa eina klukku til þess að nær sem hann
hafði nokkur málefni fyrir, þá lét hann hringja klukkunni og þó að hann færi

---

[118] The *Pass.* reads: "vnde hadde vor vele armen ghespiset" (C.iiii.b 'and had earlier
fed many poor'). The saga appears to transmit a word-for-word translation here: the in-
transitive verb *borða* is used transitively in analogy to MLG *spisen* 'to give [someone]
to eat'.

[119] The manuscript writes *að* after *hann*; it is not called for syntactically. See the par-
allel construction below: "þá léti hann mig fara."

every conceivable splendor and earthly delight. And Oswald and his wife lived a good life, piously and chastely,[13] and they ended their lives in the love of God.

It is also told that King Oswald never sat down to table before he had food prepared for many hundreds of poor people and he gave them this alms with his own hands every day.

11. Thus it happened one Easter, when the king sat at table and he had, as was his wont, first fed many poor, there came yet other poor to him and asked him for alms in God's name. The king then took the dish that stood before him and from which he himself ate and he ordered it to be broken apart and the pieces given to the pilgrims who had come.

And he said: "That would not be right if my Lord Jesus Christ came to me and I had him sent away from me, refusing him, even though he comes to me in the guise of a pilgrim rather than otherwise; for then, when I come to him, he will have me sent away with empty hands,[14] saying: 'I do not know you because you knew me not while you were living on earth'" (cf. Matthew 25:35–40).

But as the king was saying this, there sat at the table near the king a holy bishop named Aidan. This bishop took the king's arm and spoke: "See," he said, "this right arm which I am holding will never become corrupt, for many men will be both fed and supported by it."[15] And thus it has remained ever since, for his arm is still as incorrupt today as though it were on a living man and it rests in a silver shrine, which is most exquisitely ornamented, in St. Peter's church in England[16] and it is venerated there and many go on pilgrimage there with great gifts.

St. Oswald also had a bell cast so that when he had some business to discuss, he had the bell rung, and even when he traveled somewhere he always had the

---

[13] The word *hreinlega* can mean either "free from sin" or "free from sexual intercourse." I choose to translate the word with "chastely," since the narrator notes in chap. 13 that some books assert that Oswald never knew woman and that this makes sense, for there is no evidence that he had children. Regarding chaste marriage, see L. M. Weber, "Keuschheit," in *LTK*, 6:133–36.

[14] Literally: without having accomplished my mission.

[15] The entire episode derives from Bede, *HE* 3.6.

[16] According to Bede, the church was in the city named after Queen Bebba, that is, Bebbanburg or Bamburgh: "Denique in urbe regia, quae a regina quondam uocabulo Bebba cognominatur, loculo inclusae argenteo in ecclesia sancti Petri seruantur, ac digno a cunctis honore uenerantur" ('They are in fact preserved in a silver shrine in St. Peter's church, in the royal city which is called after Queen Bebba (Bamburgh), and are venerated with fitting respect by all' [3.6]).

nokkurs staðar þá lét hann flytja klukkuna ætíð með sér. So hafði hann og þá siðvenju að nær hvorutveggju[120] áttu[121] sín mál fyrir honum að kæra, ríkir og fátækir, þá lét hann ávallt hina fátæka fyrir ganga.

So finnst og skrifað að sankti Osvald[122] hafði alltjafnt stríð við þrjá konunga fyrir heilagrar trú skuld. Hinn fyrsti var einn kóngur af því ríki er heitir Forheiði; annar var kóngurinn af Britanniam[123]; þriðji var kóngurinn af því ríki sem Mericien[124] heitir og sá var þeirra þriggja mektugastur. Þessir gjörðu mikil tjón

---

[120] The manuscript writes *hvorvtheggiv*. On this form, with the first element unin-flected and the second -*tveggju* in all cases in the plural, see Bandle, 376.

[121] The manuscript writes *atte*.

[122] The manuscript combines here the Icelandic form *sankti* with the German form of the name. The *Pass*. writes: "Sunte Oswald moste stedes strijden mit dren konningen vmme den cristen louen" (C.iiii.c).

[123] The manuscript writes *Brithaniam*. Here and subsequently, with one exception, which we note, the name is rendered in what appears to be a Latin accusative. Unlike the proper name *Osvaldus*, the place name is not declined in the manuscript.

[124] The manuscript writes *Mericienn*. The Low German form in the *Pass*. is *Mericien*.

bell taken along.[17] He also had the habit that when two people had a case to plead before him, rich and poor, he always let the poor go first.

It is also written that there was constant strife between St. Oswald and three kings for the sake of the holy faith. The first was a king from the kingdom called Forheiði;[18] the other was the king of Britannia; the third was king from the kingdom called Mercia, and he was the most powerful of the three.[19] These kings

---

[17] The Icelandic passage is incomplete; presumably the Low German source was defective. According to *Pass.*, St. Oswald "leet ene clokken gheten den armen luden wen se vor em wolden. Vnde wen he de clokken horde luden. So richtede he tohant" (C.iiii.b). The point is that any poor people who wished to receive justice from the king could ring this bell, and Oswald would immediately turn his attention to them. The passage continues to report that the rich were not allowed to ring this bell (this piece of information is missing in *Pass.* but transmitted in *HL*) because St. Oswald gave judgment for the poor before he turned to the rich. And *Pass./HL* adds that rulers today don't do this, since they give preference to those who can further them, that is, the rich ("det nu lyder de vorsten nicht endoen. wente se richten eer den. dar se af ghebetert moghen werden" [C.iiii.c]).

[18] *Pass.* identifies the kings as follows: "De erste was de konnink van Vorhey. De ander van Britania. De drudde was von Mericien" (C.iiii.c). Accordingly, the first king in the Icelandic text should have been from Forey. The source of *Ósvalds saga* either had run the name *Vorhey* together with the following article *de* to generate *Vorheyde*, or else the Icelandic translator had read the two words as one.

[19] The first king cannot be identified, but the other two are Cædwalla and Penda. Bede writes: "Quo tempore maxima est facta strages in ecclesia uel gente Nordanhymbrorum, maxime quod unus ex ducibus, a quibus acta est, paganus, alter quia barbarus erat pagano saeuior. Siquidem Penda cum omni Merciorum gente idolis deditus et Christiani erat nominis ignarus; at uero Caedualla, quamuis nomen et professionem haberet Christiani, adeo tamen erat animo ac moribus barbarus, ut ne sexui quidem muliebri uel innocuae paruulorum parceret aetati, quin uniuersos atrocitate ferina morti per tormenta contraderet, multo tempore totas eorum prouincias debachando peruagatus, ac totum genus Anglorum Brittaniae finibus erasurum se esse deliberans" ('At this time there was a great slaughter both of the Church and of the people of Northumbria, one of the perpetrators being a heathen and the other a barbarian who was even more cruel than the heathen. Now Penda and the whole Mercian race were idolaters and ignorant of the name of Christ; but Cædwalla, although a Christian by name and profession, was nevertheless a barbarian in heart and disposition and spared neither women nor innocent children. With bestial cruelty he put all to death by torture and for a long time raged through all their land, meaning to wipe out the whole English nation from the land of Britain' [*HE* 2.20]). The information transmitted in the saga, however, and also *HL/Pass.*, is incorrect, for Oswald did not encounter Cædwalla in this, his final battle, but in an earlier battle, after the death of his brother Eanfrith, when Cædwalla was slain: "superueniente cum paruo exercitu, sed fide Christi munito, infandus Brettonum dux cum inmensis illis copiis, quibus nihil resistere posse iactabat, interemtus est in loco, qui lingua Anglorum Denisesburna, id est Riuus Denisi, uocatur" ('Oswald came with an army, small in numbers but strengthened by their faith in Christ, and destroyed the abominable leader of the Britons together with the immense force which he boasted was irresistible, at a place which is called in the English tongue *Denisesburn*, that is the brook of the *Denise*' [3.1]).

og forþrot og varð að þola stórt ómak bæði hann sjálfur og hans góðir menn til að frelsa sitt ríki fyrir þeirra ásóknum. En hversu mikla veraldlega sorg og áhyggju er hann hafði, þá þjónaði hann ætíð samt með allri góðfýsi og lítillæti sínum blessaða skapara með föstum og vökum, með bænahaldi og mildum ölmusum, og fyrir það var guð drottinn alltíð með honum. Og þá sem þessi styrjöld og grimmur ófriður hafði þann veg nokkura stund so verið að fyrirgreindir kóngar gjörðu áhlaup stór inn í England, ræntu og tóku allt það er þeir gátu náð, þá með þessu vildu þeir sakir þeirra illsku þó ekki láta sér þetta nægja, heldur safna þeir til samans ógrynni liðs með illþýði það versta er þeir mega og með þetta lið fara þeir inn í England og gjöra sankti Ósvaldi þau boð að koma til móts við þá með það fólk[125] er honum vilji[126] fylgja og halda opið örlög á einum[127] sléttum velli er liggur á milli Britanniam og Englands og þó nær Englandi. En vill hann það boð ekki þiggja, þá ætla þeir með herskildi og loganda eldi fara um allt England og eyða það so, en nauðga honum sjálfum að kasta heilagri trú og dýrka goð[128] þeirra. Og sem kóngur fréttir þessi boð biður hann guð af öllum hug að hann virðist til og heyra sitt ákall og vera í fylgi með sér, og sendir síðan út herör á báðar hendur og stefnir að sér öllum þeim sem á hans fund vildu koma, en fór undan með það lið er fyrst kom til hans á hendur heiðingjum.

Og um nóttina áður en stríðin átti að vera um morguninn eftir á, lá Ósvaldur kóngur alla nóttina á bænum og bífalaði sig og sína menn undir miskunn og umsjón almáttugs guðs og hans signað<rar> móður jungfrú Maríu og bað þau um að það skyldi ske sem þau vildi, og gjörði so ráð fyrir að þeir skyldi setja upp heilagt krossmark fyrir merki.

---

[125] The word is followed by og, which seems unnecessary and has been eliminated.

[126] Corrected from the manuscript, which writes vilia.

[127] Corrected from the manuscript, which writes einni.

[128] Interestingly enough, the manuscript seems to distinguish between the heathen gods and the Christian God by using only this one time goð (god in the Ms.) for the heathen gods but consistently guð (gvd in the Ms.) for the Christian God.

caused great damage and loss, and Oswald had to endure great troubles, both he himself and his good men, in order to preserve his kingdom from their attacks. But no matter how much worldly worry and anguish he had, he nevertheless served his blessed Creator at all times with great piety and humility, with fasts and vigils, in prayer and with generous alms, and for that reason the Lord God was ever with him.[20] Now when this warfare and the fierce hostilities had gone on like this for some time and the aforementioned kings continued their great assaults on England, plundering and taking all they could get their hands on, they still were not content with this on account of their malice, and so they assemble a vast force of the most depraved folk they could find and with this army they invade England and challenge St. Oswald to meet up with them with any people who wanted to accompany him and to engage in open battle on a level plain that lies between Britannia and England, yet nearer to England. But if he does not want to accept that challenge, then they intend to roam through all of England with the sword and raging flames and thus lay it waste, and they will force him to renounce the holy faith and to worship their gods. And when the king learns of this challenge, he asks God with all his heart to deign to hear his prayer and to be at his side, and he issues a call to arms all around and summons everyone who wanted to meet up with him. And he set out with the force that arrived first to wage war against the heathens.

And during the night before the morning on which the battle was to take place, King Oswald was prostrate the whole night in prayer and commended himself and his men to the mercy and providence of almighty God and His blessed mother, the Virgin Mary, and prayed that their will be done,[21] and he made provision for a sacred cross[22] to be set up as their standard.

---

[20] This is more or less a reiteration of Oswald's portrayal in the first chapter.

[21] See Bede, *HE* 3.12: "Denique ferunt, quia a tempore matutinae laudis saepius ad diem usque in orationibus persteterit, atque ob crebrum morem orandi siue gratias agendi Domino semper, ubicumque sedens, supinas super genua sua manus habere solitus sit" ('It is related, for example, that very often he would continue in prayer from matins until daybreak; and because of his frequent habit of prayer and thanksgiving, he was always accustomed, wherever he sat, to place his hands on his knees with the palms turned upwards').

[22] Bede relates (*HE* 3.2): ". . . ubi uenturus ad hanc pugnam Osuald signum sanctae crucis erexit, ac flexis genibus Deum deprecatus est, ut in tanta rerum necessitate suis cultoribus caelesti succurreret auxilio" ('. . . when he was about to engage in battle, [Oswald] set up the sign of the holy cross and, on bended knees, prayed God to send heavenly aid to His worshippers in their dire need'). In Bede this is related not about Oswald's final battle, however, but rather the battle that occurred in the place that subsequently came to be called Hefenfeld or Caelestis Campus.

En þegar um nóttina er hans lið var sofnað en hann einn vakti eftir, heyrði hann eina rödd so mælandi til sín: "Eyja, þú píslarvottur guðs og ærlegur[129] riddari Osvalde,[130] vertu ekki hryggur, heldur gleð þig,[131] þvíað þegar á morgun skaltu vera bæði sitjandi og ríkjandi með guði og hans útvöldum í himiríki og þó eigi þú einn aðeins nema líka allir þínir fylgjarar."

Af þessari röddu og fögurlegu fyrirheiti varð hann mjög glaður og lofaði guð.

12. Um morguninn snemma þegar í ár vakti kóngur allt sitt lið og taldi fyrir þeim heilaga trú og mörg önnur stórmerki drottins er hann hafði veitt og sýnt sínum ástvinum bæði fyrir hingaðburðinn og so eftir á og styrkti sitt fólk bæði með þessu og mörgu öðru.

Og mælti þá til þeirra sjálfra, so segjandi: "Heyrið þér, hinir allra sterkastir riddarar Jesu Christi; verið öruggir og styrkir í heilagri trú í þessari stríð.[132] Og stríðið mannlega á móti guðs óvinum og yðrum og fyrir það skulu þér eiga að sitja eilíft ríki með sjálfum guði og hans helgum mönnum. Hér fyrir, þér allra kærustu vinir, útréttið nú yðrar hendur og hjörtu til guðs og biðjið hann að hjálpa yður með sínum englum."

En þá sem kóngur hafði þetta mælt, þá kom ofan af himni yfir hann mikið ljós og úr því ljósinu heyrði hann rödd drottins so segjandi: "Osvalde,[133] þú verður eilíflega lifandi með mér."

Litlu eftir þetta kom á móti honum óflýjandi[134] her af ótrúöndum þjóðum og tókst þá þegar mikill bardagi og féllu af hvorumtveggjum[135] fjöldi fólks. En sakir þess að liðsmunur var ofur mikill og so þess annars að guð vildi hafa sankti Ósvald til sín í þessari reisu,[136] þá varð bæði kóngur og lið hans allt yfirunnið.

---

[129] *ærlegur* is a loan from MLG *êrlik*; see W-N, 403–4. Cf. Wolf, cxxxiv.

[130] Here, as also below in chap. 12, the name appears in the Latin vocative.

[131] *Eyja—gleð þig*: The *Pass.* writes: "Eya wes vro du merteler godes vnde tuchtighe rydder" (C.iiii.c).

[132] The gender of *stríð* vacillates. Here it seems to be construed as a feminine, but earlier in chap. 5, *í réttu stríði*, as the neuter noun one would expect.

[133] The name is here given in the Latin vocative.

[134] The manuscript has *oflyianda*, suggesting that *her* is construed as a neuter, possibly by analogy to Low German *heer*, as in the corresponding passage in the *Pass.*: "Do quam eyn groet [*corrected from* goet] heer der vnlouighen vp se" (C.iiii.c: 'Then a large army of unbelievers came upon them').

[135] On the inflection of both elements of the word, see Bandle, 376.

[136] Here the loan word *reisa* is used in its other meaning in MLG, 'time', 'occasion'; see Bandle, 344; W-N, 274–75. There is no corresponding passage in the *Pass.*

And during the night, as soon as his forces had fallen asleep, and he held vigil alone, he heard a voice speaking to him thus: "Oh, you martyr of God and honorable knight Oswald, do not be worried, rather rejoice, for already tomorrow you shall be sitting and ruling with God and His chosen in the heavenly kingdom, and not you alone but also all your followers."

On account of this voice and the beautiful promise he became very happy and praised God.

12. And early in the morning, as soon as day broke, the king awakened all his men and spoke to them of the holy faith and many other great signs the Lord had granted and shown His beloved friends both before His birth and after, and he encouraged his men both with these words and many others.

And he spoke to them, saying: "Listen, you strongest of knights of Jesus Christ, be fearless and strong in the holy faith during this battle. And fight manfully against God's enemies and yours, and in return you will enjoy eternal life with God Himself and His saints. Therefore, all you dearest of friends, extend now your hands and hearts to God and ask Him to help you together with His angels."[23]

And when the king had spoken this, a great light came down from heaven upon him and out of this light he heard the voice of the Lord, saying thus: "Oswald, you will live eternally with me."

A little after this an overwhelming host of unbelievers came against him and a great battle began at once and many were slain on either side. And because the disparity in the size of the forces was exceedingly great, but also because God wanted to take St. Oswald to Himself on this occasion, both the king and his people were completely overcome.

---

[23] Bede also includes an exhortation by Oswald, just after he has erected the cross, but this does not contain the promise of eternal life: "Flectamus omnes genua, et Deum omnipotentem, uiuum ac uerum in commune deprecemur, ut nos ab hoste superbo ac feroce sua miseratione defendat; scit enim ipse quia iusta pro salute gentis nostrae bella suscepimus" ('Let us all kneel together and pray the almighty, everliving, and true God to defend us in His mercy from the proud and fierce enemy; for He knows that we are fighting in a just cause for the preservation of our whole race' [*HE* 3.2]).

Og þá sem kóngur sá að hans fólk varð niður slegið sem annar hráviði, þá leit hann upp til himna og mælti: "Herra Jesus Christus, þú almegtugur[137] guð, tak til þín þeirra manna sálir sem hér í dag láta sitt líf fyrir þíns helga nafns skuld."

Og þegar í stað fékk hann að sjá hvar sem englar guðs komu ofan af himnum og tóku sálir hans manna jafnótt sem þeir urðu drepnir af þeirra óvinum og færðu þá[138] aftur upp með sér með miklum fagnaði og lofsöngum til eilífrar dýrðar.

Þá mælti kóngur er hann sá þetta: "Lof sé þér utan enda, drottinn minn, þvíað nú hefur ég mikinn fögnuð séð að sálir minna manna eru nú undan mér farnar til dýrðar þinnar og fyrir því er ég nú glaður til að deyja með þeim og fara úr þessum heimi og til þeirra." Síðan mælti hann: "Drottinn Jesus Christus, faðir himneskur, í þínar hendur fel ég anda minn," og gaf jafnskjótt sinn anda upp.

En guðs englar færðu sál hans með fögrum lofsöngum til eilífs fagnaðar.

Eftir það lét kóngurinn af Mericien taka hans líkama og lét höggva bæði höfuðið og báða handleggina af honum og bauð að hengja þetta hvortveggja[139] hjá almennings götu, þar sem flestir færi um, honum til háðungar.

Eftir þetta hið illa morð og manndráp sem hinu ómildu tírannir[140] höfðu framið á þessum guðs vini og hans mönnum, þá ræntu þeir og rupluðu, brenndu og niðurbrutu borgir og bæi á Englandi hvar þeir komu við og fóru eftir á í burtu aftur með það og heim til sín.

13. Einu ári eftir þetta kom einn kóngur í stað Ósvalds konungs er hét Ósvinus. Þessi kóngur lét taka sankti Ósvalds höfuð[141] og hendur og bjó um það merkilega

---

[137] W-N lists two forms deriving from MLG *almechtich*, namely *allsmektugur* and *almaktugur*. *Pass.* writes: *du almechtighe god* (C.iiii.c).

[138] The referent of the pronoun *þá* is here construed to be m. *manna* and not f. *sálir*.

[139] The manuscript writes *hvortheggia*.

[140] The word is a loan from MLG. The manuscript writes *thirranner*; in all the sixteenth-century citations, however, the word is a weak masculine, so that the nom. pl. is *tyrannar*. See W-N, 353–54, Bandle, 279.

[141] On proper names before the word governing the genitive, see *NT*, 172.

And when the king saw that his men were being mowed down like tender plants, he raised his eyes to heaven and spoke: "Lord Jesus Christ, you almighty God, take to yourself the souls of those men who lose their lives here today for the sake of your holy name."

And at once he got to see how God's angels came down from heaven and took the souls of his men the moment they were killed by their enemies and carried them back up with them to eternal glory, with much rejoicing and hymns of praise.

When the king saw this, he spoke: "Praise be to you without end, my Lord, for now I have experienced great joy, for the souls of my men have now left me for your glory, and for this reason I am now happy to die with them and to leave this earth and join them." Then he spoke: "Lord Jesus Christ, Heavenly Father, into your hands I commend my spirit" (cf. Luke 23:46), and at once he gave up his spirit.[24]

And God's angels carried his soul amidst beautiful hymns of praise to eternal joy.

After that the king of Mercia had his body taken and he had his head and both his arms cut off and ordered the head and arms hung up at the side of a busy road, where the largest number of people travel, in order to disgrace him.[25]

After this evil murder and manslaughter, which the wicked tyrants had committed against this friend of God and his men, they then plundered and raided, burned down and destroyed towns and villages in England, wherever they came, and having done so left again and went home.

13. One year after this a king named Oswy[26] succeeded King Oswald. This king had St. Oswald's head and arms taken down and properly looked after and he

---

[24] Bede has only a general observation concerning Oswald's last words: "Vulgatum est autem, in consuetudinem prouuerbii uersum, quod etiam inter uerba orationis uitam finierit; namque cum armis et hostibus circumseptus iamiamque uideret se esse perimendum, orauit pro animabus exercitus sui. Vnde dicunt in prouerbio: 'Deus miserere animabus, dixit Osuald cadens in terram'" ('It is also a tradition which has become proverbial, that he died with a prayer on his lips. When he was beset by the weapons of his enemies and saw that he was about to perish he prayed for the souls of his army. So the proverb runs, "may God have mercy on their souls, as Oswald said when he fell to the earth"' [*HE* 3.12]).

[25] Bede writes: "Porro caput et manus cum brachiis a corpore praecisas iussit rex, qui occiderat, in stipitibus suspendi" ('The king who slew him ordered his head and hands to be severed from his body and hung on stakes' [*HE* 3.12]).

[26] Oswy was Oswald's brother and ruled Northumbria from 642 to 670. See H. Vollrath, "Oswiu," in *LMA*, 6:1552.

og bauð að láta grafa með allri verðugheit[142] og so var gjört. Og guð almáttugur gjörði þar bæði margar og stórar jarteiknir fyrir síns vinar skuld, sankti Osvaldo.[143] Og enn í dag er so, að hverjir sem sækja til hans grafar og biðja hann hjálpar með réttu ákalli, hvort sem er heldur um góðs eður æru[144] eða hvað annað er menn biðja hann fulltings um, þá verður þeim það þar veitt af guði.

So finnst og í sumlegum historíum[145] af sankti Osvaldo[146] að hafi aldregi þýðst neina kvinnu utan haldið hreinlífi alla sína daga—og kemur þetta þá og vel til saman þvíað hvergi finnst það að hann hafi átt nokku<r>t barn—og so það að hann hafði fallið í stríði jafnt og hér segir.

Eftir mörgum árum frá því að sankti Ósvaldur var sleginn, þá vildi einn riddari ríða inn í Britanniam og sem hann upp kom á fjallið er sanctus Osvaldus var sleginn, þá fékk hestur hans mikla sótt so að riddarinn þenkti[147] að hann mundi sér aldrei meir að gagni verða og lagði sig niður til svefns. En áður hann sofnaði, hugsaði hann sig um hvort hann mundi ekki mega reka hann undan sér og stóð upp og gekk að hestinum og vildi koma honum á fætur, en hesturinn sneri sér á ýmsar síðurnar og leit um sig alls staðar en á fætur kom hann honum ekki, og af slíku angrast mjög riddarinn þvíað hann ætlar ekki annað en hesturinn muni endalega deyja fyrir sér, og leggur sig niður aftur og sofnar litla hríð, og er herrann vaknar sér hann að hesturinn veltur sér og er nokkuð so langt í burtu frá honum. Var hesturinn þá þar að kominn sem sankti Ósvaldur var sleginn. Þá hvíldi hesturinn sig. En þá minnst varaði þá stökk hesturinn upp og tók að bíta gras og innan litillar stundar þaðan í frá varð hann alheill. Þá varð riddarinn glaður og þakkaði guði og fékk að skilja af íblæstri ins helga anda að þar mundi einhver heilagur maður

---

[142] The word, written *verdogheit* in the manuscript, is a loan from MLG *werdicheit* 'in a worthy, reverend manner', 'festivity', 'pomp', 'ceremony' (*MNW*, 5:676; W-N does not list the word). The *Pass.*, which does not have the corresponding word here, writes: "vnde begroeff se erliken" (C.iiii.d). In the account of the translation of St. Oswald's relics, however, the *Pass.* states: "do bestedigheden se dat hyllichdom in dat munster mit groter werdicheit" (C.v.b). This is the last sentence in the account that corresponds to chap. 15 of the saga, which does not, however, transmit it.

[143] The manuscript writes *Sancte Avsvaldo*; this is another instance of the undeclinable Icelandic adjective *sankti* used with the Latin form of the name; this is in the dat., but one would expect it to be in the gen. to agree with "síns vinar."

[144] The word *æra* is a loan from MLG *êre*. Cf. W-N, 402–3; Wolf, cxxxiv. The expression "um góðs eður æru" replicates "vmme guet edder ere" in *Pass.* (C.iiii.d).

[145] *historía* is a loan from Latin *historia* via German *historie*. The Icelandic is a direct translation of *Pass.* "Ok vint men in etliken hystorien van sunte Oswalde" (C.iiii.d). See W-N, 157; Bandle, 273; Wolf, cxxii..

[146] The manuscript combines the Icelandic indeclinable adjective *sankti* with the dat. of the Latin form of the name *Osvaldus*.

[147] The manuscript writes *þeingtte*.

ordered them to be buried with all reverence, and this was done.[27] And almighty God worked there many and great miracles for the sake of His friend St. Oswald. And even to this day it still happens that anyone who seeks out his grave and asks for his help with righteous prayer, whether this be for goods or honor or whatever else people seek his help for, it is granted to them there by God.

One also reads in some accounts about St. Oswald that he never knew woman but that he preserved his virginity his entire life—and this also makes sense, for nowhere does it say that he had had a child[28]—and that he fell in battle, just as is told here.

Many years after St. Oswald had been slain, a knight wanted to ride to Britannia, and when he came up on the mountain where St. Oswald had been slain, his horse became very ill so that the knight thought it would never again be of use to him, and he lay down to sleep. But before he fell asleep, he wondered whether he might not possibly get it to move, and he got up and went to the horse and wanted to get it on its legs, but the horse rolled from side to side and looked all around, but he did not manage to get it on its feet, and because of this the knight is very upset, for he expects nothing but that the horse would die in the end, and he lies down again and falls asleep for a short time, and when the lord wakes up, he sees that the horse is rolling around and is quite far away from him. The horse had then reached the spot where St. Oswald was slain. Then the horse rested. But when it was least expected, the horse leaped to its feet and began to graze and within a short time it was completely healed. The knight rejoiced then and thanked God and realized through the inspiration of the Holy Spirit that a holy

---

[27]Bede writes: "Quo post annum deueniens cum exercitu successor regni eius Osuiu abstulit ea, et caput quidem in cymiterio Lindisfarnensis ecclesiae, in regia uero ciuitate manus cum brachiis condidit" ('A year afterwards, his successor Oswiu came thither with an army and took them away. He buried the head in a burial place in the church at Lindisfarne, but the hands and arms he buried in the royal city of Bamborough' [*HE* 3.12]).

[28]Bede informs us that he had a son named Oidiluald (Oethelwald) (*HE* 3.23; 3.24).

vera jarðaður og gjörði þar eitt glöggt mark hvar þetta var, þvíað hann var einn vísmann[148] og reið síðan til herbergis nær einum ríkum manni.

Þessi herbergisbóndinn átti sér eina dóttur sem hafði lengi legið í stórum krankleika.[149] Og sem riddarinn bæði heyrði þetta og so leit píkunnar[150] meinlæti, þá mælti hann til húsbóndans í húsinu og sagði honum hverninn að hestur sinn hafði farið bæði með það fyrsta og allt þar til er hann varð heill aftur. Þá bað bóndinn riddarann að hann vildi ríða þangað er það var að hestur hans varð heill. Það gjörir hann og höfðu jungfrúna með sér þangað. En þegar að þau voru komin í þann stað er hesturinn stökk upp þá lagði meyjan sig niður en hún sofnaði jafnskjótt. Og þegar að hún vaknaði, var hún orðin alheil af öllu sínu meini. Þökkuðu þau öll almáttugum guði og þeim guðs vini er þar hefði verið jarðaður, og fóru heim aftur síðan. Leitaðist þessi riddarinn þá eftir hver að þar mundi vera grafinn. En um síðir verður honum sagt að Ósvaldur kóngur hefði þar fallið í stríði. Þessa jarteikn segir hann öllum hvar hann fór og samaleiðis bóndinn er píkuna átti, og upp frá því gjörðist þangað mikil sókn af ýmsum löndum af krönkum[151] mönnum og fengu þeir allir bót sinna meina er þangað sóktu fyrir verðleik og árnaðarorð heilags Ósvalds kóngs.

14. Í einn tíma fóru nokkurir[152] menn af Britanniam[153] til þessa sama staðar er sankti Ósvaldur var grafinn og var þá þar að sjá mörg undarleg grös er hvergi þar í landi fundust slík með ýmsum litum. Þá var í ferðinni með þessum mönnum einn hygginn mann.

---

[148] The manuscript writes *vissmann*. Although the word *víss* with the meaning of 'wise' exists in Icelandic, in this case it may be a direct transfer into Icelandic of MLG *wîs man*. The corresponding passage in the *Passionael* reads: "wente he was ghans wijsz." Cf. n. 4.

[149] The noun *krankleiki* is formed from the adjective *krankur*, a loan from MLG. In the *Guðbrandsbiblía* the word has two forms, strong and weak, in the nominative, *krankleikur* and *krankleiki*. See Bandle, 198; Wolf, cxxiv.

[150] *píka* is a loan in Icelandic from the other Scandinavian languages but deriving ultimately from Finnish *piika*; cf. W-N, 256; Bandle, 273; Wolf, cxxviii.

[151] The word *krankur* is a loan from MLG *krank*. See W-N, 190; Bandle, 318; Wolf, cxxiv. The corresponding passage in the *Pass.* reads: "Darna quemen vele kranke mynschen in de stede" (C.v.a).

[152] On the unsyncopated nom. pl. masc., see Bandle, 369.

[153] The name has been normalized; the manuscript writes *Brithani*. The *Pass.* writes *Britania* (C.v.a).

person must be buried there and he made a distinct sign where this was, for he was a wise man, and he then rode off to take lodging with a rich man.

This master of the house had a daughter who had long suffered from a serious illness. And when the knight heard about this and saw the suffering of the girl, he spoke to his host[29] and told him what had happened with his horse, from the very beginning and all the way up to the point when it was cured. The host then asked the knight whether he would ride with him to the place where his horse was cured. He does so and they take the maiden along. And as soon as they had come to that place where the horse leaped to its feet, the maiden lay down and fell asleep immediately. And as soon as she woke up, she was completely cured of all her ills.[30] They all thanked almighty God and God's friend who was buried there and then they went home. The knight then tried to find out who was buried there. And at last he was told that King Oswald had fallen there in battle. He told everyone about this miracle wherever he went, and likewise the host who had the daughter, and from then on the place was much sought out by sick people from many lands and all who went there were cured of their ills on account of the holiness and intercession of the holy king Oswald.

14. One time some people went from Britannia to the same place where St. Oswald was buried and one could see there many strange plants which could not be found anywhere else in the country in such colors. Along on the journey with these men there was a wise man.

---

[29] In the course of time the tale got somewhat modified. Bede has the man go to an inn (*hospitium*) where the sick girl is the "niece of the patron" ('neptem patris familias' [*HE* 3.9]).

[30]The two miracles recounted here, the cure of the horse and of the ill maiden, are placed by Bede, just as here, immediately after Oswald's death (cf. *HE* 3.9).

Hann mælti: "Hvað mun því valda að þetta platz[154] er vær erum á er miklu grænna og að öllu fegra[155] en önnur jörð hér í nánd. Og sannlega trúi ég að það megi ekki annars vera nema hér hafi annaðhvort verið grafinn einhver heilagur maður eða í hel sleginn. Og fyrir víst skal ég héðan ekki fyrri fara en ég hafi reynt hvort hér er nokkur grafinn eða eigi."

Þessu verða þeir allir samþykkir. Síðan taka þeir til og grafa og finna þeir þar bein og frábærilegan ilm kenna þeir fyrir þeirra[156] nösum, so að þeir þykjast aldregi fyrr hafa kennt jafn unaðsamlegan sem þennan.

Síðan taka þeir nokkuð af beinunum og leggja í einn hreinan líndúk og búa um virkulega og sögðu sín á milli: "Þessi bein skulum vær hafa með oss alltjafnt til þess að lækna með sjúka menn hvar vær komum."

Þetta gjöra þeir og tekur sá til sín beinin að geyma sem fyrst tók til máls að grafa til þeirra. Síðan fara þeir leiðar sinnar og koma fram í einn stað. Þar var haldin mikil veisla. Þangað fara þeir og er þar fyrir mikill fjöldi fólks og voru að eta og drekka. Þessir buðu til komumönnum að eta með sér og drekka. Þeir þiggja það og er gjört við þá allt hið besta. En á meðan að sá var að eta og að drekka er beinin geymdi,[157] þá tók hann þau og hengdi með dúk og allri umbúð upp á vegginn hjá sér. En á meðan að þeir voru að þessu sinni iðju, þá kom eldur í það húsið er þeir sátu í og drukku so að það brann upp að ösku þvíað það var gjört af tré. Og þeir sem drukku í húsinu vissu ekki fyrri til en eldurinn gaus hátt upp yfir húsið og hljóp þá hver upp og út sem búinn var. En þá sem húsið var brunnið, þá fannst og enginn hlutur óbrunninn er í því húsi átti að vera, nema bein sankti Ósvalds konungs; þau voru öllu óspillt og óbrennd. Þá fréttu þeir eftir sem fundu, hver að þar mundi vera jarðaður. Þá sögðu landsmenn þar að einn ágætur kóngur af Englandi hefði þar verið sleginn og grafinn er Ósvaldur hét. Þá sögðu þeir þetta teikn fyrir mörgum mönnum og ótal fólks komu þangað og hvern hlut eða hvert mein að hver hafði og báðu guð og sankti Ósvald að létta sér eða bæta, þá fengu allir sína bæn.

15. Það var einn maður nokkuð so gemsfullur;[158] honum var og sagt frá þessum stað er sanctus Osvaldus var sleginn og grafinn. So var og honum sagt í

---

[154] The word is loaned from MLG *plâtze* (*plâtse*) and has entered modern Icelandic as *pláss*.

[155] The manuscript has the incorrect *fegre*.

[156] One would normally expect the possessive pronoun *sínum* here rather than the gen. of the personal pronoun.

[157] The manuscript incorrectly writes the plural *geymdv*.

[158] This word, which makes no contextual sense, cannot be correct, but neither Bede nor the *Pass.* offers assistance in reconstructing what the original word must have been. While Bede does not relate how Oswald's bones were found, the *Pass.* identifies the finder simply as "ein man" (C.v.a).

He said: "What could be the reason that this spot where we are is much greener and in every way more beautiful than other ground here in the vicinity? And I truly believe that this can't be for any other reason than that either a holy person is buried or has been slain here. And to be sure, I do not intend to leave here before I have investigated whether someone is buried here or not."

All agree to this. They then begin to dig and they find bones there and an extraordinary fragrance reaches their noses, so that they think they have never before experienced a fragrance as lovely as this.

They then take some of the bones and place them on a clean linen cloth and wrap it carefully, and they spoke among themselves: "We are going to take these bones along with us to cure sick people wherever we go."

They do so, and the one who first said that they should dig for them takes the bones for safekeeping. They then go their way and come to a certain place. A great banquet was being held there. They go there and a large crowd of people is there, and they were busy eating and drinking. They invited the newcomers to eat and drink with them. They accept the invitation and are treated in the best possible way. But while the one keeping the bones was to eat and drink, he took them and hung them in the cloth and its covering on the wall next to him. And while they were at this pastime, a fire broke out in the house where they were sitting and drinking so that it burned to ashes since it was made of wood. And the people who were drinking in the house did not realize this until the fire flamed up high over the house, and everyone jumped up and ran out just as they were. And when the house had burned down, there was not a single thing in the house that had not burned up, except for the bones of St. Oswald the king; they were completely unscathed and unburned. Then those who had found them asked who was buried there. Those who lived there then said that an excellent king of England had been slain there and buried and his name was Oswald. They then told many people about this miracle and a huge crowd came there and whatever the problem or injury that each had, when they prayed to God and St. Oswald to heal them or make them well, all their prayers were answered.[31]

15. There was a man who was somewhat of a prankster;[32] he was also told about this spot where St. Oswald was slain and buried. He was also told about the

---

[31] This chapter corresponds to Bede, *HE* 3.10, except that there the account is of only one person, a Briton, who comes upon the spot where Oswald was slain. He does not dig up Oswald's relics, however—after all, this is not where they are located— but merely removes some of the soil. This then, the soil in a bag together with the beam from which it is hanging, is not touched by the fire.

[32] The source of the Icelandic text must have been corrupt, for the word characterizing the man makes no sense in this context. The *Pass.* reading does not help, for there it simply says: "Ein man hoerde van der stede" ('a man heard about the place' [C.v.a]).

frá mörgum jarteiknum er guð léti birtast fyrir hans skyld. Þessi maðurinn tók sig upp til ferðar og kom til leiðis sankti Ósvalds á náttarþeli og hugsaði með sér: "Ég skal nú sjá þessa[159] undarlegu hluti sem hér birtast fyrir öllum er hér koma." En hans von varð honum eigi að öngu, þvíað so snart sem hann kom að leiðinu fann hann bein sankti Ósvalds liggjandi ofan á sléttri jörðunni. Þá varð hann harðla glaður og tók upp öll beinin er hann fann með ástúð og bjó um þau með allri virkt og flutti síðan með sér í Austurríki[160] og gaf þau drottningunni þar. En hún var bróðurdóttir Ósvalds konungs. En hún þakkaði honum stórlega þá gjöf og lét gjöra að dýrlega umbúð og hélt þau sem aðra helga dóma. Síðan flutti hún helga dóminn þennan úr því ríki er hún þá var í og í eitt annað land er heitir Lindissino. Í því[161] landi var eitt klaustur er drottningin hélt mikið til og so til þeirra herra er í klaustrinu þjónuðu og vildi hún því koma helgum dóminum þangað og so varð. Á sömu nóttinni er beinin voru komin í klaustur þetta og drottningin og hennar fylgjarar vildu ganga og skoða um beinin og so fyrir afláts[162] skyld, þá stóð hún snemma upp og gekk með sínu föruneyti til kirkju. En þegar birti guð henni fagra sýn, og þeim er henni fylgdu,[163] so að þeir sáu eina hvíta dúfu. Hún gjörði

---

[159] Corrected from the manuscript which has *þessi*.

[160] The text is corrupt, as is the text in the *Passionael*. According to Bede (*HE* 3.11), the Mercian Queen Osthryth, Oswald's niece, took the relics to the monastery at Bardney. At a stage prior to that of the German source of *Ósvalds saga*, and thus also the text in the *Passionael*, the name Osthryth became corrupt, presumably through an error in copying, and the name of the country (MHG *Ôsterrîche*, MLG *Osterîke*) was substituted together with an explanation for the translation of the relics from Austria to Lindissino, that is, the kingdom of Lindsey. See introduction, 88.

[161] Corrected from *þar* in the manuscript.

[162] The word *aflát* existed in Icelandic with the meaning of 'remission of sins'; here the word has a loan meaning, however, borrowed from MLG *aflât* 'indulgence', that is, remission of time spent in purgatory as punishment for sins (cf. *MNW*, 1:27; W-N, 4). One would expect the genitive form, *afláts*, but the genitive -s has presumably been dropped under the influence of initial s- of the following *skyld*.

[163] The manuscript incorrectly has the verb in the singular *fylde*.

many miracles that God let happen for his sake. This man set out on a journey and during the night he reached St. Oswald's road and thought to himself: "I am now going to see these wondrous things that are revealed to all who come here." And his hope was not in vain, for as soon as he came to the road he found the bones of St. Oswald lying on level ground. Then he became very happy and lovingly picked up all the bones that he found and wrapped them carefully and then took them with him to Austria and gave them there to the queen. And she was the daughter of King Oswald's brother.[33] And she thanked him greatly for that gift and had a precious receptacle made and kept them there as relics. Later she took these relics out of the kingdom she was in and to another country called Lindsey.[34] In this country there was a monastery that the queen was very fond of and also of the men who served in the monastery, and she wanted to take the relics there, and so it was done. During the same night that the relics were brought to this monastery, the queen and her companions wanted to go and look at the bones in order to gain an indulgence, and she got up early and went with her retinue to the church. And at once God granted her a beautiful vision and also to those who accompanied her, for they saw a white dove. Now and then it alighted on the

---

[33] The information is garbled. Oswald's niece Osthryth took the mutilated body to the monastery at Bardney (see D. W. Rollason, "Oswald," in *LMA*, 6:1549). Bede reports on the miracles and heavenly signs which were shown "cum ossa eius inuenta, atque ad ecclesiam, in qua nunc seruantur, translata sunt. Factum est autem hoc per industriam reginae Merciorum Osthrydae, quae erat filia fratris eius, id est Osuiu. . . . Est monasterium nobile in prouincia Lindissi, nomine Beardaneu, quod eadem regina cum uiro suo Aedilredo multum diligebat, uenerabatur, excolebat, in quo desiderabat honoranda patrui sui ossa recondere . . ." ('when his bones were discovered and translated to the church in which they are now preserved. This came about through the efforts of Osthryth, queen of Mercia, who was the daughter of Oswald's brother Oswiu. . . . There is a famous monastery in the kingdom of Lindsey called Bardney, which was greatly loved, venerated, and enriched by the queen and her husband Æthelred, and in which she wished to place her uncle's honoured bones. . . .' [*HE* 3.11]). In both *HL* and *Pass.* the name of Oswald's niece, Osthryth, is transformed into the name of a country, Austria, MHG *Ôsterrîche*, MLG *Osterîke*. Presumably the name was misread early during the German transmission of the Oswald legend and identified as the country with a similar name. Once the identification was made, the author added supplementary information to make sense of the whole. The fact that the error occurs not only in *Ósvalds saga* but also in *HL/Pass.*, indicates that the mistake already existed in the German source of these redactions. See introduction, pp. 87–88.

[34] The reference in Bede is to the monastery Bardney (Beardaneu) in the kingdom of Lindsey (Lindissi); see *HE* 3.11. Presumably because the name of Oswald's niece was mistaken for the name of a country, the subsequent identification of Lindsey as a different country came about. Wallace-Hadrill comments that it "is unknown where Oswald's bones lay between his death in 642 and their translation to Bardney c. 679" (*Bede's Ecclesiastical History*, 103).

ýmist að hún settist niður á bein sankti Ósvalds ellegar fló hún í burtu aftur. Af þessari sýn gladdist mjög drottningin og lofaði guð fyrir. Um morguninn eftir sagði drottningin og menn hennar bræðrunum í klaustrinu hvað þeir höfðu séð. Þá fögnuðu bræðurnir þessari sýn og slíkum helgum dómi er guð hafði þeim og þeirra klaustri gefið. Nokkuru seinna er bræðurnir voru í kirkju sinni og lofuðu guð eftir þeirra venju, þá sáu þeir að eitt skært ljós leið ofan af himni til og beint þar niður er sankti Ósvalds bein voru. Í þessu var einn fátækur maður þar kominn til þess ef hann mætti fá nokkura líkn síns meinlætis er hann hafði. En það var að óvinurinn bjó með honum og hafði hann af tilvísan guðs almáttugs dregist þangað er bein Osvaldus[164] voru. En er hann hafði legið þar litla hríð varð hann frelstur af þessum óvin so að hann gjörði honum aldregi[165] upp frá því og fór í burtu aftur alheill og þakkaði guði og sankti Osvald.[166] Samaleiðis gjörði og bræðurnir allir í klaustrinu er þessa sýn og jarteikn bæði sáu og heyrðu.

16. Í nokkurn tíma kom einn blindur maður þangað sem sanctus Osvaldus var grafinn þvíað honum hafði verið sagt af þeim stórmerkjum er guð lét ske fyrir heilagleik síns vinar þar. Síðan tekur hann moldina með fullri trú þeirri að hann muni fá sína sýn og ríður moldinni um augun á sér. En þegar í stað fær[167] hann sína sýn sem hann hafði aldri verið blindur. Lofar hann guð og sankti Ósvald fyrir þessa hjálp og miskunn er honum veittist.

Á þessum sama stað er þessi guðs dýrlingur var af sínum óvinum í hel sleginn, þar var einn mikill kross upp reistur. En þá sem nokkurir fátækir komu þangað til grafarinnar, þá fóru þeir til og tálguðu sér spónu af krossinum þessum og lögðu síðan í hreint vatn og gáfu eftir á öðrum sjúkum mönnum, og hvað mein sem hver hafði á sér eða innan <í> sér þá fengu allir bót sinna krankleika er þeir

---

[164] The manuscript has the undeclined Latin form *Osvalldus*. Normally the Latin form of the name appears with the proper case ending.

[165] In her edition Loth suggests that a word such as *mein* might be appropriate (1:94, 29) as object of *gjörði*, but the elliptical statement is not incomprehensible as it stands.

[166] The German form of the name occurs here. The corresponding passage in the *Pass.* does not name the saint, however: "de dankede Gode vnde dem leuen hyllighen erer gnaden" (C.v.b).

[167] The manuscript writes *fier*.

bones of St. Oswald and then flew away again. The queen rejoiced greatly at this vision and praised God for it. The next morning the queen and her people told the brothers in the monastery what they had seen. The brothers rejoiced at this vision and the relics that God had given them and their monastery. Some time after this when the brothers were in their church and were praising God, as was their wont, they saw that a bright light was shining down from heaven and straight down to where St. Oswald's bones were. At this moment a poor man came there to see whether he might get some relief for the affliction he had. And this was that he was possessed by the devil, and, guided by almighty God, he had been drawn to the spot where Oswald's bones were. And when he had lain there for a little while, he was freed of this devil so that he never again plagued him from this day on, and he went away completely cured and thanked God and St. Oswald. All the brothers in the monastery, who saw and heard about this vision and miracle, did the same.[35]

16. One time there came a blind man to the place where St. Oswald was buried,[36] since he had been told of the miracles that God granted there on account of the sanctity of his friend. He takes some earth in the full belief that he will regain his sight and he rubs the earth on his eyes. And at once he regained his sight and it was as though he had never been blind. He praises God and St. Oswald for this help and the mercy that he was granted.

At this very spot, where God's saint was slain by his enemies, a large cross was raised up.[37] And when some poor people came there to the grave, they went and cut chips off this cross and put them in clean water and gave some to other sick people, and no matter what affliction each had, either on or in the body, they were all cured of their illness when they drank from the water, and similarly other

---

[35] This chapter has a somewhat divergent account from that found in Bede *HE* 3.11. The miracle/vision of the dove does not occur in Bede, only the ray of light. Furthermore, Bede does not relate the miracle of the man possessed by the devil in the context of the translation of his relics, but rather subsequently in a monastery where soil upon which the water in which Oswald's bones were washed cures a man possessed of a devil (see the introduction, p. 86–87).

[36] This last chapter deviates from the corresponding text in Bede inasmuch as the miracles recounted did take place at Hefenfeld, but this is not, as the saga claims, the place where Oswald was slain, but rather the place where he had won an earlier battle prior to which he had raised a cross. In the German and Icelandic texts the raising of the cross is linked to Oswald's final battle.

[37] According to Bede, this is actually the cross, mentioned in chap. 11 above, that Oswald himself had raised. Bede surmises that the miracles take place there "ad indicium uidelicet ac memoriam fidei regis" ('doubtless as a token and memorial of the king's faith' [*HE* 3.2]).

drukku af vatninu ok líka fengu bót aðrar skepnur af sínum meinum þegar að þær drukku af þessu vatninu fyrir miskunn guðs.

Og þessi staður er nú síðan kallaður á latínu *caelestis locus*, en á engelsku[168] *himneskur staður*, en það er að skilja að í þeim stað skal upp hefjast og fullgjörast himneskir hlutir, bæði miklir og so undarlegir í heiður við guð sjálfan og hans útvaldan vin sanctus Osvaldus.

Nú skulum vær biðja blessaðan herra sankti Ósvald að hann þiggi fyrir oss af almáttugum guði að alla góða hluti er þessi guðs vinur megi þiggjandi verða af vorum lausnara Jesu Christo megi oss og til hjálpar koma bæði til lífs og sálar. Amen.[169]

---

[168] The adjective *engelskur* (the oblique form in the manuscript is written *eingelskv*) is borrowed from MLG *engelsch* (cf. W-N, 61). The Old and Modern Icelandic adjective is *enskr*. The corresponding passage in the *Pass.* reads: "vnde de stede heth in enghelscker sprake hemmelvelt" (C.v.b)

[169] The *Pass.* has no corresponding passage, but the prayer for St. Oswald's intercession is found in *HL*, albeit in somewhat longer form: "Nu pit wir in durch sein grosz heilikait, daz er vns vm got erwerb, daz er vns helf, daz wir hi als selikleichen leben, daz wir noch disem leben zu dem ewigen leben kumen, zu Maria, gotz muoter, vnd zu irs lieben kindes tron vnd zu sant Oswalt vnd zu seinen dinern an der engel schar. Dez helf vns der vater vnd der sun vnd der hailig gaist. Amen." ('Let us now pray to him on account of his great sanctity that he intercede for us with God to help us so that we live so worthily here on earth that after this life we come to eternal life, to Mary, God's mother, and to the throne of her dear child and to St. Oswald and to his servants, the angels. May God the Father, the Son, and the Holy Ghost help us. Amen.' [ed. Williams-Krapp, 1:368.3–8]).

creatures were healed of their injuries as soon as they drank from this water on account of the mercy of God.[38]

And this place has ever since been called in Latin *caelestis locus*, but in English *Heavenly Stead*,[39] and this means that in this place there will occur and be performed heavenly things, both great and wonderful, for the honor of God Himself and His chosen friend St. Oswald.

Now let us ask the blessed lord St. Oswald to obtain for us from almighty God that all good things which this friend of God can obtain from our Savior Jesus Christ will be of help to us for both our bodies and souls. Amen.

---

[38] This comes straight from Bede: "Nam et usque hodie multi de ipso ligno sacrosanctae crucis astulas excidere solent, quas cum in aquas miserint, eisque languentes homines aut pecudes potauerint, siue asperserint, mox sanitati restituuntur" ('And even to this day many people are in the habit of cutting splinters from the wood of this holy cross and putting them in water which they then give to sick men or beasts to drink or else they sprinkle them with it; and they are quickly restored to health' [*HE* 3.2]).

[39] The saga gives the Icelandic translation of Hefenfeld, *himneskur staður*, that is, Heavenly Stead. Bede writes: "Vocatur locus ille lingua Anglorum Hefenfeld, quod dici potest latine Caelestis Campus, quod certo utique praesagio futurorum antiquitus nomen accepit; significans nimirum, quod ibidem caeleste erigendum tropeum, caelestis inchoanda uictoria, caelestia usque hodie forent miracula celebranda" ('This place is called in English Heavenfield, and in Latin *Caelestis campus*, a name which it certainly received in days of old as an omen of future happenings; it signified that a heavenly sign was to be erected there, a heavenly victory won, and that heavenly miracles were to take place there continuing to this day' [*HE* 3.2]).

# THE LOW GERMAN LEGEND OF ST. OSWALD

The edition below is based on the text in *Dat Passionael* (Lübeck, 1492), C.ii.c–C.v.b. In the *Passionael* the superscript horizontal stroke is used to abbreviate *vnde*, to indicate double consonants (*manne*, *konnynk*) as well as medial (*ghans*, *wente*) and final nasals (*hebben*, *quam*). Infrequently, what corresponds to a superscript curved single quotation mark occurs to indicate the Latin ending *–us* (*Oswald'* = *Oswaldus*) and final *-er* (*ridd'* = *ridder*, *wedd'* = *wedder*). Occasionally the final nasal in the past singular of the verb *quemen*, that is, *quam*, is indicated by *–z* (*quaz*). All abbreviations are silently expanded. Similarly, occasional typographical errors, such as the occurrence of *n* instead of *u* in the word *bescreuen* or an aberrant letter (the first *–n-* in *heyndensch*) are silently corrected. The period is used in *Dat Passionael* for both half and full stops (once there occurs a colon), and this is retained as a punctuation device. Proper names are not consistently capitalized and occasionally periods are lacking where capitalization indicates the beginning of a new sentence. In such instances capitalization and punctuation have been introduced in this edition. To facilitate reading, quotation marks have been added to mark direct speech. The only indications of paragraph breaks occur in the miracle section. Additional paragraph breaks have been introduced, again to facilitate reading, and the initial word has been capitalized.

# Van Sunte Oswaldo
## DEME KONNINGHE

De leue here sunte Oswald was eyn gued cristen. vnde was doghentlik. vnde
hadde God leeff. vnde gaff vele almissen. vnde beschermede wedewen vnde
weyzen. vnde eerde vnde voedede de prester. vnde was hart den vnlouighen.
darumme sach em got voer. vnde wolde em tho enem konninge hebben. vnde do
men em wolde to enem konninge kresemen. do tovloet de kresem van Godes willen. wente id quam eyn rauen van dem hemmel. vnde brochte ene gulden bussen
mit kresem in deme snauele. vnde dem rauen henk eyn breeff in deme halsze. de
was beseghelt mit enem gulden kruce. vnde de rauen konde latin spreken. vnde
sprak. "Ik bringe den kresem van dem hemmele."

Do lezen se den breef. dar inne stunt ghescreuen. dat ene sunte Peter suluen
hadde ghebenedyet. vnde de rauen bleeff vortan in sunte Oswaldus hoff. Do he nu
konnink in Enghelant gheworden was. buwede he ene schone kerke in de ere des
vorsten der apostele sunte Peters. vnde settede dar prester in Gode to denende.
vnde gaff dar vele gudes to. Darna leuede he salichliken alze voer. vnde strijdede
manlyken yeghen de heyden vmme den cristen louen. vnde bedwank heren vnde
stede dat se em tyns mosten gheuen. vnde wart so mechtich. dat em alle daghe
vele grote heren bisscoppe vnde abbete deneden. Der herscop en vorhoff he sik
nicht. men he was othmodich. vnde hadde God vor oghen. vnde denede em dagh
vnde nacht mit grotem vlite. darvmme was Got mit em. Ok mosten konninghe.
hertoghen. greuen. vnde eddelmanne borghe vnde lande van em entfangen.

Do he nu so doghentlyken vnde salichliken leuede to Gode vnde den minschen.
do meneden de heren he scolde ene iuncfrouwe nemen. wente storue he ane erue. so
scolde eyn ander syn gued vnde syn rike besitten. deme yd nee sure were gheworden.
Do quam alzo drade eyn old man van deme wyllen Godes. de hadde enen grawen
langen baert. vnde droech enen palm vnde staff in synre hant. In etliken boken steyt
ghescreuen dat id eyn engel was. vnde stellede syk yft he eyn pelegrim were. Den
entfenk sunte Oswaldus ghans guetliken vnde brochte em in syn pallas.

Do sprak de olde man. "yck byn eyn prophete. vnde my sint .lxxij. lande bekant
vnde do dy kundich van Gode. dat du ene iuncfrouwe scalt nemen. de is enes heydens konnynges dochter. de heet Gaudon. vnde de iuncfrouwe heet Pia. vnde is tomale schone vnde ys de wylle Godes. dat du darumme strijdest. vnde bringest se to
deme cristen louen. dar to heft se God vtherkoren." Do sprak sunte Oswaldus. "Nu
hebbe yk nenen denre de mi de bodeschop werue. de sik in dat lant kan vntrichten."
Do sprak de gude olde man. "Sendestu dar dusent manne. de dodet der iuncfrouwen
vader alle. wente do se waert gheboren. do nam he se vp den schoet vnde lede dre
vinghere vp ere houed. vnd swoer dre eede na der heydescken ee. dat he eer num-

# ABOUT ST. OSWALD, KING

The dear lord St. Oswald was a good Christian and he was virtuous and loved God. And he gave many alms and protected widows and orphans and honored and nourished priests, and he was severe towards unbelievers. Therefore God chose him and wanted him to be a king. And when he was to be anointed king, the chrism appeared through God's will, for a raven came down from heaven and brought in its beak a golden box with chrism. And a letter hung from the neck of the raven; it was sealed with a golden cross. And the raven could speak Latin, and he said: "I am bringing chrism from heaven."

They then read the letter in which was written that St. Peter himself had blessed it. And from then on the raven stayed at St. Oswald's court. When he had now become king of England, he built a beautiful church in honor of the first apostle, St. Peter. And he appointed priests there to serve God and he gave many possessions for this. After this he lived piously as before. And he fought manfully against the heathens for the sake of the Christian faith. And he forced lords and cities to give him tribute. And he was so powerful that many great lords, bishops, and abbots served him every day. But he did not become arrogant because of his authority, but he was humble and had God ever before him. And he served Him day and night with great diligence. Therefore God was with him. And kings, dukes, counts, and noblemen had to hold cities and lands from him in fief.

When he was now living so virtuously and piously in the sight of God and men, the lords believed that he should take a wife, for if he died without heirs, someone else would possess his wealth and kingdom, someone who had never exerted himself for it. Then suddenly an old man came in accordance with God's will. He had a long gray beard and carried a palm and a staff in his hand. In some books it says that he was an angel, and he behaved as if he were a pilgrim. St. Oswald received him kindly and took him into his hall.

Then the old man spoke: "I am a prophet and seventy-two lands are known to me, and I make known to you from God that you are to take a wife. She is a heathen king's daughter. His name is Gaudon and the maiden is called Pia and she is very beautiful. And it is God's will that you fight on this account and bring her to the Christian faith. God has chosen her for this." St. Oswald then spoke: "But I have no servant who might undertake the mission and carry it out in that country." Then the good old man spoke: "Even if you send a thousand men there, the maiden's father will kill them all, for when she was born, he took her on his lap and laid three fingers on her head and swore three oaths according to heathen

mermeer enen man wolde gheuen he enwunne se denne mit dem sweerde." dat was
sunte Oswald ghans leed. vnde wiste nicht wo he doen scolde. Do sprak de olde
man. "Du hefst enen rauen in dyneme houe wol twelff iar ghetoghen. de krycht dy
vor waer de iuncfrouwen." Do heet syk Oswaldus den rauen bringen. do wolde he
nicht to em vleghen. do wart em ghans lede. Do sede de olde man. "Wes guedes
modes. God schykket dy ene drade wedder." vnd darna vloech de rauen vor den
olden man vp de tafelen. vnde sprak to em dat he synem heren willekame were.
Do sprack sunte Oswaldus. "Ik hebbe dy .xij. iaer ghehat. vnde hebbe dy nee so
mynschlyken horen spreken." daer mede vorswand de olde man.

Do screeff de leue sunte Oswaldus de .xij. stukke des hylgen louen in enen
breeff. vnde neyede den breeff dem rauen vnder syne vloghele. vnde daer to eyn
gulden vingerlin. vnde beuoel em dat he dat der iuncfrouwen des konnynghes
dochter brochte. vnde dat he er sede dat he se leuer hadde wen yennighe iuncfrouwen vp ertryke. dar mede nam de rauen orlof. Do beuoel ene sunte Oswaldus
vnseme leuen heren vnde vnser leuen vrouwen.

Do hoeff syck de rauen vp. vnde vloech hen. vnde quam in .xix. daghen to des
konnighes Gaudons borch. vnde vloech vp de tafelen. vnde nyghede em vnde der
iunghen konninghinnen. vnde sprak. "Here gheuet my orloff. yk hebbe mit iuw to
sprekende. vnde gheuet my gheleyde beth dat yk van hijr kome. dorch God vnde aller
iuncfrouwen wyllen." Do de konnink horde. dat de rauen sprak. dat was em groet
wunder van syner reede vnde ghelate. vnde sprak. "Du hefst so wol orloff ghebeden
vnde gheleyde. dat yk dy nicht weygheren enmach. Nu segge wat du wult." Do sprak
de rauen. "My heft myn here Oswaldus de konnink van Enghelant hijr ghesant. vnde
biddet iuw guetliken. dat gy em iuwe dochter gheuen. dat is Godes wylle. vnde syner
leuen moder Marien. do gy dat. so werde gy salich." Do de konnynk horde. dat de
rauen got vnde Marien syne moder nomede. Do wart he gans tornich. vnde sprak.
men scolde en dorch God vnde Marien willen vangen. vnde scolde ene doden.

Do de iuncfrouwe de bodeschop hoerde. de eer sunte Oswald hadde to entboden do krech se altohant ene grote leue vnde was er leed vmme den rauen.
vnde sprak to ereme vader. "Dodet men den voghel. so enmach yck nummer vro
werden. wente du hefst em orloff vnde gheleyde ghegheuen. is dat du dat brekest.
dat steyt dy tomale ouel." Do sprak de vader. "Leue dochter wes to vreden. hebbe
du den vogel. vnde do dar mede wat du wult."

Do wart de iuncfrouwe ghans vro. vnde nam den voghel. vnde droech ene
mit syk in ere kamer. vnde drukkede en leefliken an ere bruste. vnde sprack.
"Leue rauen segge my meer van dyneme heren Oswaldo." Do sprak he. "Nemet
enen bref vnde eyn gulden vingerlyn vth mynen vedderen. dat heft iuw myn
here ghesant. vnde heft iuw bi mi entboden. dat he iuw leuer hadde. wen yenighe
iuncfrouwen edder vrouwen vp erden." Do se in deme breue lasz. dat se dar salich
van worde. weret dat se de .xij. stukke des cristen louen louede. Do wart ere herte
tohant entfenghet van deme hyllighen gheste. dat se dat gantzliken louede. vnde

law that he would never give her to any man unless he won her with the sword." St. Oswald was quite distressed at this and did not know what he should do. Then the old man spoke: "You have now raised a raven at your court for some twelve years. He will certainly obtain the maiden for you." Oswald then ordered the raven to be brought to him, but he did not want to fly to him. He was very upset at this. Then the old man said: "Be of good spirits. God will quickly return him to you." And after this the raven flew onto the table before the old man and said to him that his lord welcomed him. St. Oswald then spoke: "I have had you for twelve years and have never heard you speak in such human fashion." At this the old man disappeared.

Dear St. Oswald then wrote the twelve articles of the holy faith in a letter and sewed the letter under the wings of the raven and also a golden ring, and he ordered him to bring that to the maiden, the king's daughter, and to tell her that he loved her more than any other maiden on earth. Thereupon the raven took leave. St. Oswald then commended him to our dear Lord and our dear Lady.

The raven then rose up and flew away and in nineteen days he came to King Gaudon's castle. And he flew onto the table and bowed down before him and the young queen and spoke: "Lord, by your leave, I must speak with you and grant me safe-conduct until I leave here, for the sake of God and all maidens." When the king heard the raven speaking, he wondered greatly at his speech and conduct, and he spoke: "You have so well asked for leave and safe-conduct that I cannot deny you this. Say now what you will." Then the raven spoke: "My lord Oswald, the king of England, has sent me here, and he kindly asks you to give him your daughter in marriage. That is the will of God and of His dear mother Mary. If you do this, you will be blessed." When the king heard the raven name God and Mary, His mother, he became very angry and said that he should be seized for the sake of God and Mary and be killed.

When the maiden heard the message that St. Oswald had sent her, she immediately was seized with great love and she was upset over the raven. And she spoke to her father: "If the bird is killed, I shall never again be happy, for you have given him leave and safe-conduct. If you take that back, things will go poorly for you." Then the father spoke: "Dear daughter, calm down; take the bird and do with it as you please."

Then the maiden became very happy, and she took the bird and carried it with her to her chamber. And she pressed it lovingly to her breast and spoke: "Dear raven, tell me more about your lord Oswald." Then he spoke: "Take a letter and a golden ring out of my feathers. My lord has sent you these, and he has told me to tell you that he loves you more than any other maiden or noble woman on earth." When she read in the letter that she would be saved if she believed in the twelve articles of the Christian faith, her heart was at once inspired by the Holy Spirit, so that she believed this completely. And she wrote him a letter in return.

screef em enen breef wedder. vnde neyede den deme rauen vnder syne vloghele. vnde dar to eyn vingerlin. vnde sprack to deme  rauen. "Dat bringe dyneme heren. vnde segghe em dar to. dat yk nenen mynschen leuer enhebbe wen em. vnde segge dat he God bidde. dat id alle schee twisscken vns beyden. dat he in deme breue vint bescreuen. dat he my in dem neghesten somer hale mit .lxxij. schepen. vnde dar to yewelken schepe neme dusent man vnde ryddere de kone sint. vnde dat se myt syck nemen vp .iij. iaer ethen vnde drinken vnde dat se dy ok to em nemen anders moghen se my nummer vth der heydenschop bringen."

Do vloech de rauen van daer vnde se beuoel ene Gode. vnde syner leuen moder Marien. In dem .ix. daghe was de rauen ouer dat meer ghevloghen. do was dar so groten wint. dat em de breeff vnde dat vingerlin in dat meer entfel. vnde dat vorslank tohant eyn visck. Do waert he ghans drouich. vnde sat vp enem steen. vnde dar vant he enen eensedel sittende. de sprak tho dem rauen. "Segghe my wat van dyneme heren sunte Oswald." De rauen sprack. "We heft iuw mynen leuen heren sunte Oswaldum bekant ghemaket." De eensedel sprak. "Dat heft ghedaen vnse leue here Jhesus Christus in dysseme iare. darumme dat yk vor em bydden scholde." Do sprak de rauen. "Ick make dy vort meer bekant. dat yck was ghesant van myneme heren in de heydenschop tho enes konninghes dochter. de heft em enen breeff ghescreuen. vnde dar tho eyn schone gulden vingerlin ghesant. dat is my in dat meer gheuallen." Do sprack de eensedel. "dat sy Gode gheclaghet. vnde synre leuen moder Marien." vnde reep God an  mit grotem ernste. vnde sloech syk suluen vmme Godes willen. Do vorhoerde God syn bed. vnde boet enem engel dat he dem viscke den breef vnde dat vingerlin neme. dat dede he. vnde brochte dat deme rauen wedder. vnde de eensedel neyede em dat wedder vnder synen vloghel vnde beuoel em vnseme leuen heren. vnde syner leuen moder Marien.

Vnde vloech .ix. daghe bet he to synem heren quam. Do wart de here ghans vro. vnde nam den rauen vnde entfenck ene guetlyken. vnde sprak. "Wat sechstu my guder tijdinghe van der konninghinnen." He sede. "nemet enen breef vnde eyn gulden vingerlin vth mynem vloghele. dat heft iuw de iunghe konninginne ghesant. vnde entbuet iuw dat se nemande leuer heft wen iuw. vnde schoelt Gode bidden. dat dat drade ghesche twisscken iuw beyden. dat in deme breue ghe-schreuen is. vnde de iuncfrouwe  heft iuw ock entboden. gy scholen se in deme neghesten somer halen mit .lxxij. schepen. vnde my mit iuw nemen. anders en-moghe gy se vth der heydenschop nicht bringen."

Do  lasz sunte Oswalt den breef. vnde leet de schepe maken vnde bereyden mit groter kostlicheyt vnde cziringhe. vnde de schepe worden ersten ouer twe iar bereydet. Do nam he grote vorsten vnde vele hertoghen vnde greuen. vnde .xij. bisscoppe. vnde .ix. abbete mit sik. vnde vele ridder vnde knechte. beth dat erer .lxxij. dusent worden. vnde leet vele kruce maken. vnde gaff yslikem eyn. dat droech he vp synen clederen. vnde trostede se vnde sprak to en allen. "Hebbet yuw wol. vnde strijdet vromeliken. wente so we van iuw steruet in mynem strijde. de scal des ewyghen leuendes seker wezen."

And she sewed it under the raven's wings and also a ring. And she spoke to the raven: "Take this to your lord and also tell him that I do not love any person more than him. And say that he should ask God that everything turn out for the two of us as he will find in the letter: that he should fetch me next summer with seventy-two ships and that on each ship he have one thousand men and knights who are brave; and that they bring along three years' worth of provisions in food and drink; and that they bring you along, otherwise they shall never be able to get me out of heathendom."

The raven then flew away from there and she commended him to God and His dear mother Mary. By the ninth day the raven had flown over the sea. There was then such a great wind that the letter and the ring fell off him into the sea, and at once a fish swallowed them. Then he was very sad and set down on a rock and there he found a hermit sitting. He spoke to the raven: "Tell me some news about your lord St. Oswald." The raven spoke: "How have you gotten to know my dear lord St. Oswald?" The hermit spoke: "Our dear Lord Jesus Christ did so this year, so that I would pray for him." The raven then spoke: "I'll let you know even more, that I was sent by my lord into heathendom to the daughter of a king. She wrote him a letter and also sent him a beautiful golden ring. These dropped off me into the sea." Then the hermit spoke: "That cries out to God and His dear mother Mary." And he called on God in great earnestness and disciplined himself for the sake of God. God then heard his prayer and commanded an angel to take the letter and ring from the fish. He did so and brought them back to the raven, and the hermit sewed this back under his wings and commended him to our dear Lord and His dear mother Mary.

And he flew for nine days until he came to his lord. He then became very happy and received the raven and welcomed him kindly and spoke: "What good news can you tell me about the queen?" He said: "Take a letter and a golden ring out from under my wings. The young queen has sent these to you and she has me tell you that she loves no one more than you and you are to ask God that what is written in the letter will quickly come to pass for the two of you. And the maiden has also told me to tell you to fetch her in the next summer with seventy-two ships and that you are to take me along. Otherwise you will not be able to take her out of heathendom."

St. Oswald then read the letter, and he had the ships built and prepared with great splendor and ornamentation. But the ships were not ready for two years. He then took great princes and many dukes and counts and twelve bishops and nine abbots with him as well as many knights and noblemen until there were 72,000 in all. And he had many crosses made and gave one to each to wear on his garments. And he consoled them and spoke to all of them: "Be of good cheer and fight bravely. And should any one of you die in my battle, he will be certain of eternal life."

Vnde voren do hen in deme namen vnses heren. vnde quemen in .xviij. weken
to dem heydenscken konninghe. Do sunte Oswald syne borch sach. do sprak he.
"Ik wil vor hen senden to der iuncfrouwen. dat se my raet gheue wo ik se moghe
kryghen." Do hadde sunte Oswalt den rauen to husz vorgheten. do wart he ghans
drouich. vnde reep vnsen leuen heren vnde vnse leue vrouwen an. vnde bad dat se
em hulpen. Do boet vnse leue vrouwe eneme engele. dat he den rauen dar brochte.
dat dede he. Do wart he ghans vro. vnde entfenk ene ghans leefliken. vnde
sande em to der iuncfrouwen in ere kameren. vnde entboet eer. efte he vmme eer
strijden scolde. dat se em dat lete weten.

Do vloech de rauen dorch eyn vinster tho der iuncfrouwen in ere kameren.
Do wart se ghans vro. vnde nam ene in eren arm. Do sede he eer. wat em sunte
Oswaldus hadde beuolen. Se sede. "Du scalt seggen sunte Oswalde dat he vor
mynes vader borch scal varen vnde dar eyn telt vpslaen. vnde scal .xij. goltsmede
mit syk bringen. vnde scal enen roden arne bouen em vp dat telt maken. de scal
wezen recht yft he leuede. vnde enwech vleghen wolde. vnde scal dar enen groten
kraem vpslaen. vnde wen men en vraghet wat se willen. so scholen se seggen dat
se hebben ghehoert. my is eyn ryke konnink gheloeut. darumme sint se hijr ghekomen. efte de iuncfrouwe yennighe vingerlinghe edder ander klenode bedorfte.
dat se van vns mochte kopen. edder maken laten."

Do nam de rauen orlof. vnde vloech tho sunte Oswalde. vnde sede em de bodeschop. Do nam konnink Oswald .xij. goltsmede mit em. vnde quam vor konnynk Gaudons borch. vnde sloech eyn telt vp. vnde makede enen aerne daer vp.
Dat sach tohant eyn heydensch man. vnde sede dat deme konninghe. Do gink he
myt synre vrouwen vnde alle syn ghesinde to deme krame vnde beseghen den
arne vnde den kraem ghans wol. Do de konnink Gaudon sach dat se altomale in
eren clederen kruce droghen. Do wart he sere tornich. vnde sprak to en. "Ik se dat
an iuwer cledinghe is eyn teken des kruces. dat bedudet dat gy alle cristen sint.
worumme sint gy in myn lant ghekomen. wente yk lathe nenen cristen leuen de
in myn lant kumpt." Do sprak sunte Oswalt. "Wy hebben ghehort. gy hebben iuwer dochter enem ryken konningk ghelauet. darumme sint wy her ghekomen. yft
de iuncfrouwe iennighe vingerlinge edder clenode bedorfte. edder efte se ychtes
wolde laten maken. behoue gy vnser nicht. so latet vns wedder henne varen."

Nu hadde konnink Oswald eyn herte. dat was vthermaten schone. vnde men
vind bescreuen. dat id ein engel was. Dat herte ansach de konnink vnde alle syn
volk. vnde beuiel en gans wol. vnde sach id gherne. Do boet de konnink alle
synem volke. dat se em dat herte hulpen vangen. vnde yaghede em na mit alle
synen denren. vnde yd berde vnderwilen yft yd syk wolde laten vangen. vnde
stunt stylle. vnde leep denne wedder drade. vnde alzo yagheden se dem herten na
beth in den wolt.

And they traveled there in the name of Our Lord, and they came in eighteen weeks to the heathen king. When St. Oswald saw his castle, he spoke: "First I want to send a messenger to the maiden to ask her to give me advice as to how I can obtain her." But St. Oswald had forgotten the raven at home. He became very sad at this and called on our dear Lord and our dear Lady and asked them to help him. Our dear Lady then ordered an angel to bring the raven there, and he did this. Then he became very happy and received him very lovingly, and he sent him to the maiden in her chamber to tell her that if he was to fight for her sake that she should let him know that.

The raven then flew through a window to the maiden in her chamber. She became very happy and took him into her arms. He then told her what St. Oswald had said. She said: "You are to tell St. Oswald that he should come to the foot of my father's castle and pitch a tent there, and he should bring twelve goldsmiths along. And he is to fasten a golden eagle to the top of the tent and it should look as though it were alive and wanted to fly off. And he is to set out much merchandise there, and if someone asks him what they wanted, they are to say that they have heard that I have been promised in marriage to a powerful king. That is why they have come here to see if the maiden needed some rings or other precious objects that she wanted to buy from us or have us make."

The raven then took leave and flew to St. Oswald and gave him the message. King Oswald then took twelve goldsmiths along and he came to the foot of King Gaudon's castle and he pitched a tent there and fastened an eagle to its top. A heathen saw this at once and told this to the king. He then went with his wife and all his retainers to the booth and they carefully looked the eagle and the merchandise over. When King Gaudon saw that they all had crosses on their garments, he became very angry, and he spoke to them: "I can see that you have a sign of the cross on your garments. That means that all of you are Christians. Why have you come into my country, when I do not allow any Christian to live who comes into my country?" St. Oswald then spoke: "We have heard that you have promised your daughter in marriage to a powerful king. That is why we have come here, to see whether the maiden needs any rings or other precious objects or if she wanted to have something made for her. But if you don't need us, then let us leave here again."

Now King Oswald had a stag which was extraordinarily beautiful, and one reads that it was an angel. The king looked at this stag as did all his people and it pleased them very much and they saw it with pleasure. The king then ordered all his people to help him catch the stag. And he pursued it with all his servants. And it behaved at times as though it wanted to be caught and it stood still, but then it quickly ran off again. And in this way they pursued the stag all the way into the woods.

Dat sach de iunghe konnynghinne vp der tynnen. vnde sprak to veer iuncfrouwen. "Ik moet dat herte ok seen. dar to mothe gy my helpen." Se spreken.
"Dat wille wy gherne doen." vnde toghen an mannes cleder. Do was de dore
mit veer yseren grindelen besloten. Do reep de iuncfrouwe vnse leue vrouwe an.
vnde sprak. "Maria du hemmelscke konninginne help my. dat yk eyn guet cristen
werde. vnde dat yk to sunte Oswalde kome." Do breken de grindele entwey. do
wart se ghans vro. vnde spracк to den veer iuncfrouwen. "Wo mochte vnse got
Machemet dat doen." vnde ghynk do to sunte Oswalde in syn telt.

Do stunt he yeghen er vp vnde was vro. vnde entfenk se seer vruntliken. vnde
sprak. "Wol vp gy heren. yk hebbe de konnynginnen. latet dat telt staen." vnde de
iunghe konninghynne hadde ere kronen mit er ghebrocht de settede se vp. vnde
hadde ok andere clenode mit er ghenomen. Do makede sik sunte Oswalt van dar
mit synem ghesinde. vnde mit syner leuen konninghinnen.

Do nu konnink Gaudon to husz quam. vnde deme herten lange na hadde ghe-
iaghet mit synem ghesinde. Do vornam he dat he syne dochter vorloren hadde.
dat was em gans leed. vnde wart sere tornich. vnde ylede sunte oswalde na mit
grotem volke. vnde vant syne dochter by em sittende. Do sprak he to em. "Gy
hebben my myne dochter van hijr ghevoert: darumme mothe gy den doet liden."
Do sprak sunte Oswalt. "Ik wil darumme mit iuw stryden." alzo streden se beth
an den drudden dagh.

Do vorfloech konnink Oswald dem konnynk Gaudon vele volkes. vnde behelt den zeghe mit der hulpe Godes. vnde sprak to konnink Gaudon. "Gy moten
iuw laten dopen. edder gy moten steruen." Do sprak konnynk Gaudon. "Ick enlate
my nicht dopen. yd en sy denne. dat gy my myn volk wedder leuendich maken."
Do reep sunte Oswald vnsen heren an mit groter andacht. Do vorhoerde em vnse
leue here van synre gude. vnde dat volk wart wedder leuendich. Do wolde syck de
konningk noch nicht laten dopen. vnde sprak he wolde anderwert mit em strijden.
vnde streden beth an den drudden dach. do behelt he echter den strijd mit der hulpe
Godes. vnde sprak echter to dem konnynghe. he scolde syk laten dopen. edder he
moste steruen. Do sprak de konnink Gaudon he wolde syk nicht laten dopen. yd
were denne dat he vth eneme stene lete water lopen. Do hoeff sunte Oswald synen
voet vp in dem namen Godes. vnde stotte an enen steen. dar vth vloet tohant eyn
schone water. vnde vth dem water dofte sunte Oswald den konnink Gaudon. vnde
heet ene konnink Symon. vnde an dem drudden daghe dofte sunte Oswald de
iunghe konninghinnen vnde syner denre vele. Dar na reet konnynk Symon wedder
to husz myt syneme heere. vnde sede dat synre vrouwen wo yd em were ghegaen.
vnde sede eer alzo vele van deme cristen louen. dat se sik ok leet dopen. vnde darna in dem .xviij. daghe dofte men alle de in syneme lande weren.

Do voerde de leue here sunte Oswald syne bruet mit gudem vrede wedder to
husz in Engellant. vnde hadde daer .xl. daghe grote warschop vnde vroude. vnde
leuede ghans ynnichliken vnde kusckliken vnde brochten ere tijd to in deme laue
Godes.

The young queen saw this from the ramparts and she spoke to four maidens: "I want to see the stag too; you'll have to help me in this." They speak: "We will gladly do so." And they put on men's clothes. The door was locked however with four iron bolts. The maiden then called upon our dear Lady and spoke: "Mary, you heavenly queen, help me to become a good Christian and to get to St. Oswald." The bolts then broke apart. Then she became very happy and spoke to the four maidens: "How could our god Mohammed ever do something like that!" And she then went to St. Oswald, into his tent.

He then got up to meet her and was happy and he received her very warmly and spoke: "Arise, you lords, I have the queen. Let the tents remain here." And the young queen had brought her crown along and she put it on her head and she had also taken along other precious objects. St. Oswald then left there with his retainers and with his dear queen.

When King Gaudon now came home after he had pursued the stag for a long time with his retainers, he realized that he had lost his daughter. He was very upset at this and became very angry and he pursued St.Oswald with a large number of people, and he found his daughter sitting at his side. He then spoke to him: "You have abducted my daughter from me; therefore you must suffer death." St. Oswald then spoke: "I want to fight with you over this." Therefore they fought until the third day.

King Oswald then put to flight many of king Gaudon's men and he was victorious with the help of God. And he spoke to King Gaudon: "You must let yourself be baptized or else you must die." Then King Gaudon spoke: "I will not let myself be baptized unless it be that you bring my men back to life." St. Oswald then called on Our Lord with great devotion. Then in His goodness our dear Lord heard his prayer and the men returned to life. But the king still did not want to let himself be baptized and he said that he wanted to fight with him again. And they fought until the third day. Then Oswald once again was victorious with the help of God, and he said once more to the king that he should let himself be baptized or else he would have to die. Then King Gaudon said that he would not let himself be baptized unless Oswald could have water run out of a rock. St. Oswald then raised his foot in the name of God and kicked the rock. At once clear water ran out of it. And with this water St. Oswald baptized King Gaudon and gave him the name King Simon. And on the third day St. Oswald baptized the young queen and many of her servants. After this King Simon rode back home with his army. And he told his wife what had happened, and he told her so much about the Christian faith that she also let herself be baptized and afterwards, on the eighteenth day, all who were in his country were baptized.

Then the dear lord St. Oswald brought his bride safely back home to England, and for forty days they had there great wedding festivities and joy. And they lived very piously and chastely and spent their lives faithful to God.

Sunte Oswald was wijsz vnde waraftich in dem gherichte. vnde was vul dogheden. vnde sath nummermer to der tafelen. he hadde denne voer vele dusent armer lude ghespyset. vnde ghaff en suluen de almissen mit synen henden.

Tho ener tijd vp den pasche dagh was he by der tafelen gheseten. vnde hadde vor vele armen ghespiset. Do quemen noch ander pelegrime de beden vmme de almissen. Do nam sunte Oswalt de sulueren schotteln dar he vth ath. vnde heet de tobreken. vnde heet se den pelegrimen gheuen. vnde sprak. "Dat is nicht guet dat myn here Jhesus Christus leddich van my gha. de in pelegrimes wyse to my ghekomen is. wente wen yk to em queme. so leet he my leddich van em ok gaen. vnde spreke. 'Ik bekenne dy nicht. wente du enhefst mi nicht bekant de wile du leuedest.'" Do he dat sprack. do sath ein hillich bysscop by em ouer der tafelen de heet Aydanus. de nam des konnynghes rechter hand. vnde kussede de. vnde sprack. "De rechter hant des konnynges scal nummermeer vorfulen. wente vele mynschen werden dorch se ghetrostet vnde ghespyset." Dat ghescach ock. wente se is noch versck. vnde in suluer bewracht vnde men bewart se in Engelant in sunte Peters munster. dar eren se de lude mit andacht.

De leue here sunte Oswald leet ene clokken gheten den armen luden wen se vor em wolden. vnde wen he de clokken horde luden. so richtede he tohant. vnde leet de clokken alletijd by syk voren. vnde hadde ok vorbaden. dat nemant de clokken moste luden. wente he richtede den armen eer wen den ryken. dat nu leyder de vorsten nicht endoen. wente se richten eer den. dar se af ghebetert moghen werden.

Sunte Oswald moste stedens strijden mit dren konningen vmme den cristen louen. De erste was de konnink van Vorhey. de ander van Britania. de drudde was van Mericien. vnde de was ghans mechtich. vnde de deden em vele vordretes. vnde moste vele mit em vmme syn lant vechten. Men wo vele wertlike sorghe he hadde. noch denede he Gode othmodichliken. mit vastende. mit bedende. vnde myt veler ander guder ouynghe. darumme was Got mit em. vnde to den lasten reden de dre konninghe in syn land. vnde entboden em dat se mit em wolden strijden in deme wyden velde by Enghelant.

Vnde do he des morghens mit den konninghen wolde strijden. do reep he des nachtes vnsen heren an. vnde beuoel syk vnde syn ghesinde vnses heren Gude vnde heet eyn kruce vpsteken. vnde do syne heren weren entslapen. Do sprak de stemme Godes to em. "Eya wes vro du marteler Godes vnde tuchtighe rydder. wente du byst morghen eyn besitter des hemmelrykes myt alle dynem ghesinde." Van der stemme waert he sere vorvrouwet. vnde trostede syn ghesinde vnde sprak. "O gy aldersterkeste ryddere Jhesu Cristi. wezet starck in deme strijde. vnde vechtet yeghen de vnlouighen. so besitte gy dat ewighe ryke. Darumme gy alderleuesten riddere. rekket iuwe hende vnde iuwe herte to Gode. vnde biddet dat he iuw helpe mit synen engelen." Do he dat mit en hadde ghesproken. do openbarde syk eyn groet lycht vp em. vnde de stemme Godes sprak to em. "Du

St. Oswald was wise and righteous in judgment and he was ever virtuous, and he never sat down at table before he had fed many thousand poor people, and he himself gave them alms with his own hands.

One time on Easter Day he was seated at table and he had earlier fed many poor. But more pilgrims came and asked for alms. St. Oswald then took the silver bowl out of which he himself ate and had it broken into pieces and given to the pilgrims. And he spoke: "It is not right that my Lord Jesus Christ should go from me emptyhanded, when He comes to me in the guise of a pilgrim, for when I come to Him, He will also have me go emptyhanded from Him, and He will say: 'I do not know you, since you did not know Me when you were living'" (cf. Matthew 25:35–40). As he was saying this, a holy bishop whose name was Aidan sat at his side at table. He took the king's right hand and kissed it and spoke: "The right hand of the king will never decay, for many people were consoled and fed by it." And that is what happened, for it is still incorrupt and preserved in silver, and it is kept in St. Peter's church in England. There people venerate it with devotion.

The dear lord St. Oswald had a bell cast for the poor people who wanted to appear before him. And when he heard the bell ring, he immediately gave judgment. And he had the bell always taken along with him, and he had also forbidden anyone to ring the bell unless he had first judged the poor before the rich. Unfortunately the princes do not do this nowadays, for they judge first those from whom they might derive profit.

St. Oswald constantly had to fight with three kings on account of the Christian faith. The first was the king of Vorhey, the other of Britain, the third was from Mercia, and he was very powerful. And they did him much wrong and he had to fight much for the sake of his country. But no matter how many worldly cares he had, he nonetheless served God humbly, with fasting and prayer and with many other pious devotions. Therefore God was with him. And in the end the three kings rode into his country and sent him a message that they wanted to fight with him on the level plain near England.

And when he was to fight with the kings the next morning, he called on Our Lord during the night and commended himself and his retainers to our Lord God. And he ordered a cross to be erected. And when his lords had fallen asleep, the voice of God spoke to him: "Be happy, you martyr of God and brave knight, for tomorrow you shall possess the kingdom of heaven with all your retainers." He rejoiced greatly on account of this voice and he consoled his retainers and spoke: "O you most strong knights of Jesus Christ, be strong in combat and fight against the unbelievers, for then you will possess the eternal kingdom. Therefore, most dear knights, raise your hands and hearts to God and ask Him to help you with His angels." When he had spoken this to them, a great light shone upon him and the voice of God spoke to him: "You will live eternally with Me." Then

werst ewichliken mit my leuende." Do quam eyn groet heer der vnlouighen vp se. vnde bunden sunte Oswalde swarlyken. vnde vorsloghen vele van synem heere. Do de leue here sunte Oswald dat sach. do sach he vp to Gode. vnde sprack. "Here Jhesu Christe du almechtighe God. nym ere zelen to dy. de syk vmme dynen hillighen namen hebben ghegheuen in den doed." Tohandes sach he de enghele syner denre zelen vroliken voren in dat ewyghe ryke mit groten vrouden. Do de leue here sunte Oswald dat sach. do sprack he vnde sede. "Nu sterue yck deste vrolyker. wente yk see myner denre zelen vor my in dat ewighe leuent varen." Unde sede darna. "Here Jhesu Criste du almechtighe God. yck beuele dy mynen ghest." vnde starf do in God.

Do leet de konnynk van Mericien syn houed vnde de arme aff houwen. vnde henk se schentliken by den wech. Eyn iar darna quam de konnynk Oswinus in sunte Oswaldus stede. vnde nam sunte Oswaldus houed vnde syne arme. vnde begroeff se erliken. vnde got dede grote teken dorch synen willen. vnde trostet noch alle de mynschen de to syneme graue komen. wente so we to syneme graue komen vnde ene mit ernste anropen. dat sy vmme guet edder ere. efte wat en schadet. dat werd en alle entwidet.

Ok vint men in etliken hystorien van sunte Oswalde. dat he nee ene vrouwe hadde. men he leuede kuscklyken de daghe synes leuendes. vnde trostede de ar- men. vnde dede en vele gudes to allen tijden. vnde starff in deme strijde vmme des cristen louen willen als voer ghesecht is.

Darna ouer vele iare do sunte Oswald wart gheslaghen. do wolde ein ridder to enem berghe rijden. do he vp dat velt quam. dar sunte Oswald wart gheslaghen. do wart syn pert ghans krank. dat he yd moste vor syk driuen. vnde lede syk nedder. vnde kerde syk hen vnde her van groten smerten. do was de ridder ghans wemodich. vnde mende id scolde drade steruen. Do id syk lange hen vnde her gheworpen hadde. do quam id an de stede. dar sunte Oswald was ghemartert vnde begrauen. do rouwede it ene wile. vnde stunt do vp. vnde beet an dat grone gras. vnde wart drade ghesunt van allem ghebreke. Do wart de ridder ghans vro. vnde dankede Gode. vnde vornam wol. dat in der stede ein hyllich mynsche were begrauen. wente he was ghans wijsz. vnde merkede de stede. vnde reth to ener herberghe. De weerd hadde ene dochter de lach yn groter krankheit. Do he dat horde vnde sach. do sede he en. wo syn pert in der stede ghesunt were worden. Do beden se den ridder. dat he mit en to der stede reede. dat dede he. vnde se voerden de iuncvrouwen in de stede. dar waert se entslapen. vnde do se ene wile hadde gheslapen. do makede se sunte Oswald ghesunt. Do entwakede se. vnde stunt vroliken vp. vnde dankede Gode synre gnaden. vnde voer mit eren vrunden wedder to husz. vnde sede dat teken allen mynschen. darna quemen vele kranke mynschen in de stede. vnde worden alle ghesunt van synre hyllycheyt.

To ener tijd quemen etlike manne van Britania in de suluen stede dar sunte Oswalt was begrauen. vnde seghen dat de plaen ghans grone vnde schone was. Do

a great army of unbelievers came upon them and they vehemently united against St. Oswald and killed many in his army. When our dear lord St. Oswald saw that, he looked up to God and spoke: "Lord Jesus Christ, you almighty God, take to Yourself the souls of those who have died for the sake of Your holy name." At once he saw the angels happily leading the souls of his retainers into the eternal kingdom with great joy. When the dear lord St. Oswald saw that, he spoke and said: "Now I die all the more joyfully, for I see the souls of my retainers go into eternal life before me." And after this he said: "Lord Jesus Christ, you almighty God, I commend my spirit to you" (cf. Luke 23:46). And he died in God.

The king of Mercia then had his head and arms cut off and hung shamefully by the road. One year after this King Oswinus succeeded Oswald, and he took Oswald's head and arms and buried them reverently. And by God's will there were great signs, and he still consoles all the people who come to his grave, for when we go to his grave and earnestly call on him, be that for the sake of possessions or honor or for whatever pains one, everyone is heard.

And in some legends about St. Oswald it says that he never had a wife but lived chastely his entire life. And he consoled the poor and did them much good at all times, and he died in battle for the sake of the Christian faith, as was told above.

Many years after St. Oswald had been slain, a knight wanted to ride to a mountain. When he came onto the plain where St. Oswald had been slain, his horse became so ill that he had to push it in front of him, and it lay down and rolled back and forth in great pain. The knight became very sad at this and thought it was soon going to die. After it had tossed back and forth for a long time, it reached the place where St. Oswald had been martyred and buried. There it rested for a while and then stood up and grazed in the green grass and it was quickly healed of all its ills. The knight then became very happy and thanked God, and he realized that at this place a holy person was buried, for he was very wise. And he remembered the place and rode to an inn. The innkeeper had a daughter who lay in bed quite ill. When he heard and saw this, he told him about the place where his horse had been healed. They then asked the knight to ride with them to that place. He did so and they led the maiden to that place. There she fell asleep, and after she had slept for a while, St. Oswald healed her. She then woke up and stood up joyously and thanked God for His mercy. And she went back home with her friends and told everyone about the miracle. After this many sick people came to this place and they were all healed on account of his holiness.

One time some men from Britain came to the same place where St. Oswald was buried and they saw that the plain was very green and beautiful. There was a

was eyn wijsz man mank en de sprak. "Dat de anger so grone is vor deme anderen velde dat is vmmer ein teken.  dat dar eyn hyllich mynsche gheslaghen  vnde begrauen is." vnde groeff do sunte Oswaldes bente en deel her vth. vnde dede se in enen doek. vnde dachte in syk. "Ik wil dar mede vele mynschen ghesunt maken."  vnde quam darna to enre groten  warschop. dar weren vele mynschen de ethen vnde drunken. vnde entfengen ene guetliken. vnde beden em. dat he mit en ethe. do henghede he dat ghebeente mit dem doke an de want. vnde ath mit en. Do se so seten vnde ethen vnde drunken. do wart  dat husz entbernende dar se inne seten. dat dat vuer hogh bouen dat husz vpsloech. wente id was van holte. Do se dat ghewaer worden. do vorschrekkeden se sere. vnde vloen vth deme husze. Do it alle vorbrant was. do vunden se noch sunte Oswaldus ghebeente in dem doke vngheserighet. Do se dat teken seghen. do bevragheden se. we in der stede gheslaghen were. vnde vornemen dat dar de leue  here sunte Oswald gheslaghen vnde begrauen were. Do seden se dat teken allen mynschen. vnde quemen vele mynschen  to der stede vmme trostes wyllen. vnde wat se van em begherden. dat wart en ghegeuen.

Ein man hoerde van der stede vnde van den tekenen de sunte Oswald dar dede. vnde quam enes nachtes dar vnde dachte. "yk wyl beseen yft de wunderte-ken by dem graue wol moghen ghescheen." Do he dar quam. do vant he altohandes sunte Oswaldes  ghebeente bouen vp deme graue liggende. Do wart he ghans vro. vnde nam dat ghebeente mit groter andacht. vnde gaff id der konninginnen van Osterike de was sunte Oswaldes broder dochter. de nam dat myt groten vrouden. vnde voerde dat to husz. vnde leet eyn schonen sark dar to maken dar in lede se dat hyllychdoem myt groter werdicheyt. vnde voerde dat in dat lant Lindissino. dar inne was eyn closter vnde ein munster. vnde de konninghinne hadde de heren in deme closter ghans leeff. vnde se wolde eres omes hyllighedom in deme clo-ster hebben vnde in der suluen nacht do de konnynghynne vnde eer  ghesinde to deme sarcke ghingen. do seghen se ene schone witte duuen van deme hyllichdom vpvaren vnde wedder aff. Des tekens  worden se ghans vro. vnde seden dat den broderen in dem closter. do vrouweden se syk des hyllichdomes gans sere. Darna quam ein licht van dem hemmele. dat scheen vp sunte Oswaldes beente. vnde ein mynsche was by dem sarcke. de was beseten. de wart tohant vorlozet van syner hyllicheyt. de dankede Gode vnde dem leuen hyllighen erer gnaden. Unde do de brodere dat teken seghen. do bestedigheden se dat hyllichdom in dat munster mit groter werdicheit.

To den tijden quam ein blynd man. de hoerde de teken  de God dorch sunte Oswaldes dede. vnde quam to synem graue vnde nam dar aff erden. vnde be-streek dar mede syne oghen. vnde bad ene mit groter andacht. dat he em van Gode vorworue. dat he seende worde. altohant wart he seende. vnde dankede Gode vnde sunte Oswalde.

wise man among them and he spoke: "The reason that the meadow is green compared to the other field is certainly a sign that a holy person was slain and buried here." And he dug up some of St. Oswald's bones and put them in a cloth and he thought to himself: "I want to heal many people with these." And after this he came to a large inn where there were many people who were eating and drinking. And they received him kindly and invited him to eat with them. He then hung the bones in the cloth on the wall and he ate with them. As they were sitting, eating and drinking, the house in which they were sitting caught fire and the flames shot up high above the house, for it was of wood. When they became aware of this, they were very frightened and fled out of the house. When it had burned down completely, they nevertheless found St. Oswald's bones unscathed in the cloth. When they saw this miracle, they asked who had been slain in that place, and they learned that the dear lord St. Oswald had been slain and buried there. They then told everyone about the miracle and many people came to the place seeking consolation. And whatever they desired of him, that was granted.

A man heard about the place and the miracles that St. Oswald worked there. And one night he came there and thought: "I want to see whether miracles really take place at the grave." When he got there, he at once found St. Oswald's bones lying on top of the grave. He then became very happy and picked up the bones with great devotion. And he gave them to the queen of Austria; she was the daughter of St. Oswald's brother. She accepted them with great joy and took them home and had a beautiful shrine made for them and laid the relics in it with great reverence. And she took it to the country called Lindsey. There was a monastery there and a monastery church. And the queen was very fond of the monks in the monastery and she wanted to have her uncle's relics in the monastery. And during the same night when the queen and her retinue went to the shrine, they saw a beautiful white dove fly up from the relics and back down. They rejoiced greatly at this miracle and told the brothers in the monastery about it. They were very happy to have the relics. After this a light from heaven came down and shone on St. Oswald's bones. And there was a man near the shrine who was possessed by the devil, and he was immediately freed from him on account of Oswald's holiness. And he thanked God and the dear saint for their mercy. And when the brothers saw this miracle, they translated the relics to the church with great ceremony.

At this time a blind man came who heard about the miracles God worked on account of St. Oswald. And he came to his grave and took some of the soil from it and smeared it over his eyes and prayed with great devotion that God bring it about that he receive his sight. At once he could see and thanked God and St. Oswald.

In der stede dar sunte Oswald van den konninghen vorslaghen wart. dar
heet he ein kruce vpsteken. Darna quemen etlike mynschen to dem kruce vnde
sneden dar spone van vnde leden de in eyn water. dar drunken de kranken minschen vnde dat quyk van. vnde worden dar aff ghesunt van der gnaden Godes.
vnde de stede heth in enghelscker sprake hemmelvelt. vnde in dem latine Celestis locus. dat bedudet. dat in der stede eyn hemmelsch teken scal vp gherichtet
werden vnde ghescheen.

At the place where St. Oswald was slain by the kings, he had a cross raised up. Afterwards some people came to the cross and cut pieces of wood from it and laid them in water. Many sick people and cattle drank this and they were healed through the grace of God. And this place is called in the English language Heavenfield and in Latin *Celestis locus*. This means that in this place a heavenly sign will be raised up and a miracle occur.

# BIBLIOGRAPHY

Icelandic names have been alphabetized by given name rather than patronymic.

## Editions and Translations

*Acta Sanctorum.* Augusti, 2: 5-12. Aug. 5: 83-103: "De S. Oswaldo rege ac mart."
_____. Octobris: 1, 46-47: "Vita Remigii."
*Analecta Hymnica Medii Aevi.* 13. *Historiae Rhythmicae. Liturgische Reimoffi-
cien.* Zweite Folge. Ed. Guido Maria Dreves. Leipzig: O. R. Reisland, 1892;
repr. New York: Johnson Reprint Co., 1961.
Baesecke, Georg, ed. *Der Münchener Oswald. Text und Abhandlung.* Germanis-
tische Abhandlungen 28. Breslau: M. & H. Marcus, 1907.
_____. *Der Wiener Oswald.* Heidelberg: Carl Winter, 1912.
Bayart, P. "Les Offices de Saint Winnoc et de Saint Oswald d'après le Manu-
scrit 14 de la Bibliothèque de Bergues." *Annales du Comité flamand de
France* 35 (1926): 1–132; 36 plates.
Bede. *Ecclesiastical History of the English People.* Ed. Bertram Colgrave and
R. A. B. Mynors. Oxford: Clarendon Press, 1969.
_____. *Historia Ecclesiastica gentis Anglorum, Historia abbatum, Epistola
ad Ecgbertum una cum Historia abbatum auctore anonymo.* Ed. Charles
Plummer. Oxford: Clarendon Press, 1896; repr. 1969.
*Breta sögur.* In *Hauksbók udgiven efter de Arnamagnæanske Håndskrifter No.
371, 544 og 675, 4⁰ samt forskellige Papirhåndskrifter.* Copenhagen: Det
kongelige nordiske Oldskrift-Selskab, 1892-1896.
Curschmann, Michael, ed. *Der Münchner Oswald. Mit einem Anhang: die ost-
schwäbische Prosabearbeitung des 15. Jahrhunderts.* Altdeutsche Textbib-
liothek 76. Tübingen: Max Niemeyer, 1974.
_____. "'Sant Oswald von Norwegen': Ein Fragment eines Legendenepos."
*Zeitschrift für deutsches Altertum* 102 (1973): 101–114.
Ebernand von Erfurt. *Heinrich und Kunegunde.* Ed. Reinhold Bechstein. Bib-
liothek der gesamten deutschen National-Literatur 39. Quedlinburg and
Leipzig: Gottfr. Basse, 1860.
Einar Ól. Sveinsson, ed. *Brennu-Njáls saga.* Reykjavík: Hið íslenzka fornritafé-
lag, 1954.
*Fredegarii et aliorum chronica. Vitae sanctorum.* Ed. Bruno Krusch. MGH,
Scriptores rerum Merovingicarum 2. Hannover: Hahn, 1888.

Geoffrey of Monmouth. *The Historia Regum Britanniae of Geoffrey of Monmouth*. Ed. Acton Griscom. London: Longmans, 1929; repr. Geneva: Slatkine Reprints, 1977.

_____. *The Historia Regum Britannie of Geoffrey of Monmouth*. V. *Gesta Regum Britannie*. Ed. and trans. Neil Wright. Cambridge: D. S. Brewer, 1991.

Gierach, Erich, ed. *Das Märterbuch. Die Klosterneuburger Handschrift 713*. Berlin: Weidmannsche Buchhandlung, 1928.

Gregory of Tours. *Historiarum Libri Decem*. I: Libri I-V; II: VI-X. Darmstadt: Wissenschaftliche Buchgesellschaft, 1989.

_____. *The History of the Franks*. Translated with an Introduction by Lewis Thorpe. Harmondsworth: Penguin, 1974.

_____. *Opera*. Ed. W. Arndt and Br. Krusch. I. *Historia Francorum*. MGH, Scriptores rerum Merovingicarum 1. Hannover: Hahn, 1885.

_____. *Zehn Bücher Geschichten*. I: *Buch 1–5*. Ed. Rudolf Buchner, 5th rev. ed. Darmstadt: Wissenschaftliche Buchgesellschaft, 1977.

_____. *Zehn Bücher Geschichten*. II: *Buch 6–10*. Ed. Rudolf Buchner. 4th rev. ed. Darmstadt: Wissenschaftliche Buchgesellschaft, 1955.

Haupt, M. "Oswalt." *Zeitschrift für deutsches Altertum* 13 (1867): 466–91.

"Hendrek og Kunegundis." In *Reykjahólabók: Íslandske helgenlegender*, ed. Agnete Loth, 1:35–70. Editiones Arnamagnæanæ A 15. Copenhagen: Munksgaard, 1969.

Jacobus a Voragine. *Legenda Aurea vulgo Historia Lombardica dicta*. Ed. Th. Graesse. 3rd ed. Bratislava: Koebner, 1890; repr. Osnabrück: Otto Zeller Verlag, 1969.

_____. *The Golden Legend. Readings on the Saints*. Trans. William Granger Ryan. 2 vols. Princeton: Princeton University Press, 1993.

Jón Sigurðsson, ed. "Saga Ósvalds konúngs hins helga." *Annaler for nordisk Oldkyndighed og Historie* (1854): 3-91.

Köpke, Karl, ed. *Das Passional. Eine Legenden-Sammlung des dreizehnten Jahrhunderts*. Quedlinburg and Leipzig: Gottfr. Basse, 1852.

Leo of Ostia. *Chronica monasterii Casinensis*. MHG, Scriptores 7. Hannover: Hahn, 1846.

Loth, Agnete, ed. "Et islandsk fragment fra reformationstiden. AM 667, X, 4to." *Opuscula* 4, 25–30. Bibliotheca Arnamagnæana 30. Copenhagen: Munksgaard, 1970.

Luther, Martin. "Die Lügend von S. Johanne Chrysostomo. 1537." In *D. Martin Luthers Werke*. Kritische Gesamtausgabe, 50: 48–64. Weimar: Hermann Böhlaus Nachfolger, 1914.

"The Munich Oswald." In *The* Strassburg Alexander *and the* Munich Oswald. *Pre-Courtly Adventure of the German Middle Ages*, trans. J. W. Thomas, 83–118. Columbia: Camden House, 1989.

"Osvaldr." In *Reykjahólabók: Íslandske helgenlegender*, ed. Loth, 1:71–95.

"Oswald." In *Der Heiligen Leben*, vol. I: *Der Sommerteil*, ed. Margit Brand, Kristina Freienhagen-Baumgardt, Ruth Meyer, and Werner Williams-Krapp, 358-68. Tübingen: Max Niemeyer, 1996.

"De S. Oswaldo rege ac mart." *Acta Sanctorum.* Augusti: 2, 5-12 (Aug. 5).

Overgaard, Mariane, ed. *The History of the Cross-Tree Down to Christ's Passion.* Editiones Arnamagnæanæ B 26. Copenhagen: Munksgaard, 1968.

*Reykjahólabók: Íslandske helgenlegender.* Ed. Agnete Loth. 2 vols. Editiones Arnamagnæanæ A 15, 16. Copenhagen: Munksgaard, 1969, 1970.

*Sanctuarium seu Vitae Sanctorum.* Ed. Boninus Mombritius. Paris: Albert Fontemoing, 1910; repr. Hildesheim and New York: Georg Olms, 1978.

Storm, Gustav, ed. *Islandske Annaler indtil 1578.* Christiania: Det norske historiske Kildeskriftfond, 1888.

Unger, C. R., ed. *Heilagra Manna søgur.* Christiania: B. M. Bentzen, 1877.

"Vita S. Oswaldi Regis et Martyris." In *Symeonis monachi Opera Omnia. Historia Ecclesiæ Dunhelmensis*, ed. Thomas Arnold, 1: 338-85. London: Longmans, 1882-1885; repr. Nendeln: Kraus, 1965.

"Vitae Heinrici et Cunegundis Impp." Ed. G. Waitz. MGH Scriptores IV, 787-828. Hannover: Hahn, 1841.

Vizkelety, A. "Der Budapester Oswald." *Beiträge zur Geschichte der deutschen Sprache und Literatur* (Halle) 86 (1964): 107–88.

Williams, Ulla. *Die >Alemannischen Vitaspatrum<. Untersuchungen und Edition.* Tübingen: Max Niemeyer Verlag, 1996.

Wolf, Kirsten, ed. *Saga heilagrar Önnu.* Stofnun Árna Magnússonar á Íslandi 52. Reykjavík: Stofnun Árna Magnússonar á Íslandi, 2001.

Würth, Stefanie, trans. *Isländische Antikensagas.* I. Munich: Eugen Diederichs Verlag, 1996.

## Secondary Literature:

Ásgeir Blöndal Magnússon. *Íslensk orðsifjabók.* [Reykjavík]: Orðabók Háskólans, 1989.

Baker, E. P. "St. Oswald and his Church at Zug." *Archaeologia* 93 (1949): 103-23.

Bandle, Oskar. *Die Sprache der Guðbrandsbiblía: Orthographie und Laute. Formen.* Bibliotheca Arnamagnæana 17. Copenhagen: Ejnar Munksgaard, 1956.

Bornholdt, Claudia. Engaging Moments: *The Origins of Medieval Bridal-Quest Narrative,* Ergänzungsbände zum *Reallexikon der Germanischen Altertumskunde* 46. New York: Walter de Gruyter, 2005.

Cormack, Margaret. *The Saints in Iceland: Their Veneration from the Conversion to 1400.* Subsidia Hagiographica 78. Brussels: Société des Bollandistes, 1994.

Bräuer, Rolf. "Die drei Fassungen des Legendenromans vom heiligen Oswald und das Problem der sogenannnten Spielmannsdichtung." *Wissenschaftliche Zeitschrift der Ernst-Moritz-Arndt-Universität Greifswald* 15 (1966): 551-55.

_____. *Das Problem des "Spielmännischen" aus der Sicht der St.-Oswald-Überlieferung.* Berlin: Akademie-Verlag, 1969.

Curschmann, Michael. *Der Münchener Oswald und die deutsche spielmännische Epik. Mit einem Exkurs zur Kultgeschichte und Dichtungstradition.* Münchener Texte und Untersuchungen zur deutschen Literatur des Mittelalters 6. Munich: C. H. Beck, 1964.

_____. "Münchner Oswald." In *Die deutsche Literatur des Mittelalters. Verfasserlexikon*, 2nd rev. ed. Kurt Ruh et al., 6:766–72. New York: Walter de Gruyter, 1987.

_____. "'Oswald' (Prosafassungen)." *Die deutsche Literatur des Mittelalters. Verfasserlexikon*, 2nd rev. ed. Kurt Ruh et al., 7:126–28. New York: Walter de Gruyter, 1989.

Delehaye, Hippolyte. *Les Légendes hagiographiques.* 3rd rev. ed. Brussels: Société des Bollandistes, 1927.

_____. *The Legends of the Saints: An Introduction to Hagiography.* Intro. Richard J. Schoeck; trans. V. M. Crawford. 1907; South Bend: University of Notre Dame Press, 1961.

Dünninger, J. "St. Oswald und Regensburg. Zur Datierung des Münchener Oswald." In *Gedächtnisschrift für Adalbert Hämel*, 17-26. Würzburg: Konrad Triltsch Verlag, 1953.

Edzardi, A. Ph. *Untersuchungen über das Gedicht von St. Oswald.* Hannover: Carl Rümpler, 1876.

Elliott, Dyan. *Spiritual Marriage: Sexual Abstinence in Medieval Wedlock.* Princeton: Princeton University Press, 1993.

*Enzyklopädie des Märchens. Handwörterbuch zur historischen und vergleichenden Erzählforschung.* Ed. Kurt Ranke et al. Berlin: Walter de Gruyter, 1977– .

Folz, Robert. "Saint Oswald roi de Northumbrie: Étude d'hagiographie royale." *Analecta Bollandiana* 98 (1980): 49-74.

_____. "La légende liturgique de saint Henri II empereur et confessor." In *Clio et son regard: Mélanges d'histoire de l'art et d'archéologie offerts à Jacques Stiennon à la occasion de ses vingt-cinq ans d'enseignement à l'Université de Liège*, ed. Rita Lejeune and Joseph Deckers, 245–58. Liège: Pierre Mardaga, 1982.

_____. *Les Saints rois du Moyen Âge en Occident (VIᵉ– XIIIᵉ siècles)*. Subsidia Hagiographica 68. Brussels: Société des Bollandistes, 1984.

_____. *Les Saintes reines du Moyen Âge en Occident (VIᵉ – XIIIᵉ siècles)*. Subsidia Hagiographica 76. Brussels: Société des Bollandistes, 1992.

Günter, Heinrich. *Kaiser Heinrich II., der Heilige*. Kempten and Munich: Jos. Kösel'sche Buchhandlung, 1904.

Guth, Klaus. *Die Heiligen Heinrich und Kunigunde. Leben, Legende, Kult und Kunst*. Bamberg: St. Otto-Verlag, 1986.

*Handwörterbuch des deutschen Aberglaubens*. Ed. Hanns Bächtold-Stäubli et al. 10 vols. Berlin: Walter de Gruyter, 1927–1942.

Haug, Walter. "Das Komische und das Heilige. Zur Komik in der religiösen Literatur des Mittelalters." *Wolfram-Studien* 7 (1982): 8-31; repr. in idem, *Strukturen als Schlüssel zur Welt. Kleine Schriften zur Erzählliteratur des Mittelalters*, 257-74. Tübingen: Max Niemeyer, 1989.

Heffernan, Thomas J. *Sacred Biography: Saints and Their Biographers in the Middle Ages*. New York and Oxford: Oxford University Press, 1988.

Irtenkauf, Wolfgang. *Stuttgarter Zimelien. Württembergische Landesbibliothek. Aus den Schätzen ihrer Handschriftensammlung*. Stuttgart: Württembergische Landesbibliothek, 1985.

Jón Helgason. *Málið á nýja Testamenti Odds Gottskálkssonar*. Safn Fræðafjelagsins 7. Copenhagen: Hið íslenska Fræðafjelag, 1929; repr. [Reykjavík]: Málvísindastofnun Háskóla Íslands, 1999.

*Kaiser Heinrich II. 1002–1024*. Ed. Josef Kirchmeier, Bernd Schneidmüller, Stefan Weinfurter, and Evamaria Brockhoff. Veröffentlichungen zur Bayerischen Geschichte und Kultur 44. Augsburg: Bayerisches Staatsministerium für Wissenschaft, Forschung und Kunst, 2002.

Kalinke, Marianne. "*Reykjahólabók*: A Legendary on the Eve of the Reformation." *Skáldskaparmál* 2 (1992): 239-69.

_____. "The Icelandic Legend of the Hairy Anchorite." In *Sagnaþing helgað Jónasi Kristjánssyni sjötugum 10. apríl 1994*, 2: 485-96. Reykjavík: Hið íslenska bókmenntafélag, 1994.

_____. "Maríu saga og Önnu." *Arkiv för nordisk filologi* 109 (1994): 43-99.

_____. "Þa kom þar þessi forbrende Lavrencivs: Two versions of *Laurencius saga*." *Maal og Minne* (1994): 113-34.

_____. "*Stefanus saga* in *Reykjahólabók*." *Gripla* 9 (1995): 133-87.

_____. *The Book of Reykjahólar: The Last of the Great Medieval Legendaries*. Toronto: University of Toronto Press, 1996.

Klauser, Renate. *Der Heinrichs- und Kunigundenkult im mittelalterlichen Bistum Bamberg*. Bamberg: Selbstverlag des Historischen Vereins, 1957.

Klockhoff, Oskar. "Om Osvalds saga." In idem, *Små Bidrag till nordiska Literaturhistorien under Medeltiden*, 1–22. Upsala: E. Edquist, 1880.

Kruse, Norbert, et al., eds. *Weingarten. Von den Anfängen bis zur Gegenwart.* Weingarten: Biberacher Verlagsdruckerei, 1992.

Kunze, Konrad. "Die Hauptquelle des Märterbuches." *Zeitschrift für deutsche Philologie* 88 (1969): 45-97.

_____. "'Buch der Märtyrer' (Märterbuch)." In *Die deutsche Literatur des Mittelalters. Verfasserlexikon*, 1:1093–95. Berlin: de Gruyter, 1978.

*Lexikon für Theologie und Kirche.* Ed. Josef Höfer and Karl Rahner. 10 vols. 2nd rev. ed. Freiburg: Verlag Herder, 1957-1965.

Masser, Achim. *Bibel- und Legendenepik des deutschen Mittelalters.* Grundlagen der Germanistik 19. Berlin: Erich Schmidt, 1976.

Mertens, Volker. "Verslegende und Prosalegendar. Zur Prosafassung von Legendenromanen in 'Der Heiligen Leben'." In *Poesie und Gebrauchsliteratur im deutschen Mittelalter. Würzburger Colloquium 1978*, ed. Volker Honemann, Kurt Ruh, Bernhard Schnell, and Werner Wegstein, 265–89. Tübingen: Max Niemeyer, 1979.

Miller, Nikolaus. "Brautwerbung und Heiligkeit. Die Kohärenz des *Münchner Oswald.*" *Deutsche Vierteljahresschrift* 52 (1978): 226–40.

Ó Riain-Raedel, Dagmar. "Edith, Judith, Mathilda: The Role of Royal Ladies in the Propagation of the Continental Cult." In *Oswald: Northumbrian King to European Saint*, ed. Clare Stancliffe and Eric Cambridge, 216-22. Stamford: Paul Watkins, 1995.

Pizarro, Joaquín Martínez. *A Rhetoric of the Scene: Dramatic Narrative in the Early Middle Ages.* Toronto: University of Toronto Press, 1989.

Rollason, D. W. "Oswald." In *Lexikon des Mittelalters*, 6:1549–50. Munich and Zurich: Artemis & Winkler, 1993.

Salzer, Anselm. *Die Sinnbilder und Beiworte Mariens in der deutschen Literatur und lateinischen Hymnenpoesie des Mittelalters. Mit Berücksichtigung der patristischen Literatur. Eine literar-historische Studie.* Seitenstetten: Programm des k. k. Ober-Gymnasiums zu Seitenstetten, 1886–1894; repr. Darmstadt: Wissenschaftliche Buchgesellschaft, 1967.

Schiller, Karl, and August Lübben. *Mittelniederdeutsches Wörterbuch.* 5 vols. Bremen: J. Kühtmann, 1875–80; repr. Vaduz: Sändig, 1986.

Schröpfer, Hans-Jürgen. *"Heinrich und Kunigunde". Untersuchungen zur Verslegende des Ebernand von Erfurt und zur Geschichte ihres Stoffs.* Göppingen: Alfred Kümmerle, 1969.

Silvas, Anna. *Jutta and Hildegard: The Biographical Sources.* Medieval Women: Texts and Contexts 1. Turnhout: Brepols, 1998.

Stancliffe, Clare, and Eric Cambridge, eds. *Oswald: Northumbrian King to European Saint.* Stamford: Paul Watkins, 1995.

Storm, Gustav, ed. *Islandske Annaler indtil 1578.* Christiania: Det norske historiske Kildeskriftfond, 1888.

Thacker, Alan. *"Membra Disjecta*: The Division of the Body and the Diffusion of the Cult." In *Oswald: Northumbrian King to European Saint*, ed. Stancliffe and Cambridge, 97–127.

Veturlíði Óskarsson. *Middelnedertyske låneord i islandsk diplomsprog frem til år 1500*. Bibliotheca Arnamagnæana 43. Copenhagen: C. A. Reitzel, 2003.

Vollmann-Profe, Gisela. *Geschichte der deutschen Literatur von den Anfängen bis zum Beginn der Neuzeit*. I/2: *Wiederbeginn volkssprachiger Schriftlichkeit im hohen Mittelalter (1050/60 — 1160/70)*. 2nd rev. ed. Tübingen: Niemeyer, 1994.

Wallace-Hadrill, J. M. *The Long-Haired Kings and Other Studies in Frankish History*. New York: Barnes & Noble, 1962.

_____. *Early Germanic Kingship in England and on the Continent*. Oxford: Clarendon Press, 1971.

_____. *Bede's Ecclesiastical History of the English People: A Historical Commentary*. Oxford: Clarendon Press, 1988.

Westergård-Nielsen, Christian. *Låneordene i det 16. århundredes trykte islandske litteratur*. Bibliotheca Arnamagnæana 6. Copenhagen: Ejnar Munksgaard, 1946.

Widding, Ole, and Hans Bekker-Nielsen. "En senmiddelalderlig legendesamling." *Maal og Minne* (1960): 105–28.

_____. "Low German Influence on Late Icelandic Hagiography." *Germanic Review* 37 (1962): 237–62.

Williams, Charles Allyn. *The German Legends of the Hairy Anchorite*. With Two Old French Texts of *La vie de saint Jehan Paulus*. Ed. Louis Allen. Illinois Studies in Language and Literature 18. Urbana: University of Illinois Press, 1935.

Williams-Krapp, Werner. *Die deutschen und niederländischen Legendare des Mittelalters. Studien zu ihrer Überlieferungs-, Text-, und Wirkungsgeschichte*. Tübingen: Max Niemeyer Verlag, 1986.

Wolf, Kirsten, ed. *Saga heilagrar Önnu*. Stofnun Árna Magnússonar á Íslandi 52. Reykjavík: Stofnun Árna Magnússonar á Íslandi, 2001.

Würth, Stefanie. *Der "Antikenroman" in der isländischen Literatur des Mittelalters. Eine Untersuchung zur Übersetzung und Rezeption lateinischer Literatur im Norden*. Beiträge zur nordischen Philologie 26. Basel: Helbing & Lichtenhahn, 1998.

Zingerle, Ignaz V. *Die Oswaldlegende und ihre Beziehung zur deutschen Mythologie*. Stuttgart and Munich: Gebrüder Scheitlin, 1856.

# INDEX

Icelandic names have been alphabetized by given name rather than patronymic